The Changing Japanese Political System

Japan's political stability was shattered after the general election of July 1993 when the conservative Liberal Democratic Party's thirty-eight year domination ended in defeat. This book examines the impact the 1993 general election had on Japanese politics. Although the LDP regained the position of a ruling party within a year, Hori questions whether the Japanese political system has managed to maintain the same efficacy as it had prior to 1993.

Using institutional analysis, Hori argues that this fundamental change caused three institutional transformations; a decline in the importance of LDP organizations in the decision-making process of the government and the Diet, weakened management of the LDP through factions, and detached attitudes of LDP members to Ministry of Finance bureaucrats. Hori analyses three cases, one prior and two after the 1993 election, illustrating just how ineffective the close cooperation between MOF bureaucrats, LDP executives and faction leaders became.

The general election of 1993 was epoch-making in Japanese politics. *The Changing Japanese Political System* is a welcome addition to the current political and public administration literature, providing an illuminating explanation of why Japanese politics has gone adrift.

Harumi Hori spent ten years as a government barrister and judge before leaving to study politics at the London School of Economics and Political Science. She gained her doctorate at the University of Oxford and is now a researcher at the Japan Research Institute.

The Nissan Institute/Routledge
Japanese Studies Series

Editorial Board

Other titles in the series:

The Changing Japanese Political System

The Liberal Democratic Party and the Ministry of Finance

Harumi Hori

Routledge
Taylor & Francis Group

LONDON AND NEW YORK

First published 2005
by Routledge
2 Park Square, Milton Park, Abingdon, Oxon OX14 4RN

Simultaneously published in the USA and Canada
by Routledge
270 Madison Ave, New York, NY 10016

Routledge is an imprint of the Taylor & Francis Group
© 2005 Harumi Hori

Typeset in Times New Roman by
Florence Production Ltd, Stoodleigh, Devon
Printed and bound in Great Britain by
MPG Books Ltd, Bodmin

British Library Cataloguing in Publication Data
A catalogue record for this book is available from the British Library

Library of Congress Cataloging in Publication Data
A catalog record for this book has been requested

ISBN 0–415–37241–0

Contents

Figures

Tables

Acknowledgements

This book is based on my doctorate thesis, *Changes in the Japanese Political System after 1993: Incapacitated Cooperation between the Liberal Democratic Party and the Ministry of Finance*. It would not have been completed without the kindness and help of some remarkable people, and I would like to acknowledge them here.

My thanks go first and foremost to my parents for their unfailing support and understanding.

I wish to express my deep gratitude to my supervisors, Professor J. A. A. Stockwin and Professor Desmond King. Professor Stockwin shared his deep and vast knowledge of Japanese politics with me and patiently encouraged and supported a student who had much to learn about political science. Professor King gave me profound advice on theoretical arguments and persistently helped me to develop logical thinking.

I would especially like to thank the interviewees I met in Japan, although I cannot mention their names here. Without their cooperation this book would not have been possible, and they gave me inspiration and insight in many respects.

Last and not least, I am very grateful to the staff of the Bodleian Japanese Library for their kind assistance.

This book is dedicated to my parents, who have always supported my decisions.

Abbreviations

BOJ   Bank of Japan (Nippon Ginkō)
CAR   Council on Administrative Reform (Gyōsei Kaikaku Kaigi)
CGP   Clean Government Party (Kōmeitō)
CP   Conservative Party (Hoshutō)
CPB   Cabinet Planning Board
DP   Democratic Party (Minshutō)
DRP   Democratic Reform League (Minshu Kaikaku Rengō)
DSP   Democratic Socialist Party (Minshatō)
EC   Executive Council (Sōmukai)
FA   Financial Agency (Kin'yūchō')
FRC   Financial Reconstruction Commission
FSA   Financial Supervisory Agency (Kin'yū Kantokuchō)
FTC   Fair Trade Commission (Kōsei Torihiki Iinkai)
G-2   Military Intelligence of the GHQ
GDP   Gross domestic product
GHQ   General Headquarters' Office
GS   Government Section of the GHQ
GTSRC   Government Tax System Research Council (Seifu Zeisei
            Chōsakai)
HC   House of Councillors (Sangiin)
HOAR   Headquarters' Office on Administrative Reform of the LDP
            (Jimintō Gyōsei Kaikaku Honbu)
HR   House of Representatives (Shūgiin)
JCP   Japanese Communist Party
JNP   Japan New Party (Nihonshintō)
JRP   Japan Renewal Party (Shinseitō)
LDP   Liberal Democratic Party (Jiyūminshutō)
LDP TSRC   Tax System Research Council of the LDP (Jimintō Zeisei
            Chōsakai)
LP   Liberal Party (Jiyūtō)
LTCBJ   Long-Term Credit Bank of Japan (Nihon Chōki Shin'yō
            Ginkō)

MAFF	Ministry of Agriculture, Forestry and Fisheries (Nōrin Suisanshō)
MCI	Ministry of Commerce and Industry
MHA	Ministry of Home Affairs (Naimushō)
MITI	Ministry of International Trade and Industry (Tsūshō Sangyōshō)
MOF	Ministry of Finance (Ōkurashō)
NCB	Nihon Credit Bank (Nihon Saiken Shin'yō Ginkō)
NFP	New Frontier Party (Shinshintō)
NHP	New Harbinger Party (Shintō Sakigake)
ODA	official development assistance
PARC	Policy Affairs Research Council (Seimu Chōsakai)
PMO	Prime Minister's Office (Sōrifu)
PR	Peace and Reform (Heiwa Kaikaku)
RCB	Resolution and Collection Bank
SESC	Securities and Exchange Surveillance Commission
SDL	Social Democratic League (Shakai Minshu Rengō)
SCAP	Supreme Command for the Allied Powers
TSRC	Tax System Research Council
VAT	value-added tax

1 Introduction

Japan has maintained political stability since 1955. The Liberal Democratic Party (LDP) has dominated the Diet, monopolizing the position of a ruling party since its foundation in 1955. Political processes in the Diet and administration were established on the basis of the single party dominance by the LDP, and for more than 30 years they did not suffer from fundamental changes. Japanese politics gave 'the impression of stultifying immobilism' (Stockwin 1988: 325). Such stability, however, was shattered after the general election of July 1993.

On 18 June 1993, opposition parties called for a no-confidence resolution against the Miyazawa Cabinet; 39 out of 274 LDP members voted for this no-confidence resolution, and 18 LDP members abstained. The no-confidence resolution passed the House of Representatives (HR), and a general election was held on 18 July 1993. The LDP gained 223 seats out of 511. As a result, and for the first time since its foundation in 1955, it could not maintain its majority in the HR. On 30 July 1993, eight parties[1] reached an agreement that they would vote for the leader of the Japan New Party (JNP), Hosokawa Morihiro, as the next Prime Minister. On 9 August 1993, the Hosokawa Coalition Cabinet was established, and the LDP became an opposition party for the first time since its foundation in 1955. This event, the formation of a coalition cabinet excluding the LDP, was epoch-making in Japanese politics.

The leading article of the *Asahi Shinbun* of 30 July 1993 described the establishment of the Hosokawa Coalition Cabinet as 'the third large-scale change following the Meiji Restoration (1868) and the defeat in the Second World War' and as 'an epoch-making event in Japanese history' (*Asahi Shinbun*, 30 July 1993). The Hosokawa Coalition Cabinet, however, did not last one year. On 8 April 1994, Prime Minister Hosokawa suddenly announced his resignation and, on 25 April 1994, the Hosokawa Coalition Cabinet resigned en masse. On 30 June 1994, the Murayama Coalition Cabinet, which consisted of the LDP, the Japan Socialist Party (JSP) and the New Harbinger Party (NHP), was established, and the LDP regained the position of a ruling party. The result of an opinion poll conducted by the *Asahi Shinbun* after the establishment of the Murayama

Cabinet showed that 67 per cent of respondents answered that Japanese politics would not change (*Asahi Shinbun*, 20 July 1994).

Did the result of the general election of July 1993 bring about important effects on Japanese politics? And, if it did affect Japanese politics, to what extent and how has the Japanese political system changed? Although the LDP regained the position of a ruling party within a year, does a political system that functioned under LDP dominance still maintain the same efficacy it had under LDP dominance?

These are questions which I explore in this book. I argue that the result of the July 1993 general election brought about a fundamental change in Japanese politics, including the end of LDP hegemony in the Diet. This fundamental change caused institutional changes in the weight of LDP organizations in the decision-making process of the government, the management system of the LDP and the relationship between LDP politicians and bureaucrats, especially those of the Ministry of Finance (MOF). The *Asahi Shinbun* reported these events in the following terms:

> [the series of political events (the approval of the no-confidence vote and the dissolution of the HR)] has clearly divided the LDP. It is an epoch-making event, which has ended one-party dominance by the LDP which has persisted since its foundation in 1955. From now on, it can be said that Japanese politics will become unstable. A new era of Japanese politics will begin, in which fundamental reorganisations of the Japanese political system will occur.
>
> (*Asahi Shinbun*, 19 June 1993)

On the one hand, the fundamental change created by the ending of LDP dominance brought about coalition cabinets, which enabled other political parties to expand their influence on political processes. On the other hand, it caused political confusion. Under LDP dominance, an issue settling system based on close cooperation between LDP executives, faction leaders and bureaucrats had existed, and had successfully dealt with political and economic issues. The effectiveness of this issue settling system, however, significantly declined because of institutional changes after 1993. The issue settling system was supported by three factors: the important positions of LDP organizations in the decision-making process of the government; the strict management system of the LDP through factions; and the close relationships between LDP politicians and bureaucrats. The collapse of the hegemony of the LDP in the Diet after 1993 brought about changes in these three factors. The importance of LDP organizations in the decision-making process of the government was reduced. Factional control over LDP members was weakened. The attitudes of LDP politicians towards bureaucrats, especially MOF bureaucrats, became detached. Consequently, close cooperation between LDP executives, faction leaders and bureaucrats did not function as it had functioned under LDP dominance and, as a result, the issue settling system became ineffective. The decline in the importance of LDP organizations and the weakened management system of the LDP had effects on all policy areas. Accordingly, the malfunction of the issue settling system can be observed ubiquitously in all policy areas. The change in the relationship between LDP politicians and bureaucrats, however, is particularly significant regarding MOF bureaucrats, and political confusion was especially conspicuous regarding the MOF because the MOF had been regarded as the most competent and powerful ministry. I therefore limit my argument about the malfunction of the issue settling system to the administration of the MOF.

I adopt a historical institutional approach to analyse the above argument. Analysing Japanese politics in terms of institutions and institutional relationships gives us a clear understanding of the structure of Japanese politics. In a political field, individuals' behaviour and propensity are affected by institutions in which they are incorporated, and decision-making processes consist of interactions of institutions. A historical aspect is important because institutions and institutional relationships in Japanese politics, such as the Diet, the cabinet system, the bureaucracy and the political party system, were established in the Meiji era (1868–1912), and they have maintained their structure, characteristics and dispositions in spite of political changes. Accordingly, it is crucial to explore the original political settings of those institutions and institutional relationships in order to achieve a precise understanding of present Japanese politics.

From the viewpoint of historical institutionalism, I expound my argument by examining the Japanese bureaucracy and its relationship with party politicians from the Meiji era to the present. The characteristic of the relationships between LDP politicians and bureaucrats – whereby bureaucrats planned policies and used party politicians to put those policies into practice and politicians delegated policy-making to bureaucrats – was observed not only under LDP dominance. A mechanism based on such roles of bureaucrats and party politicians was consolidated in the Meiji era, and has been maintained, adapting itself by incremental adjustment to political circumstances. These include the Taishō Democracy (from the 1910s to the beginning of the 1930s), political reforms after the Second World War and LDP dominance after 1955. The issue settling system under LDP dominance, based on close cooperation between LDP executives, faction leaders and bureaucrats, is the result of such adaptation of the mechanism to the monopolization of the ruling position in the Diet by the LDP after 1955. The mechanism functioned effectively by adapting itself to political changes; however, it has not been able to adjust to the new political circumstances manifest since 1993.

Three cases are analysed: one before 1993 (the introduction of the consumption tax) and two after 1993 (financial crises and MOF reform in the latter half of the 1990s), to illustrate the issue settling system under LDP dominance worked successfully before 1993 and inefficiently after 1993.

The MOF has tightly controlled financial institutions by issuing directives and executing administrative guidance, and it was proud of having allowed no financial institution to fail since 1945. LDP politicians have safely put financial policies into the hands of the MOF and refrained from intervening in this policy area. MOF bureaucrats and LDP politicians have thus maintained a smooth relationship regarding financial policies. It therefore seemed most unlikely that cooperation between MOF bureaucrats, LDP executives and faction leaders should not have functioned effectively and that political confusion should have been brought about in this policy area. However, regarding the failure of the Jūsen and the Long-Term Credit Bank of Japan (LTCBJ), LDP politicians did intervene in the processes of making liquidation plans for the Jūsen and the LTCBJ, and those processes were thrown into political turmoil because of severe conflicts and lack of control in the LDP. Although the MOF relied on the issue settling system, it could not put its original liquidation plans into practice, and the liquidation processes were significantly delayed because of the political confusion.

Regarding MOF reform, LDP politicians had refrained from intervening in organizational and personnel matters of the MOF bureaucrats. From the 1950s to the beginning of the 1960s, LDP politicians had attempted to reform the MOF, and all such attempts had failed. Since then no significant plan for MOF reform had been put on the political agenda. LDP politicians had preferred to obtain beneficial treatments in budget compilation by cooperating with MOF bureaucrats, and they left organizational and personnel matters, which would affect the interests of MOF bureaucrats directly, in the hands of the MOF bureaucrats themselves. As a result, close cooperation between LDP politicians and MOF bureaucrats had been maintained, and both LDP politicians and MOF bureaucrats had obtained benefits from this cooperation. MOF bureaucrats put their plans into practice efficiently, and LDP politicians secured their seats in the Diet by distributing public works and subsidies among their supporters.

It therefore seemed highly unlikely that LDP politicians would harm such a profitable relationship by intervening in organizational and personnel matters of the MOF. Nevertheless, in 1998 the jurisdiction of the inspection and supervision of financial institutions was split away from the MOF, and the Financial Supervisory Agency (FSA) and Financial Reconstruction Commission (FRC) were established. The MOF exerted its influence on legislation processes through the issue settling system by drafting bills and negotiating LDP politicians and faction leaders over those drafts. The legislation process relating to MOF reform was supposed to follow the same procedure. MOF bureaucrats attempted to shift the movement of MOF reform in a direction more favourable to themselves through the issue settling system, as it had done in the past under LDP dominance. The MOF made drafts of the bills and negotiated with LDP executives and faction leaders. However, the main venue of government decision-making had shifted from LDP organizations to organizations consisting of ruling coalition parties, and in those organizations, the LDP was forced to change its decisions and make compromises with other ruling coalition parties.

Furthermore, regarding the establishment of the FRC, the 'new policy-oriented' politicians of the LDP, who were actually in charge of revising the Financial Revitalization Bill, did not seek support from the MOF with regard to creating the draft Bill, and the MOF was also excluded from the revising process. Thus, in the case of MOF reform, the political processes followed a different procedure from that followed under LDP dominance in which the issue settling system fully functioned. Consequently, the MOF lost its means of exerting influence on the process of legislating the above law. The Financial Revitalization Bill was created to rescue the Japanese financial intitutions that had serious financial difficulties and to restore the Japanese financial systems. The legislative process of this law will be explained in Chapter 6.

As well as the above two cases, I chose the introduction of the consumption tax case in 1989 to confirm the effectiveness of the issue settling system before 1993. The introduction of a new tax system, the consumption tax, was supposed to affect Japanese taxpayers as a whole. This policy was extremely unpopular among the Japanese electorate and difficult to put into practice, and it was therefore expected that LDP politicians would have an extremely strong interest and would be willing to intervene. Tax system reform had been executed immediately after the Second World War following the Shoup Proposals of 1949,[2] and no substantial tax reform had been executed since then until the introduction of the consumption tax in 1989. Therefore, it was highly unlikely to introduce a new tax that would be imposed on the whole Japanese taxpayers. Nevertheless, the MOF succeeded in legislating the consumption tax plan by fully exploiting the issue settling system, which confirms the proposition that the issue settling system functioned effectively before 1993.

2 The Japanese political system

A historical institutional approach

Historical institutional approach

Historical institutionalists analyse structural consistencies behind the persistence of particular patterns of policy by focusing on institutions and institutional relationships (Hall 1986: 18). They examine institutions and institutional relationships, exploring their political and economic development in historical context. Therefore historical institutionalism can explain why a specific pattern of institutional configuration persists in a particular political area by examining the process of its development. For example, Kathleen Thelen studied the resilience of wage bargaining organizations in advanced industrial countries to the pressures of globalization in the 1980s, which divided the bargaining power of skilled workers from that of unskilled workers (Thelen 1999: 398–9). She explains that wage bargaining institutions in Denmark and Sweden experienced substantial reconfiguration in the 1980s whereas in Germany such pressures did not bring about significant changes in those institutions. She explores the difference between the Danish and Swedish cases and the German case by examining how 'ideological and material foundations sustained these institutions prior to the onset of these new pressures' (Thelen 1999: 398). Danish and Swedish models, she argues, were characterized by a high degree of egalitarianism. Denmark and Sweden had overarching national wage bargaining institutions, and, facing the above change in labour markets in the 1980s, those egalitarian institutions were significantly subverted. On the other hand, the German system, which accommodated the diversity of labour markets such as the skilled worker market and the unskilled worker market, had accepted the inequalities between different labour markets. As a result, contrary to the Danish and Swedish cases, the German system did not experience significant changes (Thelen 1999: 399). This example shows how political and social circumstances determine the structure of institutions and institutional relationships that shapes the reactions of institutions. A historical aspect is therefore essential to clarify the reactions of institutions and institutional arrangements.

The institutional aspect of historical institutionalism

Historical institutionalism offers two arguments regarding institutions. The first is that institutional factors shape the objectives of political actors. The individual is a satisficer who is motivated by 'satisficing' values expressed in rules, routines or established procedures. Individuals have incomplete and fragmented knowledge, and their attention is limited. Therefore individuals cannot select the best behaviour, comparing all the alternatives that are available for them, nor can they precisely predict the outcome of their decisions (Parsons 1995: 278). Under such 'bounded rationality', individuals behave according to rules, routines or established procedures given by institutions in which they are incorporated. Thus, institutions provide individuals with an interpretation of their interests or a direction of their action through rules, routines or established procedures (Hall and Taylor 1996: 939). In other words, individuals form the goals and preferences of their political activities through education and experiences that are based on the formal or informal rules and systems of institutions in which they are incorporated. For instance, with respect to the Japanese bureaucracy, bureaucrats are promoted within the ministry in which they are first employed, and they accumulate expertise and learn formal and informal rules through on-the-job training. As a result, bureaucrats achieve loyalty to their ministry and the pattern of behaviour and preferences that is unique to their ministry. This pattern of behaviour and preferences constrains their future behaviour. Individuals can behave rationally and strategically. However, institutions limit choices that individuals can select by moulding the patterns of individuals' behaviour and purposes. Thus individuals' rational or strategic behaviour is limited by institutional circumstances.

The other argument offered by historical institutionalism is that institutional relations and interactions structure the distribution of power among political actors (Thelen and Steinmo 1992: 3). For instance, Peter Hall explains the direction of British economic policy by analysing the distribution of power in political economy in terms of institutional relationships. In order to explain the course of the nation's economic policy, he presents five sets of structural variables – the organizations of labour, capital, the state, the political system and the structural position of the country within the international economy – and he argues that these factors interact with each other (Hall 1992: 259–61). He argues that the power of the trade unions peaked in 1974–1975, and from 1976 to 1977 pressure from the financial market was intensified, which urged the Thatcher government to take up policies of monetarism (Hall 1992: 100).

As for the concept of institutions, institutions constrain not only the strategies of individuals but also their goals and preferences through education and experiences. In this context, the concept of institutions includes not only formal organizations but also those that structure the relationship between political actors and constitute education and experiences, such as formal rules, compliance procedures and standard operating practices (Hall 1986: 18–19).

The historical aspect of historical institutionalism

Historical institutionalism emphasizes the origins of institutions and institutional relationships. It 'sees institutions as the legacy of concrete historical process' (Thelen 1999: 382). In other words, institutions preserve a persistent character, which is embedded and developed in specific circumstances (Hall and Taylor 1996: 940–1). Institutions and institutional arrangements adopt a set of paths when they are formed and then evolve along those paths, so a historical aspect is crucial to understanding their reactions and behaviour. Accordingly, institutions and institutional arrangements are path-dependent and evolve by incremental changes, and such path dependency and incremental changes are intelligible in terms of historical analysis (North 1990: 95–6), therefore 'preceding steps in a particular direction induce further movement in the same direction' (Pierson 2000a: 252).

Path dependency originates from the study of economics, and Douglass C. North argues that this concept can be applied to institutions and institutional relationships. According to him, the factors of path dependency, large set-up costs, learning effects, coordination effects and adaptive expectations can be applied to institutions and institutional relationships in a political field (North 1990: 95). Large set-up costs are necessary to create new political institutions. In a political field, actors 'constantly adjust their behaviour in the light of how they expect others to act' (Pierson 2000a: 258). Therefore whether political actors join a new political institution or contribute their resources to a potential institution depends 'to a considerable degree on their confidence that a large number of other people will do the same' (Pierson 2000a: 258). In order to attract a large number of potential members, a new institution requires a high level of resources.

As for learning effects, individual members of institutions are constrained by the rules of the institutions in which they are incorporated, and institutions themselves are constrained by the rules that regulate institutional relationships. They therefore invest in achieving the specialized skills that are required by such rules and develop an identity that is unique to that institution or institutional relationship. As a result, transaction costs from existing rules to hypothetical alternatives become quite high, and the attractiveness of existing institutional arrangements increases. Consequently the constraint of existing rules on individuals and institutions is reproduced or strengthened. Furthermore, such constraints promote coordination between individuals and institutions according to existing formal and informal rules. About adaptive expectations, complexity and opacity, which are intrinsic characteristics of politics, result in individuals and institutions adhering to established mind-sets and understandings presented by existing rules and institutional arrangements (North 1990: 95, Pierson 2000a: 257–60).

Furthermore, Paul Pierson argues that characteristics of political institutions such as the absence or weakness of efficiency-enhancing mechanisms of competition and learning, the shorter time horizons of political actors and the strong status quo bias built into institutions strengthen the path dependency of institutions and institutional relationships in a political field (Pierson 2000a: 257). Contrary to economic markets, 'Political institutions rarely confront a dense environment of competing institutions that will instantly capitalize on inefficient performance' (Pierson 2000a: 261). In economic markets, because of fierce competition, inefficient performances are replaced by more efficient ones. On the other hand, in political fields, such fierce competition does not usually happen, and although a particular set of paths may become less effective, it will not be replaced by a new set immediately.

Once a particular path is consolidated, switching costs from the existing path to alternatives are borne in the short term while the benefits of such change will generally materialize in the long term. Political actors, especially politicians, are generally interested in the short-term consequences of their behaviour; therefore, once a particular path is established, political actors have a strong propensity to choose an existing path (Pierson 2000a: 261). In addition, those who establish institutions or institutional arrangements tend to create rules and arrangements in order to protect the existing institutions or institutional arrangements they have consolidated, which results in the status quo bias of political institutions (Pierson 2000a: 262).

These factors bring about the increase in transaction costs from existing arrangements to new alternatives, which result in path-dependent behaviour. Consequently, 'some original ordering moment triggered particular patterns, and the activity is continuously reproduced even though the original event no longer occurs' (Pierson 2000a: 263).

The path dependency of institutions and institutional arrangements does not mean that they permanently react by following a particular path selected at the first stage: they follow an evolving process. Pierson divided this process into three stages. According to him, institutions and institutional arrangements follow a path-dependent process that consists of three stages in a temporal sequence: the initial critical juncture; the period of reproduction; and the end of the path (Pierson 2000b: 76).

In the initial critical juncture, 'events trigger movement toward a particular "path" or trajectory out of two or more possible ones' (Pierson 2000b: 76), and a particular set of paths is selected. The political setting of the initial stage in which a particular institutional arrangement is selected determines the structure of the arrangement that constitutes its reproduction mechanism. For example, when the Japanese bureaucracy was established in the Meiji era, political circumstances were highly unstable, and those who executed the Meiji Restoration faced strong demands for political participation in the decision-making processes from those who were excluded from the Meiji government. Such political circumstances affected the structure of the Japanese bureaucracy, which had a highly autonomous meritocratic career system that was supposed to protect the vulnerable government by strengthening autonomy and enhancing the competence of administrative organizations. And this structure determined the reproduction mechanism of the Japanese bureaucracy, which reinforced its precedents and the current systems and reproduced its monopolization of information and expertise in policy-making.

In the second stage, the period of reproduction, positive feedback reinforces the path initiated in the first stage. This explanation, however, does not imply that an institution is permanently locked in to a particular path following a self-reinforcing sequence. Institutions experience changes, but they are bounded, incremental changes. The experiential learning processes of an institution take place within its 'pre-established patterns of moral and causal beliefs, behavioral routines, structural capabilities, and resources' (Olsen and Peters 1996: 12) that were determined by the historical background of the institution. Therefore institutions 'tend to refine existing paradigms, technologies, and competences rather than to fundamentally re-examine them' (Olsen and Peters 1996: 9–10). Responding to new information, institutions evolve by continuing such incremental changes in a trial-and-error fashion (Olsen and Peters 1996: 69). If the initial response of an institution to a particular event is inadequate, it searches other means and adapts itself to a new situation. Thus institutions produce continuous incremental changes by learning within an established set of core beliefs, behaviours and structures. Institutions continue such incremental adjustments. Some events, however, may disrupt the reproduction mechanism and trigger institutional breakdown, which leads to the third stage, the end of the path.

In the third stage, a long-lasting equilibrium is dislodged (Pierson 2000b: 76), and a new institutional equilibrium is consolidated. The reproduction mechanism of institutions is disrupted, and institutional breakdown occurs, which triggers a shift to a new institutional equilibrium.

Historical institutionalism is criticized on the ground that its model is too static and has difficulties in explaining political changes. Such criticism places too much emphasis on only one side of path dependency, its reproducing processes.

In Figure 2.1, I illustrate two kinds of reactions of institutions, incremental adjustments in the second stage and institutional innovation in the third stage of the process of path dependency. Criticism of historical institutionalism pays attention only to the second stage of path-dependent processes, the period of reproduction, and overlooks dynamic institutional innovation that causes a disruption of an existing institutional equilibrium and a shift to a new one in the third stage, the end of the path. For example,

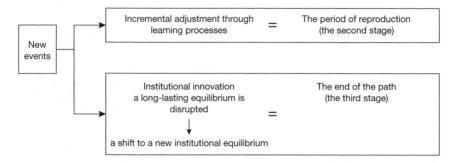

Figure 2.1 Institutional changes in the second and third stages of Pierson's path dependency model

the defeat of the Tokugawa Bakufu in the Boshin War (1868) against the Chōshū and Satsuma *han* (fief) decisively injured the prestige of the Tokugawa Bakufu and the Tokugawa Shogun. The base of the reproduction mechanism of the Tokugawa Bakufu administration system that had been maintained more than 250 years, namely that the Tokugawa Shogun governed the *daimyō* (feudal lords) as their master, was broken down. As a result, the Tokugawa Bakufu was replaced by a new political system, the Meiji government, which had the Emperor as a sovereign.

Not only in the third stage but also in the second stage, institutions are not constantly locked in to the same pattern. They evolve themselves by repeated incremental changes. The mechanism established in the Meiji era, which was based on the bureaucrats' superiority regarding policy-making and the cooperation between bureaucrats and party politicians, adapted to new political circumstances after 1955, namely LDP dominance in the Japanese political process, by establishing close connections with LDP organizations and politicians. Thus path dependency explains 'both continuity and (structured) change' of institutions (Thelen 1999: 384).

Some criticize historical institutionalism by suggesting that its substantive argument is not really different from conventional wisdom. Such criticism, however, overlooks the merits of historical institutionalism in presenting a framework to explain the differences in the reactions of institutions and to understand institutional changes in their evolving processes.

Japanese politics and historical institutionalism

A historical aspect is essential for understanding the Japanese political system. Political institutions, especially the Japanese bureaucracy, have preserved their structure and characteristics since the Meiji era. For instance, the employment system and promotion system of the Japanese bureaucracy (a qualifying examination, a closed career system, a seniority rule and on-the-job training) have hardly been changed since the Meiji era. The first qualifying examination was held in 1894. Since then, the qualifying examination has been held every year (except from 1944 to 1946). Each ministry has used its own discretion in employing applicants who passed the qualifying examination. Furthermore, if the academic knowledge required for the qualifying examinations before and after the Second World War are compared, the requirements have scarcely changed. The Higher Civil Officials' Examination (after 1918, the administrative field of the Higher Examination) was held as a qualifying examination for career officials before the Second World War. After the Second World War, from 1948, the Higher Class of the National Civil Servants' Examination has been held as a qualifying examination. Comparing subjects in the Higher Civil Officials' Examination with subjects in the Higher Class of National Civil Servants' Examination (in the law field, which has mainly supplied career officials for non-technical work), it is apparent that there is no significant difference between them. Although a multiple-choice paper was added to the latter examination, the same subjects – constitutional law, administration law, civil law, international law, criminal law, commercial law and economics – constitute both examinations, so it is clear that both examinations require the same academic knowledge.

After being hired, bureaucrats are promoted in the ministry that first employs them, based on a seniority rule. As for the training system, in the MOF, the training system for newly employed officials has not fundamentally changed since the Meiji era. In the Meiji era, they had an apprentice training in the first year. They were assigned to the Counsellor's Office of the Minister's Secretariat as an apprentice. Their task as an apprentice was to observe senior colleagues' work. While they were reading and copying drafts that their senior colleagues had created, they were supposed to understand the unique atmosphere of the MOF and its way of dealing with tasks. This training system has been maintained to the present. Newly employed officials are assigned as an apprentice to the Secretarial Division or the Overall Coordination Division of the Minister's Secretariat or the Coordination Division of each bureau (Naiseishi Kenkyūkai 1971: 3, Sakakibara 1977: 41).

Such continuity can be understood when viewed within the context of the path dependency of the Japanese bureaucracy. The structure of the Japanese bureaucracy reinforced its path-dependent characteristics. The closed career system and on-the-job training system has allowed bureaucrats to monopolize information and the expertise of policy-making. Through those systems, their monopoly of information and expertise has been reproduced and strengthened, which has brought about further expansion of, and strength to, the existing structure of the Japanese bureaucracy. Early commitment is required of applicants for career official positions because of the competitive qualifying examination system and the closed career system. Bureaucrats have accumulated the knowledge of existing rules and precedents through on-the-job training and the promotion system within one ministry. They have also developed loyalty to their ministry through the closed career system and promotion system. The strict seniority rule and the closed career system have made them cooperate with each other in following existing rules and precedents. Thus early commitment, learning effects, strong loyalty and mutual cooperation have increased the transaction costs for bureaucrats to move from existing rules and precedents to new hypothetical alternatives. For bureaucrats, following the existing rules and precedents has been cost-effective; therefore existing institutional arrangements have been reproduced and strengthened.

Not only the Japanese bureaucracy but also the mechanism of the Japanese political system has maintained path-dependent characteristics. In Japanese politics, a mechanism in which bureaucrats initiated and created policies and cooperated with party politicians in the legislative process was consolidated in the Meiji era. Both bureaucrats and party politicians obtained benefit from this mechanism. Bureaucrats could bring into effect their policy plans and budgets effectively by cooperating with party politicians. Party politicians could concentrate on their election campaigns because bureaucrats undertook policy-making. Thus bureaucrats and party politicians have regarded this mechanism as effective, and as a result it has been reproduced, using repeated incremental adjustments to react to new political circumstances. During the Taishō Democracy (from the 1910s to the beginning of the 1930s), some bureaucrats became members of a political party, the Seiyūkai. Nevertheless, their organizational autonomy and relationships with party politicians regarding policy-making – bureaucrats' superiority in policy-making and cooperation between bureaucrats and party politicians in the legislative process – did not experience significant change.

After the Second World War, in spite of political reforms conducted by the General Headquarters' Office (GHQ), this mechanism survived, adjusting itself incrementally. The GHQ required the system of the Japanese bureaucracy and the cooperation of the bureaucrats to implement its reform plans. Furthermore, after the GHQ executed a massive purge of politicians, military officers and business leaders from their public position, only bureaucrats remained in the Japanese political system. The Japanese bureaucracy succeeded in preserving its organizations, employment system and personnel system. Thus, it preserved its monopoly of expertise and information and secured its autonomous organizations. Bureaucrats strengthened their relationship with political parties in order to put their policies into legislation under the Constitution of 1946, which provided that the Diet should monopolize authority over legislation. Under LDP dominance after 1955, bureaucrats adapted this mechanism to a new political circumstance – the monopoly of the ruling position in the Diet by the LDP – by concentrating on establishing close connections with LDP executives and faction leaders while they maintained their superiority in policy-making and organizational autonomy. Thus, under LDP dominance, the issue settling system (whereby bureaucrats planned policies and negotiated with LDP executives and faction leaders to submit their plans as bills in the Diet, while LDP executives negotiated with opposition parties to let those bills pass the Diet smoothly) was established, and this system dealt with political issues successfully.

The confusion of Japanese politics after 1993 may be described as the third stage of the path dependent process of this mechanism. The end of LDP dominance and the beginning of the era of coalition cabinets impaired the effectiveness of the issue settling system. Close cooperation between LDP executives, faction leaders and bureaucrats could not bring about immediate settlement of political and economic issues, and this eroded the reproduction process of the issue settling system. Nevertheless, cooperation between LDP politicians and bureaucrats was so firmly institutionalized that the mechanism could not adjust itself to a new political circumstance, the era of coalition cabinets, by incremental adjustment. The long-lasting institutional equilibrium was dislodged, and a new institutional equilibrium – a decision-making system that can replace the issue settling system – has not been established. This issue, the mechanism in the third stage after 1993, is examined in detail in Chapter 8, Conclusion.

Bureaucratic autonomy

The mechanism by which bureaucrats initiated and created policies and cooperated with party politicians in the legislative process of those policies has determined the responses of the government to political and economic issues in Japan. This mechanism is based on autonomous bureaucracy. Since the Meiji era, the Japanese bureaucracy has exerted overwhelming power in policy-making by monopolizing information and expertise. Therefore exploring bureaucratic autonomy is essential to any analysis of this mechanism and of the Japanese political system.

The historical aspect of bureaucratic autonomy

Exploring the original institutional setting of the Japanese bureaucracy in the Meiji era is essential to understanding bureaucratic autonomy in Japan because it determined the structure of Japanese bureaucracy that has been inherited by the present bureaucracy. As Bernard S. Silberman describes, the political circumstances following the Meiji Restoration (1868) were characterized as those of high uncertainty. Leaders of the Meiji Restoration had to consolidate an administrative system to replace the Tokugawa Bakufu administration system, which had ruled Japan for more than 250 years. Lower rank *samurai* (military men) of four *han* (feudal clans; Satsuma, Chōshū, Tosa, Hizen) that played a main role in the Meiji Restoration dominated the political process at that time. Therefore former *samurai* and *daimyō* (feudal lords) of other *han* accumulated dissatisfaction with the leaders of the Meiji Restoration. Such dissatisfaction broke out in rebellions, such as the Seinan Rebellion in 1877, and, later, in a political movement, the Jiyūminken undō (the People's Rights Movement), whose members demanded participation in the political process. Under such uncertain political circumstances, the leaders of the Meiji Restoration had to establish 'the organizationally oriented pattern of bureaucratic organization' in which the leaders' status and power were provided in organizational rules and the autonomy of the administrative role was preserved in order to protect the leaders from the volatility of political circumstances (Silberman 1993: 46–64). They established administrative organizations and the system of bureaucracy by Imperial Ordinance, such as the Imperial Ordinance on the Ministry System (1886), and the Imperial Ordinance on Civil Officials Employment (1893). Furthermore, the leaders had to establish some criteria in order to legitimize their leadership and to centralize expertise in policy-making on administrative organizations responding to a political movement that demanded participation in the political process. They established a criterion 'based on the ability to achieve high standards of some measurable characteristics' (Silberman 1993: 51) and the system to keep expertise in policy-making with administrative organizations. They established Tōkyō Imperial University as an institution to educate applicants for career officials, and introduced a closed career system based on a competitive qualifying examination. On the other hand, those who were dissatisfied with the administration of the leaders of the Meiji Restoration formed political parties as opponents of the government. As a result, when political parties were formed, party politicians could not participate in the policy-making process of the government. Thus historical circumstances determined the structure of the Japanese bureaucracy and its relationship with party politicians; in other words, it was highly autonomous and superior to politicians in policy-making. The present Japanese bureaucracy inherited this institutional structure – the closed career system based on a qualifying examination system, the personnel system consisted of a seniority rule and on-the-job training. The institutional relationship between bureaucrats and politicians, in which bureaucrats take initiatives to create policies, has also been inherited by the present Japanese bureaucracy.

The factors of bureaucratic autonomy

The organizational factors of bureaucratic autonomy

An autonomous social entity 'not only acts on its preferences, in addition, its preferences are internally or self-generated' (Nordlinger 1981: 25). The characteristic of the autonomy of a social entity lies in independence in forming and acting on its own preferences.

Considering the above definition of autonomy, I argue that two organizational factors are required for achieving bureaucratic autonomy in the Japanese setting. One is organizational integrity. The preferences of a bureaucratic agency should be self-generated and unique to the agency. In order to have such self-generated unique preferences, bureaucratic organization should be differentiated from other political actors and obtain patterns of preference or behaviour that are unique to the organization. The other is organizational ability. The bureaucratic agency should be capable of forming and implementing policies according to its own preferences.

The Japanese bureaucracy retained organizational integrity and ability from the beginning. Regarding organizational integrity, bureaucrats have achieved patterns of preferences and behaviour that are unique to their ministry through on-the-job training based on the closed career system. Most career officials have been graduates of the Law Faculty of Tōkyō Imperial University, which was established by the government as an institute to educate applicants for bureaucratic careers. Therefore career officials have shared the same academic background. Additionally, their promotion has been based on a strict seniority rule in the ministry that first employed them; this has generated a strong loyalty to their ministry. Thus the employment system and the personnel system of the Japanese bureaucracy has brought about homogeneous and integrated bureaucrats who are loyal to their ministry and who have achieved the patterns of preferences and behaviour unique to their ministry. For instance, career officials of the Ministry of Home Affairs, especially the Local Administration Bureau, had the motivation to be Bokuminkan, local administrative officials who commit themselves to the welfare of subjects in their administrative jurisdiction (Mizutani 1999: 203).[1] With regard to organizational ability, the highly competitive qualifying examination system and closed career system created competent bureaucrats who monopolized the expertise of policy-making.

The relational factors of bureaucratic autonomy

Bureaucratic autonomy should be explored from the viewpoint of not only the structures of bureaucracy but also the relationships of bureaucracy with other political actors. The essential issues of bureaucratic autonomy – to what extent and in what ways bureaucrats realize their preferences regardless of other political actors' preferences – are determined by the relationships between bureaucracy and other political actors such as political parties, interest groups and the electorate.

My argument focuses on the relationship between party politicians and bureaucrats; I therefore limit the argument of the relational factors in this book to the relationship between bureaucrats and party politicians. In democratic countries, the authority of legislation belongs to a parliament that consists of elected politicians. In order to put their preferences into practice, bureaucrats therefore need deference from politicians with regard to policy-making. The questions to what extent and in what ways bureaucrats put their preferences into practice determine the degree and content of the autonomy of bureaucracy. These questions can be investigated by exploring the balance of ability to plan policies and the closeness (cooperation with and infiltration into each other) between bureaucrats and party politicians. For instance, according to Daniel P. Carpenter, in America, the Congress exercises overwhelming power over the bureaucracy. 'Bureaucracies are created, empowered, and founded by the legislature; they owe their existence to the Congress.' (Carpenter 2001a: 14–16). The American bureaucracy has had to construct from scratch its reputation for planning policies. In addition, the Republican Party and the Democratic Party have competed for the position of ruling party in the Congress, and presidents have been elected from both parties. Therefore in order to obtain trust from politicians with regard to its ability to plan policies, the American bureaucracy has constructed multiple and diverse networks that 'enhance the agency's appearance of neutrality' (Carpenter 2001a: 365). Contrary to the American case, the Japanese bureaucracy was created and empowered by Imperial Ordinances that did not require the approval of the Imperial Diet, and bureaucrats obtained their ability and established their autonomy from the beginning. There was therefore no necessity for the Japanese bureaucracy to form multiple and diverse networks in order to achieve bureaucratic autonomy.

Path dependency and the factors of bureaucratic autonomy

In the analysis of the organizational and relational factors of bureaucratic autonomy, the aspect of path dependency, which I argued as a particular characteristic of institutions, is essential. In the previous section, I explained that the structure of the Japanese bureaucracy, which has supported the two organizational factors (organizational integrity and organizational ability), reinforced the path-dependent characteristics of the Japanese bureaucracy.

The relational factor is also path dependent. I argue that two indicators constitute the relational factor of the autonomy of the Japanese bureaucracy: bureaucrats' superiority in policy-making compared to party politicians; and cooperation between bureaucrats and party politicians. I also argue that they are path dependent. The monopoly of expertise and information about policy-making by bureaucrats has been reproduced through the personnel and employment systems of the Japanese bureaucracy. The expertise in and information about policy-making were inherited by junior officials from senior officials within ministries through on-the-job training systems. The meritocratic closed career system, whereby every year each ministry employed new officials from those who had passed the highly competitive qualifying examination, not only maintained the high competence of bureaucrats but also excluded non-bureaucrats from taking positions in ministries, and this enabled the Japanese bureaucrats to keep their expertise and knowledge to themselves. Compared with the American bureaucracy, in which many executives of administrative organizations are politically appointed and private organizations supply human resources capable of planning policies to party politicians and administrative organizations, the Japanese bureaucracy has reproduced a monopoly on information and expertise much more easily. The strict seniority rule and the promotion system (bureaucrats have, in general, been promoted within the ministry that first employed them) brought about bureaucrats' loyalty to their ministry, thus strengthening their unity and the monopoly on expertise. In this way, the superiority in policy-making of bureaucrats over party politicians has been reproduced. As for cooperation between bureaucrats and party politicians, both bureaucrats and party politicians have regarded such cooperation as effective to achieve the benefits they want. By such cooperation bureaucrats have been able to put their plans and budgets into legislation efficiently. Meanwhile, party politicians have been able to concentrate on election campaigning because bureaucrats were undertaking the policy-making. Consequently, cooperation between bureaucrats and party politicians in the legislative process has been reproduced since the Meiji era.

Conclusion

Analysing the temporal sequence of institutions and institutional relationships is important to understand changes in them, and historical institutionalism provides a suitable framework for such an analysis. A historical institutional approach is also the most appropriate to analyse the Japanese political system. The mechanism based on autonomous bureaucracy and cooperation between bureaucrats and party politicians has followed a path-dependent process since its establishment in the Meiji era. Therefore a historical perspective, exploring its original political settings and following its incremental adaptation, is crucial in order to examine whether the mechanism has been dislodged since 1993 and if so, why such a disruption happened. The basis of the mechanism, bureaucratic autonomy, can be analysed by focusing on organizational and relational factors. Therefore in order to explore bureaucratic autonomy, an institutional perspective, examining the institutional structure of bureaucratic organizations and institutional relationships between bureaucrats and politicians, is essential. These institutional structures of the Japanese bureaucracy and institutional relationships between bureaucrats and politicians are historically embedded in the Japanese political system. Their structure and characteristics have been preserved in the present Japanese bureaucracy and its relationship with politicians. Because of such path-dependent characteristics, in order to understand the autonomy of the present Japanese bureaucracy and its relationship with politicians, a historical approach, exploring the political backgrounds in the beginning of the Meiji era and the process of their incremental adjustment, is crucial. A historical institutional approach can appropriately explain the structure of the present Japanese political system and the disruption of the mechanism after 1993.

3 The Japanese political system from the Meiji era to 1993

The Japanese political system under the Meiji Constitution

Political parties under the Meiji Constitution

After the Meiji Revolution, in the 1870s and the 1880s, while the Hanbatsu[1] government controlled the Japanese political system, a political movement that demanded a parliamentary system grew up. The Hanbatsu government could not neglect the surge of such public demands, and in 1882, an Imperial Mandate was promulgated that proclaimed that the Imperial Diet would be established in 1890. Responding to this Mandate, two political parties, Jiyūtō and Rikken Kaishintō, were formed in 1882. The two parties were known as 'Mintō' (People's Parties, as distinct from Government Parties), and they confronted the Hanbatsu government.

Table 3.1 shows the number of seats held by each political party in the First, Second and Third Sessions of the HR. When the first election of the HR was held in July 1890, two parties, Jiyūtō and Rikken Kaishintō, between them obtained a majority in the HR (174 seats out of 300). There were political parties that supported the Hanbatsu government, such as Taiseikai and Chūōkōshōbu, which were called 'Ritō (Government's Party)'; however, they were overwhelmed by the Mintō in the HR.

As Table 3.1 shows, from the beginning the Mintō took the majority of the HR, and they challenged the Hanbatsu government. For instance, in the First Session of the HR, the Mintō strongly opposed the budget of the 1891 fiscal year (83 million yen), and the Hanbatsu government was forced to slash the budget by 6.310 million yen. In the Second Session (opened on 21 November 1891), the confrontation between the Mintō and the Hanbatsu government was so severe that the HR was dissolved on 25 December 1891 and the budget of the 1892 fiscal year was shelved. In February 1893, a bill to impeach the second Itō Cabinet passed the HR. While the Mintō were confronting the Hanbatsu government in the HR, leaders of the Mintō sought a compromise with the Hanbatsu government. For example, Ōkuma Shigenobu, the actual leader of Rikken Kaishintō, obtained the post of

Table 3.1 The House of Representatives of the
Imperial Diet from the First to the
Third Session

The First Session

Political party	Number of seats
Jiyūtō	131
Rikken Kaishintō	43
Taiseikai	85
Others	41
Total	300

The Second Session

Political party	Number of seats
Jiyūtō	90
Rikken Kaishintō	43
Jiyū Club	33
Dokuritsu Club	20
Tomoe Kurabu	17
Taiseikai	46
Tōhoku Dōmeikai	5
Others	5
Vacancy	1
Total	260

The Third Session

Political party	Number of seats
Jiyūtō	92
Rikken Kaishintō	38
Dokuritsu Club	25
Chūōkōshōbu	84
Tōhoku Dōshikai	9
Others	52
Total	300

Source: Shūgiin and Sangiin eds, 1990.

Foreign Minister in the Kuroda Cabinet (1888). Also, the Hanbatsu government realized that it could not ignore the importance of political parties.
Some Hanbatsu politicians, such as Itō Hirobumi, sought to form a political
party in which Hanbatsu politicians could take the initiative, and he formed
Rikken Seiyūkai (Seiyūkai) in 1890.

Although political parties were formed as opponents to the Hanbatsu government in the 1890s, changes in their membership and strategies had occurred by the 1910s. Young enthusiasts who predominated among party members in the 1890s were replaced by those who had successful careers in business, journalism and bureaucracy (Duus 1968: 12–13). For instance, the number of the leaders of Seiyūkai who had experience of business steadily increased from 38 (1900–1904) to 50 (1917–1920), whereas the numbers of those from local politics declined from 77 (1900–1904) to 24 (1917–1920) (Duus 1968: 14).

As the membership of political parties changed, the strategies of political parties also changed. They tried to participate in the decision-making of the government and to obtain posts in administrative organizations by cooperating with the Hanbatsu government. For example, in 1898 the Kenseitō supported the Yamagata Cabinet legislative programme in the Diet in return for the government's financial support for the expansion of Kenseitō's local strength. However, the cooperation broke down after the Diet session was over, and the Yamagata Cabinet issued an Imperial Order that reduced the accessibility of party members to the higher positions of administrative ministries, such as the Ministry of Home Affairs (Duus 1968: 10).

During the Taishō Democracy, from the beginning of the Taishō era (1912) to the 15th May Event[2] in 1932, the president of a ruling party in the HR was generally appointed as the Prime Minister. Table 3.2 shows the names of the Prime Ministers and their political parties from 1906 to 1932. However, the era of party politics lasted for only a short period. After the 15th May Event in 1932, in which the then Prime Minister Inukai Tsuyoshi was assassinated by a group of junior military officials, the era of party cabinets ended and all political parties were dissolved in 1940.

Japanese bureaucracy under the Meiji Constitution

The Japanese bureaucracy was gradually systematized in the 1870s and the 1880s. Immediately after the Meiji Restoration, Chōshi (those recruited by the Hanbatsu government from each *han* (fief)) and Kōshi (those seconded from each *han*) were engaged in the administration of the Hanbatsu government. Since an administration system was not fully organized and a parliamentary system had not been introduced, administrative officials in the early stage of the Meiji era had characteristics both of politicians and of bureaucrats. For instance, influential politicians, such as Yamagata Aritomo, Itō Hirobumi, and Inoue Kaoru, were actually engaged in practical administration as bureaucrats (Sasaki 2000: 105).[3]

The Ordinance of 1869 provided for the organization of an administrative system (Dajōkansei; the administrative system of two offices and six ministries), and classified bureaucrats into three categories, Chokujukan, Sōjukan and Hanjukan (later renamed Chokunin-kan, Sōnin-kan and

Table 3.2 Prime Ministers from 1906 to 1932

No	Prime Minister	Term	Political party
12	Saionji Kinmochi	07.01.1906 to 14.07.1908	Rikken Seiyūkai
13	Katsura Tarō	14.07.1908 to 30.08.1911	
14	Saionji Kinmochi	30.08.1911 to 21.12.1912	Rikken Seiyūkai
15	Katsura Tarō	21.12.1912 to 20.02.1913	
16	Yamamoto Gonnohyōe	20.02.1913 to 16.04.1914	
17	Ōkuma Shigenobu	16.04.1914 to 09.10.1916	
18	Terauchi Masatake	09.10.1916 to 29.09.1918	
19	Hara Kei	29.09.1918 to 04.11.1921[1]	Rikken Seiyūkai
20	Takahashi Korekiyo	13.11.1921 to 12.06.1922	Rikken Seiyūkai
21	Katō Tomosaburō	12.06.1922 to 25.08.1923[2]	
22	Yamamoto Gonnohyōe	02.09.1923 to 07.01.1924	
23	Kiyoura Keigo	07.01.1924 to 11.06.1924	
24	Katō Takaaki	11.06.1924 to 28.01.1926[3]	Kenseikai
25	Wakatsuki Reijirō	30.01.1926 to 20.04.1927	Kenseikai
26	Tanaka Giichi	20.04.1927 to 02.07.1929	Rikken Seiyūkai
27	Hamaguchi Osachi	02.07.1929 to 14.04.1931[4]	Rikken Seiyūkai
28	Wakatsuki Reijirō	14.04.1931 to 13.12.1931	Rikken Seiyūkai
29	Inukai Tsuyoshi	13.12.1931 to 16.05.1932[5]	Rikken Seiyūkai

1 Uchida Yūya (temporary): 4.11.1921–13.11.1921 (Hara Kei was assassinated on 4.11.1921)
2 Uchida Yūya (temporary): 25.8.1923–2.9.1923
3 Wakatsuki Reijirō (temporary): 26.1.1926–30.1.1926
4 Shidehara Kijūrō (temporary): 15.11.1930–9.3.1931
5 Takahashi Korekiyo (temporary): 16.5.1932–26.5.1932 (Inukai Tsuyoshi was assassinated on 15.5.1932)

Han'nin-kan respectively). In 1886, a cabinet system was introduced, and the administrative system was reorganized into 10 ministries: Imperial Household, Foreign Affairs, Home Affairs, Finance, Army, Navy, Justice, Education, Agriculture and Commerce, and Post and Communication. In 1886, the ministry system was systematized and the Administrative Vice Minister, the Secretary, the Directors and the Councillors were inaugurated in each ministry.

As the ministry system was organized, the employment system of career officials changed from free appointment to a qualifying examination system. As explained above, civil officials were classified into 3 categories, Chokunin-kan, Sōnin and Hannin, according to their grades. The classification consisted of 15 grades, and Chokunin-kan, the highest rank (the Administrative Vice Ministers or the Directors General) was above third grade, Sōnin (career officials lower than the Chiefs of a division) was from seventh to fourth grade, and Hannin, the lowest rank, was from fifteenth to eighth grade. At first, officials were freely recruited and appointed by each ministry. However, the Hanbatsu government realized the necessity of a recruiting system of career officials (Sōnin level) based on a qualifying examination, in order always to be able to employ competent officials. In 1886, the Imperial University (later renamed Tōkyō Imperial University) was established in order to educate candidates for career officials, and the first Civil Officials' Examination (Bunkan Shiho Saiyō Shiken) was held in 1888.

After the discontinuation of this examination in 1891, the Civil Officials' Appointment Ordinance (Bunkan Nin'yōrei) of 1893 established a new appointment system based on a new qualifying examination. The first Higher Civil Officials' Examination (Bunkan Nin'yō Kōtō Shiken) was held in 1894, and the examination was subsequently held once a year until 1942. Figure 3.1 shows the appointment system based on the Ordinance of 1893.

As the examination system became fully established, the percentage of career officials who passed the examination increased. The percentage of Directors General of Bureaux who were examination-qualified rapidly increased from 33 per cent in 1910 to 82 per cent in 1920. From 1918 to 1945 every Vice Minister in every ministry was examination-qualified (Spaulding Jr 1971: 41).

The personnel system of career officials was also organized. Since the Higher Civil Officials' Examination was a qualifying examination, each ministry maintained its right to employ new officials from those who passed the examination. Each ministry employed new officials once a year from new university graduates (most of them were graduates of the Law faculty of Tōkyō Imperial University) who passed the examination (a closed-career system). And each ministry also had the right to promote its officials. The

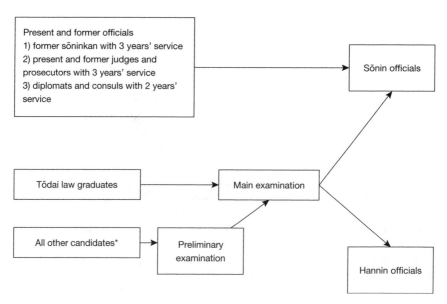

Figure 3.1 Appointment system of the Ordinance of 1893

* After 1918, graduates of Kōtō Gakkō (High Schools) and Daigaku Yoka (Preparatory Course of Private Universities) were exempted from taking the preliminary examination.

Source: Spaulding Jr 1967: 104.

promotion of career officials was generally based on a seniority rule. They were promoted according to the year in which they were first employed. Table 3.3 shows the names of Administrative Vice Ministers of Finance and the years when they were first employed by the MOF. It shows that a seniority rule was strictly followed in the MOF, and the order of the years of employment shows that, in general, a new Administrative Vice Minister would be appointed from officials who were employed later than his predecessor.[4]

As stated above, the structure of the Japanese bureaucracy, its organization (ten ministries and the ministry system) and its personnel system (the qualifying examination system, the closed career system and a

Table 3.3 Administrative Vice Ministers of Finance from 1903 to 1945

Name	Date of appointment	Year of employment
Sakatani Yoshirō	05.12.1903	1884
Wakatsuki Reijirō	08.01.1906	1892
Mizumachi Kesaroku	13.04.1907	1891
Sakurai Tetsutarō	03.06.1908	not known
Wakatsuki Reijirō	17.07.1908	1892
Hashimoto Keizaburō	08.09.1911	1897[1]
Shōda Kazue	21.12.1912	1895
Hamaguchi Osachi	16.04.1914	1895
Sugawara Michitoshi	02.07.1915	1895
Shōda Kazue	09.10.1916	1895
Ichiki Otohiko	16.12.1916	1896
Kanno Katsunosuke	02.10.1918	1896
Nishino Gen	14.06.1922	1902
Ono Giichi	11.06.1924	1903
Den Akira	12.08.1924	1904
Kuroda Hideo	22.03.1927	1905
Kawada Isaoi	04.07.1929	1908
Kuroda Hideo	14.12.1931	1905
Fujii Sadanobu	21.05.1934	1909
Tsushima Juichi	10.07.1934	1912
Kawagoe Takeo	13.03.1936	1910
Kaya Okinori	02.02.1937	1917
Ishiwata Sōtarō	05.06.1937	1916
Ōno Ryūta	06.01.1939	1917
Hirose Toyosaku	22.07.1940	1917
Taniguchi Tsuneji	25.07.1941	1919
Matsukuma Hideo	24.03.1944	1921
Tanaka Yutaka	23.02.1945	not known
Yamagiwa Masamichi	13.04.1945	1925

Notes: Date of appointment: the date of appointment as an Administrative Vice Minister of Finance
Date of employment: the date of first employment as an official of MOF
1 Appointed an assistant officer of the Cabinet Legislation Bureau in 1890

Sources: Ōkurashō Zaisei Shitsu 1998: 454; Hata and Senzenki Kantyōsei kenkyūkai 1981.

seniority rule) was established by the 1900s. As a result of this, the Japanese bureaucracy fulfilled two organizational prerequisites for bureaucratic autonomy: organizational integrity and organizational ability.

With regard to organizational integrity, independent administrative organizations were systematized and the homogeneity of bureaucrats who shared the same quality, academic backgrounds, inclination and behavioural patterns were produced. The administrative organizations (which consisted of ten ministries) and the ministry system were established by an Imperial Ordinance, which did not require the approval of the Imperial Diet. Therefore the Japanese bureaucracy did not owe its establishment and its existence to the Imperial Diet. The personnel system and the employment system accentuated the homogeneity of bureaucrats. Each ministry employed new offcials only from applicants who had passed the Higher Civil Officials' Examination. New officials who passed this examination were almost all graduates of the Law Faculty of Tōkyō Imperial University, and the proportion of graduates of the Law faculty who passed the examination from 1894 to 1943 was about 60 per cent (Hata 1983: 17). Bureaucrats were generally promoted in the ministry that had originally employed them, and they accumulated expertise through on-the-job training. As a result, they achieved the pattern of thinking and behaving that was unique to their ministry. The educational background, the closed career system and the on-the-job training system brought about a unique culture and homogeneity in each ministry.

Concerning organizational ability, the highly competitive examination and the monopolization of expertise gave bureaucrats an outstanding ability to plan policies. The Higher Civil Officials' Examination was a formidable barrier. Almost every year about 90 per cent of applicants failed the examination (Spaulding Jr 1971: 41). Furthermore, a closed career system based on the competitive qualifying examination and on-the-job training enabled bureaucrats to keep the expertise and information of policy-making to themselves, which definitely distinguished bureaucrats from other political actors in terms of their ability to plan policies.

The relationship between politicians and bureaucrats under the Meiji Constitution

Bureaucrats' attitude towards politicians: transcendentalism

When the Imperial Diet was established and the Mintō obtained a majority in the HR, bureaucrats took on an independent attitude towards party politicians. Such an attitude was called 'transcendentalism'. Transcendentalism originated from a speech that Prime Minister Kuroda Kiyotaka presented to prefectural governors in 1890. He addressed them as follows: 'The Government must always steadfastly transcend and stand apart from the political parties and thus follow the path of righteousness' (Banno 1971: 9). Later, the meaning of transcendentalism expanded from the denying of party cabinets to the 'ignoring of the legislature by the executive' (Banno 1971: 31). Tsuzuki Keiroku, an official of the Ministry of Home Affairs (MHA) at that time, insisted in his article 'Transcendentalism' (1892) that government officials were responsible only to the Sovereign and not to the Diet or the people, so that they should execute the 'national interest'. It was an outspoken declaration of the 'absolute superiority of the executive to the legislature' (Banno 1971: 32).

The highly competent self-image and reputation based on a qualifying examination system, a closed-career system and an independent personnel system (as explained in the previous section) constituted the bureaucrats' privileged status and strengthened 'transcendentalism'. Bureaucrats considered that only they themselves represented national interests as the Emperor's servants. Tsuzuki Keiroku openly declared in his essay 'Minseiron' (Civil Government) that the members of the House of Representatives had no expertise to deal with national political issues, and that they followed public opinion blindly (Banno 1971: 34–5).

From confrontation to cooperation – the establishment of the mechanism

From the 1890s to the beginning of the 1900s, the political parties, which were excluded from the decision-making process of the government, and the Hanbatsu government fiercely confronted each other. Bureaucrats took a transcendental attitude towards political parties, and they did not seek party politicians' cooperation in legislation during this period. On the other hand, through severe confrontation between political parties and the Hanbatsu government in the House of Representatives of the Imperial Diet, some Hanbatsu politicians began to accept political parties as an inevitable part of the political process. The establishment of the Seiyūkai in 1900 by Itō Hirobumi, a prominent Hanbatsu politician, reflected such a change in the attitude of Hanbatsu politicians.

The increase of military expenditure due to the Sino-Japanese War (1894–1895) and the Russo-Japanese War (1904–1905) forced the Hanbatsu government to compromise with political parties. Under the Meiji Constitution, the government could execute the previous fiscal year's budget when the House of Representatives did not pass the budget (Article 71 of the Meiji Constitution). Nevertheless, the budget of the previous fiscal year was not enough to cover the increasing military expenditure. It was necessary for the Hanbatsu government to pass the current year's budget. As for political parties, by the 1910s, their membership and strategies had changed. The young enthusiasts who had been the party members in the 1890s were replaced by party members who had successful careers in business, journalism and bureaucracy. Those who had experience in the government as career officials or in a business field took over the party leadership (Duus 1968: 12–15). As the composition of party membership changed, the strategies of political parties also changed from confronting the Hanbatsu government to participating in the decision-making process of the government. On the one hand, bureaucrats had to compromise with party politicians in order to implement the budget that covered increasing military expenditure; on the other hand, party politicians sought to cooperate with bureaucrats in order to participate in the decision-making process of the government and to obtain some positions of ministries. Thus a mechanism was consolidated in which bureaucrats initiated and created policies and cooperated with party politicians to put those policies into legislation.

Politicians' intervention in bureaucrats' personnel matters during the era of party cabinets

Although the Japanese bureaucracy established its independent personnel system, party politicians tried to intervene in the bureaucrats' personnel matters in order to expand their political power. During the Taishō Democracy (from the beginning of the 1910s to the beginning of the 1930s), ruling parties frequently intervened in personnel matters of the Ministry of Home Affairs (MHA). The jurisdiction of the MHA included regulation of election campaigns and the allocation of public works, areas closely related to politicians' interests. The Police and Security Bureau of the MHA had authority in the personnel matters of the Chief of the Police Headquarters in each prefecture, and the Chiefs of Police Headquarters in each prefecture who were responsible for the regulation of election campaigns. The Public Construction Bureau and the governor of each prefecture, who was appointed by the MHA, had the authority to decide on public works and contractors. Therefore ruling parties tried to intervene in the appointments of the Director General of Police and Security Bureau, the Superintendent General of the Metropolitan Police and governors of a prefecture, in order to win the next election (Mizutani 1999: 173). For example, Hara Kei (Seiyūkai) was appointed the Minister of Home Affairs three times – in the First and the Second Saionji Cabinet (1906–1908, 1911–1913) and the First Yamamoto Cabinet (1913–1914) – and he promoted MHA officials who had been ordered to take leave of absence or who had been relegated under anti-Seiyūkai cabinets. Suzuki Kisaburō, Minister of Home Affairs of the Tanaka Cabinet (1927–1929), dismissed or ordered to take leave of absence 17 governors who were regarded as anti-Seiyūkai. Adachi Kenzō, Minister of Home Affairs of the Hamaguchi Cabinet (Minseitō, 1929–1931) gave 12 officials leave of absence, dismissed 16 officials and relegated 39 officials (Mizutani 1999: 191–3). In order to protect their positions or their promotion, some MHA officials voluntarily cooperated with the Seiyūkai and became its members. However, many MHA officials and some governors resisted excessive intervention by the Seiyūkai. They formed anti-Seiyūkai groups in order to protect bureaucrats' autonomy.

The several revisions of the Civil Officials' Appointment Ordinance reflect the conflicts between bureaucrats and party politicians over the MHA's personnel matters. In 1898 the second Yamagata Cabinet revised the Ordinance and abolished free appointment with respect to the posts of Director General of Police and Security and the Superintendent General of the Metropolitan Police, in order to protect these posts from intervention by politicians. In 1913, the First Yamamoto Cabinet revised the Ordinance and increased the number of posts of free appointment. In 1914, after the First Yamamoto Cabinet resigned following a political scandal, the Ordinance was revised again, and free appointment was abolished for the posts of Director General of Police and Security and the Superintendent General of the Metropolitan Police. In 1920, the first substantial party cabinet, the Hara Cabinet (Seiyūkai), revised the Ordinance and the two posts became free appointment posts. However, after the 15th May Event in 1932, which ended the era of party cabinets, the Ordinance was revised yet again and free appointment was abolished for the two posts.

Unlike the MHA, the MOF avoided such interventions. MOF officials were regarded as cautious about having contacts or cooperating with party politicians publicly (Mizutani 1999: 193). The personnel system of the MOF was based on the results of university examinations and the Higher Civil Officials' Examination, and it was operated on a strict seniority rule. In addition, budget compilation was regarded as highly technical. Therefore party politicians lacked a strong motive to intervene in the personnel matters of the MOF (Mizutani 1999: 196).[5]

Although party politicians intervened in the personnel matters of the MHA, such intervention occurred only in a limited period from 1906 to 1932. As the details of the revision of the Civil Officials' Appointment Ordinance illustrates, intervention by politicians faced resistance from bureaucrats determined to protect their autonomy in their personnel matters. Furthermore, the area of such intervention was limited to particular positions in the MHA, such as the governor of each prefecture or the Director General of the Police and Security Bureau, and other ministries succeeded in protecting their independence from party politicians.[6]

Therefore, in general, until 1945 bureaucrats maintained autonomy in their personnel matters. Table 3.4 shows the names of Directors General of the Local Administration Bureau of the MHA and the years when they were first employed. Although politicians' interventions in personnel matters of the MHA were the most frequent and conspicuous compared with other ministries, the appointment of the Director General of the Local Administration Bureau, one of the key posts of the MHA, was generally based on a seniority rule. Table 3.4 shows that, in general, each new Director General of the Local Administration Bureau was appointed from the group of officials who were first employed later than that Director General's predecessor.

Table 3.4 Directors General of the Local Administration Bureau of the MHA from 1902 to 1945

Name	Date of appointment	Year of employment
Yoshihara Saburō	08.02.1902	1889[1]
Tokonami Takejirō	17.01.1906	1890[2]
Mizuno Rentarō	04.09.1911	1893[3]
Yuasa Kurahei	22.12.1912	1898
Kobayashi Ichita	01.06.1913	1898
Watanabe Shōzaburō	28.04.1914	1897
Soeda Keiichirō	17.12.1917	1898
Kobashi Ichita	05.10.1920	1898
Tsukamoto Seiji	09.10.1920	1904
Tsukamoto Seiji	21.04.1921	1904
Ushio Shigenosuke	01.11.1922	1908
Ushio Shigenosuke	16.05.1928	1908
Sagami Shin'ichi	25.05.1928	1911
Tsugita Daizaburō	05.07.1929	1910
Minabe Chōji	15.04.1931	1911
Ōno Rokuichirō	18.12.1931	1913
Kawarada Kakichi	29.01.1932	1910
Yasui Eiji	04.03.1932	1916
Okada Shūzō	15.01.1935	1915
Ōmura Seiichi	13.03.1936	1918
Saka Chiaki	10.02.1937	1919
Hazama Shigeru	17.04.1939	1920
Tomeoka Yukio	24.07.1940	1919
Narita Ichirō	20.10.1941	not known
Furui Yoshimi	15.06.1942	1925
Arai Zentarō	01.07.1943	1923
Nadao Hirokichi	18.04.1944	1924
Irie Seiichirō	09.04.1945	1926

Note: Date of appointment: the date of appointment as Director General of Local Administration Bureau
Year of employment: the year of first being employed by the MHA
1   employed by Provisional Secretariat of the Imperial Diet
2   employed by the MOF
3   employed by the Ministry of Agriculture and Commerce

Source: Hata and Senzenki Kanryōsei Kenyūkai 1981.

Bureaucrats' superiority in policy-making

Bureaucrats monopolized policy-making expertise from the beginning of the Meiji era. Immediately after the Meiji Restoration, many bureaucrats were also politicians and they executed political and economic reforms. Bureaucrats inherited the characteristic of a politician as a policy-maker. Bureaucratic systems were structured to protect the vulnerable government from pressure from outside, especially from political parties, which were demanding political participation. Expertise and information about policy-making was centralized in administrative organizations by adopting a closed career system and an on-the-job training system. The independence of administrative organizations from the Imperial Diet was preserved by the Meiji Constitution, which provided that the Emperor had the authority to determine the organizations of administrations and to appoint and dismiss officials (Article 9). As a result, the Japanese bureaucracy secured its independence from political parties, and their monopoly of expertise and information was reinforced through a closed career system based on a competitive qualifying examination.

On the other hand, party politicians generally lacked experience and expertise in policy-making. When the Imperial Diet was established, political parties were formed as opponents to the Hanbatsu government. Although political parties demanded their participation in policy-making processes, they were excluded from the decision-making process of the government. During the Taishō Democracy, party politics flourished; however, its duration was relatively short (from the beginning of the 1910s to 1932), and the areas in which party politicians were interested – such as public works, public security and police works – were ones that affected the results of elections and were also limited. Many party politicians were regarded as representing the interests of particular influential groups in their constituencies.[7]

In general, party politicians did not commit themselves to initiating policy innovation.[8] For example, bills submitted by the government were usually drafted by bureaucrats and then approved by the cabinet to submit to the Imperial Diet. The proportion of bills submitted by members of the HR that were passed by the Imperial Diet during the Taishō Democracy (from the 30th to the 60th session) remained remarkably low – 6.21 per cent – compared with the proportion of bills submitted by the cabinet (mostly created by bureaucrats) that were passed by the Imperial Diet – 80.22 per cent. Furthermore, this proportion is lower than both that of previous sessions (from the 1st to the 29th sessions, 13.5 per cent) and the average rate (9.26 per cent).

Bureaucrats' superiority in policy-making was also reflected in the appointment of Ministers. It was not unusual for ex-career officials to be appointed as Ministers. For instance, with regard to the past Ministers of Finance from 1885 to 1945, 25 out of 51 Ministers were ex-MOF officials. Following Sakatani Yoshirō (from 7 January 1906 to 14 January 1908), all Ministers of Finance who were ex-MOF officials had had experience in the position of Administrative Vice Minister of Finance.

While bureaucrats prided themselves that they were the only actors who were pursuing the national interest and who had the ability to plan policies, party politicians were criticized as corrupt and representing a particular interest group, *zaibatsu* (big business groups). As the franchise was extended, the cost of election campaigns rapidly increased from 4,976,672 yen in 1915 to 21,910,689 yen in 1924 (Duus 1968: 19). Because of this inflation of election costs, the ability to fundraise became important for party leaders, and they increasingly depended on big business groups – such as the Seiyūkai and Mitsui *zaibatsu*, and the Minseitō and Mitsubishi *zaibatsu* – for political funds. Such dependence on *zaibatsu* caused criticism among the public that political parties represented the interests of *zaibatsu*. First Lieutenant Koga Kiyoshi, one of the leaders of the 15th May Event, accused party politicians: 'Japan now faces a serious circumstance. Politicians should implement reforms. However, they are absorbed in pursuing their own benefits by cooperating with the zaibatsu. Politicians ignore their duties . . .' (Hayashi and Tsuji 1981: 281).

After the 15th May Event in 1932, the era of party cabinets ended and bureaucrats came to the fore of Japanese politics. Gordon Mark Berger argues that the main cause for the decline of party power and prestige in the 1930s was that the ability of party politicians to deal with sophisticated policies, such as the control of the national economy, was widely questioned (Berger 1977: 59). For instance, Minobe Tatsukichi, a distinguished professor of the Law Faculty of Tōkyō Imperial University, was a highly respected intellectual and his theory of the Meiji Constitution supported the growth of party politics from the 1920s to the beginning of the 1930s; however, he publicly questioned the ability of party politicians in an article published in 1934:

> The Imperial Diet has, in general, dealt with political issues, such as the freedom of assembly and speech or the extension of the franchise. . . . Only common sense was required to decide issues which the Imperial Diet has dealt with. Therefore, party politicians, who have had training and obtained common sense through discussion in the Imperial Diet, could manage to decide national policies. . . . However, political and economic circumstances have changed. The control on finance, production, and labour has become the most important national issue. . . . Such economic issues, especially control of economic activities can be decided appropriately only by those who have specialised knowledge not by those who have plain common sense. The deliberation in the Imperial Diet, which consists of several hundreds of politicians who are 'amateur' regarding economic issues, is not an appropriate way to decide such economic issues, and party politicians, who have only plain common sense, are not qualified to deal with those issues.
>
> (Minobe 1934: 10–11)

Although party politicians in general had not committed themselves to planning policies since the Meiji era, the capacity of party politicians to engage in policy-making was publicly questioned when the Japanese economy experienced the serious depression and the financial crisis that began in 1927.

Conclusion: the relationship between politicians and bureaucrats under the Meiji Constitution

From the beginning of the Meiji era the Japanese bureaucracy achieved the two organizational factors of bureaucratic autonomy: organizational integrity and organizational ability. Its structure – the closed career system based on the competitive qualifying examination and the independent personnel system, established in the early Meiji era – enhanced and reproduced its integrity and ability. Japanese bureaucrats under the Meiji Constitution committed themselves to initiating and planning policy innovation, regarding themselves as the only actors to pursue the national interest. Bureaucrats maintained their superiority over party politicians in policy-making. Nevertheless, under the parliamentary system, the cooperation of party politicians was indispensable to putting plans and budgets drafted by bureaucrats into effect. On the other hand, party politicians could not get the opportunity to accumulate experience and expertise to plan policies since political parties were formed in opposition to the government. Accordingly, the mechanism – based on bureaucrats' superiority in policy-making and cooperation between bureaucrats and party politicians in the legislative process of policies created by bureaucrats – was consolidated. Although party politics were put into practice during the Taishō Democracy and party politicians intervened in the personnel matters of bureaucrats, party politicians in general did not commit themselves to initiating and planning policies. Thus the mechanism was maintained under party cabinets during the Taishō Democracy.

The Japanese bureaucracy after the 15th May Event

Immediately after the 15th May Event in 1932, which ended the era of party cabinets, the army did not intend to assume the political power of the parties. As a result, there was 'a power vacuum into which career bureaucrats soon moved' (Spaulding Jr 1970: 53). For example, under the Okada Cabinet (from July 1934 to March 1936), led by the Minister of Home Affairs, Gotō Fumio, who had been a prominent bureaucrat, Committees on Election Campaign Discipline were established in each town, village and prefecture. Through these committees, control by the MHA penetrated into the smallest unit of association in every town and village (Hashikawa 1965: 254). After the 26th February Event[9] in 1936, the army increasingly expanded its power and attempted to permeate civil administration. Rather than the relationship with party politicians, it was the relationship with the army that became crucial to understanding the Japanese bureaucracy from 1936 to the end of the Second World War.

The theme of this book, however, is the relationship between party politicians and bureaucrats. Therefore, in this section I present only a brief description of the Japanese bureaucracy's relationship with the army during this period, which shows the tenacious structure of the Japanese bureaucracy in spite of persistent intervention by the army.

The Japanese bureaucracy from 1936 to the end of the Second World War in 1945 can be described from two aspects: expansion of bureaucratic power and intervention by the army.

With regard to the expansion of bureaucratic power, increasing demand for state control of economic and social activities brought about the penetration of bureaucratic power into those areas. After the war in Manchuria (1931) and in China (from 1937), the necessity of regulating economic and social activities was advocated by the army and bureaucrats to prepare for a total war. To win a total war, a nation is required to devote all kinds of resources, not only military resourses but also economic and social resources. The government's intervention in those areas greatly increased, and this brought about considerable expansion of bureaucratic power. In 1938, the Imperial Diet passed two important laws: the National Mobilization Law (Kokka Sōdōinhō), which provided 'a sweeping delegation of authority to impose economic controls on labour and capital by executive ordinance alone' (Spaulding Jr 1970: 64); and the Electric Power Control Law (Denryoku Kanrihō), which nationalized the electric power industry. The passage of those laws symbolized an expansion of bureaucratic power. Following the National Mobilization Law, 42 ordinances[10] were enacted, which enabled bureaucratic power to penetrate every aspect of economic, social and cultural activities (Shibagaki 1979: 298). According to the Ordinance of Organizations of Key Industries (Jūyō Sangyō Tōseirei), organizations (Tōseikai) were established from 1941 to 1942 in order to form a cartel in each key industry, through which the government regulated key industries. As will be explained later in this chapter, the wide-ranging regulatory administration during this period remained after the Second World War, and this sustained the expansion of bureaucratic power.

The other aspect to be described – the intervention by the army in the civil administrative area – took two forms: attempts to take the leadership regarding national mobilization policies; and attempts to reform administrative organizations.

With respect to the leadership in national mobilization policies, the Army Ministry strongly supported the establishment of the Cabinet Planning Board (CPB) in 1937. After the war with China broke out in July 1937, the CPB was established to plan general policies of mobilization. In the CPB, the appointing of army and navy officers on active duty to staff positions was permitted, which breached the traditional barrier between the civil and military services. The Army attempted to make the CPB the central organization to control national mobilization policies being under the direct control of the Prime Minister. The Army intended to take the leadership in national mobilization policies through this organization. However, not only bureaucrats but also the Navy strongly opposed the Army's intention. As a result, the superiority of the CPB to other ministries was denied. Article 1 of the Ordinance of the Cabinet Planning Board provided that, with respect to important issues presented by other ministers to the cabinet meeting, the CPB could report its opinions through the Prime Minister to the Cabinet. The ordinance gave the CPB only the opportunity to report its opinions, and it did not provide it with authority to supervise other ministries. Although the CPB succeeded in legislating the National Mobilization Law, drafting concrete plans and their implementation were delegated to established ministries, and the CPB did not necessarily take the leadership. For instance, in the process of enacting the Ordinance of Organizations of Key Industries, the CPB fiercely confronted the Ministry of Commerce and Industry (MCI). The CPB insisted on enacting an ordinance regarding each industry, while the MCI insisted on one ordinance which would be applied to all industries. The CPB made a concession to the MCI, and an Ordinance of Organizations of Key Industries that would be applied to all key industries was enacted (Shibagaki 1979: 312).

Concerning attempts at administrative reform, the army attempted to integrate the personnel matters of bureaucrats into a central organization in order to control appointments and promotion of civil officials. In 1936, the Hirota Cabinet (March 1936 to February 1937) put the reform of administrative organizations on its political agenda, and the Ministers of Army and Navy presented 'Guidelines for Reform of Administrative Organizations'. It proposed the establishment of a central organization that would have the authority to decide the personnel matters of bureaucrats. Bureaucrats of every ministry 'were singularly united in adamant opposition to a centralized civilian personnel bureau' (Spaulding Jr 1970: 74). Although six successive cabinets[11] attempted to enact an Ordinance that would establish a Cabinet Personnel Bureau, all attempts failed. The Army's attempt to establish a central personnel organization 'vanished into thin air' (Ide 1974: 158) because of strong opposition from bureaucrats. Indeed, so-called 'revisionist bureaucrats'[12] were 'much more willing than other bureaucrats to act . . . across the line between the civil and military services' (Spaulding Jr 1970: 61) Nevertheless, the relationship between revisionist bureaucrats and army was not necessarily harmonious. Young extremists in the Army's Imperial Way (Kōdō) faction[13] 'put the civil service on the list of their enemies' (Spaulding Jr 1970: 57), and 'by 1935 they no longer regarded revisionist bureaucrats as exceptions to the rule' (Spaulding Jr 1974: 70). At the beginning of 1936, the army attempted to separate the Trade Bureau of the Ministry of Foreign Affairs and to make an independent Trade Ministry. Bureaucrats fiercely opposed this plan. After negotiations between the CPB, the Cabinet Legislative Bureau, the MOF and the MHA, the Cabinet approved a revised plan. The Trade Bureau Chief and more than a hundred officials of the Ministry of Foreign Affairs resigned in protest. As a result, the Trade Ministry Ordinance was withdrawn, the officials then withdrew their resignations and the Army abandoned its plan

(Spaulding Jr 1974: 73). Even revisionist bureaucrats were 'staunchly opposed to appointing non-career men to chokunin positions (career officials' positions)' (Spaulding Jr 1974: 75). Kazami Akira, the Cabinet Secretary of the First Konoe Cabinet, wrote in his memoirs:

> [When he (Konoe) began to revise the Imperial Ordinance of Civil Officials Appointment] four or five revisionist bureaucrats (Kakushin Kanryō) came to see me. I thought they agreed with the revision and came to encourage me. To my surprise, their attitudes were quite opposite. They absolutely opposed the revision and they came to see me to tell their strong opposition.
>
> (Kazami 1950: 153)

The influence of the Army during this period is not deniable, but the failure of the Army's attempts to take the leadership in mobilization policies and to reform administrative organizations highlights the strong resilience of the Japanese bureaucracy.

The activities of the CPB and the revisionist bureaucrats seemed to be conspicuous during this period. However, the strict state control policies executed during this period were not necessarily the innovations of revisionist bureaucrats. Rather, changes of political and economic circumstances pressured the government to take such policies (Spaulding Jr 1970: 60). Political circumstances greatly changed after the outbreak of the war in China in 1937. The Japanese government began to prepare for a total war against the United States or Russia, and in order to make the most of limited resources, changing political, economic and social systems became urgent issues for the Japanese government (Spaulding Jr 1970: 61–2). It can therefore be said that state control of economic and social activities was not necessarily a policy innovation by revisionist bureaucrats. It was planned and implemented by bureaucrats (not always revisionist bureaucrats) as required measures responding to the political and economic circumstances at that time, which demanded preparation for a total war.

Political reforms after the Second World War

After the Second World War, the Supreme Command for the Allied Powers (SCAP) and the General Headquarters' Office (GHQ) executed political, social and economic reforms. The New Constitution was enacted in 1946 as the symbol of the new Japanese political and social system. The Emperor became the symbol of the State and lost his position as Supreme Sovereign.

The New Constitution declares that the Diet has supreme sovereignty of the nation (Article 41), and it monopolizes the legislative authority and the approval of the next year's budget (Articles 41, 83). The leader of a majority party in the Diet is supposed to be appointed Prime Minister by an election in the Diet. The status of bureaucrats changed from that of Emperor's servants to that of public servants (The National Public Service Law, Article 96). The Cabinet and Ministers control civil officials by having the authority to appoint Ministry officials (The National Public Service Law, Article 55).

In spite of such political reforms after the Second World War, continuity can be observed in the political institutions and institutional relationships before and after the Second World War. The following sections examine structural continuity in the Japanese bureaucracy – in its organizations and its personnel system – and in the relationships between politicians and bureaucrats.

The continuity in the Japanese bureaucracy before and after the Second World War

Despite the reform of the civil service system executed by the GHQ, the structure and characteristics of the Japanese bureaucracy before the Second World War remained under the New Constitution.

The GHQ adopted 'an indirect governing style' (Kansetsu Tōchi Hōshiki). Instead of implementing economic, social and political reform by itself, the GHQ decided to govern by using Japanese administrative organizations. The GHQ needed both the expertise and the help of Japanese bureaucrats to implement reform, so 'reform of the bureaucracy itself had to take second place in the scale of priorities' (Stockwin 1999: 106). A division in the GHQ over the principle of occupation was also advantageous to Japanese bureaucrats. The Government Section of the GHQ (GS) advocated thorough reform to achieve complete democratization of Japan; on the other hand, the Military Intelligence of the GHQ (G-2) gave priority to maintaining public order in consideration of the political tension surrounding Japan after the Second World War. When the GS created a list to purge politicians, businessmen, military and civil officials from their positions, this was strongly opposed by the G-2, who insisted that the number and range of civil officials to be purged should be substantially limited (Mastuda 1996: 8–9). As a result, the number of bureaucrats purged from their positions was significantly limited (1,809) as compared to the number of politicians (about 35,000) and military officials (about 167,000) (Mizutani 1999: 302–3). In the Japanese establishment, only bureaucrats remained almost unharmed by the purge.

As for administrative organizations, all ministries, except for the Ministries of Army, Navy and Home Affairs (MHA), survived. The MHA was divided into several organizations, such as the Ministry of Construction, the Prime Minister's Agency and the National Public Safety Commission. However, in 1960, organizations whose jurisdiction was local administration were reintegrated and restored as the Ministry of Home Affairs.

Concerning the personnel system of bureaucrats, the autonomy of each ministry in its personnel matters was hardly damaged by the GHQ's reform. The GHQ attempted to integrate the authority to decide bureaucrats' personnel matters into the National Personnel Authority. However, each ministry succeeded in protecting its actual authority to recruit its new officials independently. Since 1949 the National Civil Servants' Examination has been held once a year, and each ministry has independently employed new officials from those who pass the examination. The majority of career officials has consisted of graduates from Tōkyō University (Tōkyō Imperial University was renamed Tōkyō University after the Second World War). The proportion of graduates of Tōkyō University who were employed by the MOF (Higher Class Officials) from 1949 to 1963 was 83 per cent, which illustrates the fact that in the MOF, graduates of Tōkyō University greatly outnumbered those of other universities (Hata 1983: 54). Thus the closed career system based on a qualifying examination and the university from which most career officials graduated scarcely underwent any changes in spite of reforms conducted by the GHQ. With regard to the promotion of bureaucrats, a seniority rule also remained.

Furthermore, bureaucrats maintained their influence on economic and social activities. The GHQ implemented its policies through the Japanese bureaucracy. Immediately after the Second World War, the Japanese economy was largely destroyed, and Japan lacked capital, infrastructure, energy and facilities to restore its economy. To achieve rapid economic recovery, the government depended on administrative regulation to utilize limited resources. Noguchi Yukio refers to the Japanese economic and social systems after the Second World War as 'the 1940s system', since the strict regulation of economic and social activities introduced in the 1940s remained in place after the Second World War (Noguchi 1995: 234–5). As explained in the previous section, from the end of the 1930s, various regulations were introduced in order to expand the production capacity of military supplies by making the most of limited capital and resources. For instance, the Foreign Exchange Control Law was entirely revised in 1941. The trade in foreign exchange was completely regulated by the government, and the ordinance of the MOF provided the details of regulation. This comprehensive regulation of foreign exchange generally remained after the Second World War. According to the Ordinance of Organization of Key Industries (Jūyō Sangyō Tōseirei), organizations (Tōseikai) were established from 1941 to 1942 in order to form a cartel in each key industry. The government regulated key industries through those organizations. Noguchi Yukio argues that this way of regulation, i.e. through Tōseikai, remained after the Second World War as a way of regulation through organizations of major industries (Noguchi 1995: 40–1). Such extensive regulation of economic and social activity expanded and strengthened the bureaucrats' power.

Despite the reforms executed by the GHQ, the Japanese bureaucracy succeeded in protecting its institutional structure, its organizations and its personnel systems established under the Meiji Constitution. As B. C. Koh describes, 'the old patterns of Japanese bureaucracy' were 'singularly resilient' (Koh 1989: 65) so the two organizational factors of bureaucratic autonomy – organizational integrity, and organizational ability – were hardly damaged. The Japanese bureaucrats retained their high prestige as the most competent actors in the Japanese political system.

The relationship between politicians and bureaucrats

Whereas many military officials and party politicians were accused of responsibility for the Second World War and purged from their public ositions, bureaucrats remained as almost the only actors in the Japanese establishment. In addition, the Japanese bureaucracy succeeded in protecting its autonomous meritocratic personnel and employment systems, which had reinforced their monopoly of expertise in policy-making. Under the Meiji Constitution, bureaucrats were regarded as servants of the Emperor, who represented the state. They were proud of representing national interests as the Emperor's servants. Although the bureaucrats' status changed from that of the Emperor's servants to that of civil servants, bureaucrats still regarded themselves as the only actors to pursue the national interest. The political circumstances surrounding bureaucrats (outlined above) strengthened their self-pride.

Sakakibara Eisuke, an ex-MOF bureaucrat who became known as 'Mr Yen' to the mass media after he served as Vice Minister of Finance for International Affairs, admits in his book, *Nihon wo Enshutsu suru Shin Kanryōzō* (*New Bureaucrats who lead Japan*): '[bureaucrats] sometimes despise party politicians in their heart. Many bureaucrats are confident that it is not party politicians but bureaucrats who are "real statesmen". For bureaucrats, "political neutrality" means "not submitting to unreasonable demands from political parties"....' (Sakakibara 1977: 114). He openly states in this book: 'Bureaucrats actually control Japanese politics. For bureaucrats, deliberation in the Diet and demands from interest groups are nothing but obstacles that bureaucrats have to get over in order to execute "politics in the true sense"' (Sakakibara 1977: 114). 'Transcendentalism', as described by Tsuzuki Keiroku, was inherited by the bureaucrats after the Second World War.

As for party politicians, political parties such as Nihon Jiyūtō, Nihon Shinpotō and Nihon Kyōdōtō were formed at the end of 1945. However, the GHQ purged many politicians in February 1946 and January 1947. In January 1946, the GHQ executed the first purge of politicians, civil and military officials, and business leaders from public service. Many influential senior politicians were purged. As for Nihon Shinpotō, 260 out of 274 members were purged, and for Nihon Jiyūtō, 30 out of 43 members were

purged. The number of purged politicians amounted to 35,000, 16.8 per cent of the total number purged. As a result, the existing political parties were seriously damaged, and politicians who won the first general election of April 1946 were almost all new junior members (Kitaoka 1995: 33–4). Newly elected politicians in the election of 1946 lacked ability and experience in policy-making. On the other hand, as mentioned before, the number of purged bureaucrats was only 1,809 (0.9 per cent) (Mizutani 1999: 302–3). As a result, bureaucrats, who monopolized expertise and information from the GHQ, were in a dominant position in policy-making. One ex-MOF bureaucrat (an official of the Budget Bureau of the MOF at that time) illustrated party politicians' lack of expertise under the Katayama Cabinet (from 24 May 1947 to 10 March 1948): 'bureaucrats attended the Cabinet Meeting', and issues were settled 'by negotiations between bureaucrats who attended the Cabinet Meeting' (Mizutani 1999: 304). Under the Ashida Cabinet (from 10 March 1948 to 15 October 1948), bureaucrats still attended and took the lead in discussion at Cabinet meetings (Mizutani 1999: 305).

Furthermore, bureaucrats expanded their influence on political parties by supplying ex-bureaucrats as candidates for general elections. The purge of many politicians brought about a serious shortage of professional politicians. Such a shortage resulted in a rapid increase in the number of ex-bureaucrats in political parties (especially the Jiyūtō). The Prime Minister Yoshida Shigeru vigorously recruited bureaucrats as candidates of the Jiyūtō, and appointed them Ministers or party executives. For example, Satō Eisaku (an ex-bureaucrat of the Ministry of Transportation) was appointed Chief Cabinet Secretary of the second Yoshida Cabinet (1948–1949), Ikeda Hayato (an ex-bureaucrat of the MOF) was appointed Minister of Finance of the third Yoshida Cabinet and the Minister of International Trade and Industry of the fourth Yoshida Cabinet (1952–1953).

The purge of 1946 and 1947 seriously damaged political parties, but scarcely damaged bureaucrats. They maintained self-confidence as the only actors representing national interests, and they succeeded in protecting their organizations and their autonomy in personnel matters, which had strengthened their high prestige and transcendental attitudes. As a result, from immediately after the Second World War to the 1950s, bureaucrats were in a dominant position in the Japanese political system.

The Japanese political system under LDP dominance

After defeat in the Second World War, political parties were restored. In November 1945, the Nihon Shakaitō, the Nihon Jiyūtō and the Nihon Shinpotō were established, and in December 1945 the Nihon Kyōdōtō was formed. Three conservative parties, the Nihon Jiyūtō, the Nihon Shinpotō and the Nihon Kyōdōtō, were integrated into two parties, the Jiyūtō (Liberal Party) and the Minshutō (Democratic Party) by 1955. In 1951, the Nihon

Shakaitō divided into two groups, a left-wing group and a right-wing group. Nevertheless, they increased their number of seats in the HR,[14] and, in October 1955, they merged into one party, the Nihon Shakaitō (Japan Socialist Party, JSP). Competing with this consolidation, two conservative parties, the Jiyūtō and the Minshutō were integrated into the Jiyūminshutō (Liberal Democratic Party, LDP) in November 1955. When the LDP was consolidated, the number of its seats in the HR and the House of Councillors (HC) were 299 (out of 467) and 118 (out of 250) respectively. Subsequently, the LDP kept a majority in the Diet until 1993. Table 3.5 shows the number of seats which the LDP won in general elections from 1958 to 1993.

LDP dominance in the Diet had significant effects on the structure of political institutions and institutional relationships, especially in the LDP and in the relationship between LDP politicians and bureaucrats.

The structure of the LDP under LDP dominance

The personnel system of the LDP

Although a seniority rule has been applied to personnel matters in the LDP since its foundation in 1955, there were several exceptions. Some junior members of the LDP were appointed Ministers or LDP executives in the 1950s, for instance, the Minister of Posts and Telecommunications, Tanaka Kakuei, in the First Kishi Cabinet (July 1957), the Secretary General of the LDP, Fukuda Takeo, in the second Kishi Cabinet (January 1959) and the Cabinet Secretary, Ōhira Masayoshi, in the First Ikeda Cabinet (July

Table 3.5 The number of seats held by the LDP after the general elections from 1958 to 1993

Number of election	Date of general election	Number of seats held by LDP	Total seats in HR
28	22.05.1958	298	467
29	20.11.1960	300	467
30	21.11.1963	294	467
31	29.01.1967	280	486
32	27.12.1969	300	486
33	10.12.1972	284	491
34	05.12.1976	260	511
35	07.10.1979	258	511
36	22.06.1980	287	511
37	18.12.1983	267	511
38	06.07.1986	310	512
39	18.02.1990	286	512
40	18.07.1993	228	511

Source: Asano 1997: 285–9.

1960). However, as the LDP obtained a stable position as a ruling party, a seniority rule was established in the personnel system of the LDP.[15] Figure 3.2 illustrates the distribution of LDP members according to the times of winning an election after the general elections of December 1976 and October 1979. It shows that the number of LDP members who won an election enough times to be appointed as a Minister (about five times) became stable. Thus the condition for adopting a seniority rule was completed, and LDP politicians who have won elections five or six times have been constantly appointed as ministers.

In addition to a seniority rule, the rule of allocating posts in proportion to factions' power (Habatsu Kinkō Jinji) was also established as the personnel system of the LDP.[16] Table 3.6, Table 3.7 and Figure 3.3 illustrate that ministerial posts were allocated to factions according to the number of their members after the 1980s. Table 3.6 shows the difference in each faction between the proportion of factional members and the proportion of ministerial posts with regard to the third Ikeda Cabinet (from 9 December 1963 to 8 November 1969) and the second Ōhira Cabinet (from 9 November 1979 to 16 July 1980). Both Table 3.6 and Table 3.7 show the absolute values of the difference between the proportion of the number of ministers' posts and the proportion of the number of members with respect to each faction, and the total of those values. The less the total value, the more the posts are allocated in proportion to the number of factional members. Compared with the third Ikeda Cabinet (total value 46.97), the posts of the second Ōhira Cabinet (total value 12.91) were allocated much more in proportion to each faction's power. Table 3.7 shows the values of the total in comparison with the following cabinets,

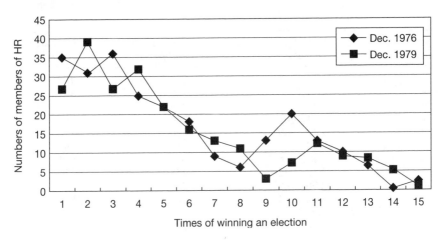

Figure 3.2 Distribution of LDP members according to times of winning an election

Table 3.6 The difference between the proportion of the number of factional members and the proportion of the number of ministerial posts

The Third Ikeda Cabinet

Name of faction	A	B	C	D	E
Ikeda	4	60	14.49	23.53	9.04
Satō	3	91	21.98	17.65	4.33
Ōno	3	40	9.66	17.65	7.99
Kawashima	2	20	6.28	11.76	5.58
Kōno	2	67	16.18	11.76	4.42
Fujiyama	1	34	8.21	5.88	2.33
Ishii	1	28	6.76	5.88	0.88
Miki	1	49	11.03	5.88	5.15
Kishi	0	5	1.20	0	1.20
Fukuda	0	20	4.83	0	4.83
Total	17	414			45.75

The Second Ōhira Cabinet

Name of faction	A	B	C	D	E
Ōhira	4	70	20.90	22.22	1.32
Tanaka	4	85	25.40	22.22	3.18
Fukuda	4	75	22.39	22.22	0.17
Nakasone	3	48	14.33	16.66	2.33
Miki	2	42	12.54	11.11	1.43
Mizuta	0	5	1.49	0	1.49
Nakagawa	0	10	2.99	0	2.99
Total	17	335			12.91

A: number of ministerial posts (except posts that were allocated to LDP members who did not belong to any faction)
B: number of members (total of the House of Representatives and the House of Councillors)
C: proportion of factional members (%) = number of its members divided by total number of LDP members × 100
D: proportion of ministerial posts (%) = number of its ministerial posts divided by total number of ministerial posts × 100
E: difference between the proportion of factional members and proportion of ministerial posts = |C–D|

Source: Kitaoka 1995, Satō and Matsuzaki 1986.

and Figure 3.3 illustrates the data in Table 3.7. The figure indicates that, by the end of the 1970s, this rule – allocating posts in proportion to the power of each faction – was established in the LDP. (Although the total value of the third Nakasone Cabinet reaches 23.5, the difference was caused by allocating 8 out of 19 ministers' posts to the Tanaka faction, which was the largest faction at that time and played a crucial role in establishing the Nakasone Cabinet.)

Table 3.7 The totals of the difference between the proportion of the number of factional members and the proportion of the number of ministerial posts

Name of cabinet	Date of formation	Total value
3rd Ikeda	09.12.1963	46.97
2nd Satō	17.02.1967	43.35
1st Tanaka	07.07.1972	35.87
2nd Tanaka	22.12.1972	37.90
Miki	09.12.1974	26.18
Fukuda	24.12.1976	28.69
2nd Ōhira	09.11.1979	12.91
Suzuki	17.07.1980	18.06
2nd Nakasone	27.12.1983	5.40
3rd Nakasone	22.07.1986	23.50
Takeshita	06.11.1987	11.36
2nd Kaifu	28.02.1990	12.15

Total value: total of the difference of each faction between the proportion of factional members and the proportion of ministerial posts = total of E

E = difference between the proportion of factional members and the proportion of ministerial posts = |C–D|

C: proportion of factional members (%) = number of its members divided by total number of LDP members × 100

D: proportion of ministerial posts (%) = number of its ministerial posts divided by total number of ministerial posts × 100

Sources: Kitaoka 1995, Satō and Matsuzaki 1986, Ishikawa 1984.

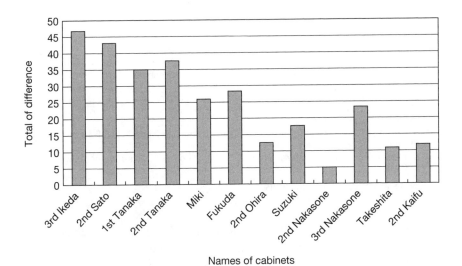

Figure 3.3 The totals of the difference between the proportion of the number of factional members and the proportion of the number of ministerial posts

Sources: Kitaoka 1995, Satō and Matsuzaki 1986, Ishikawa 1984.

The decision-making system of the LDP

Under LDP dominance, the decision-making system of the LDP was systematized. Figure 3.4 shows the organizations of the LDP. Key organizations of the decision-making process of the LDP are the Policy Affairs Research Council (PARC) and the Executive Council (EC). The PARC has Divisions which correspond to ministries (for example, the Agriculture and Forestry Division corresponds to the Ministry of Agriculture, Forestry and Fisheries). In the decision-making process of the LDP, each division of the PARC scrutinizes drafts of bills or discusses political and economic issues, and then its decisions are examined at the general meeting of the PARC. Finally, the EC approves them.

As the decision-making system of the LDP was systematized, the importance of LDP organizations in the decision-making process of the government increased. Members of each division of the PARC, the so-called

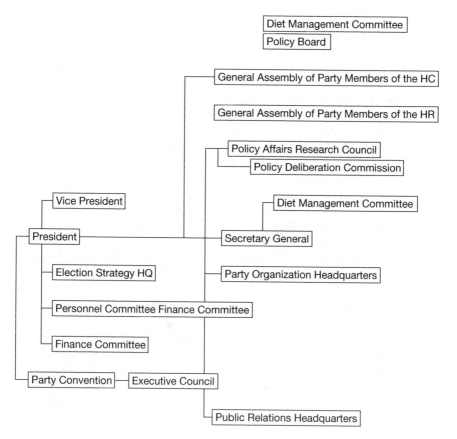

Figure 3.4 Organizations of the LDP

Source: Satō and Matsuzaki 1986: 189

'zoku', strengthened connections with a ministry that corresponded to their division. For instance, members of the Agriculture and Forestry Division of the PARC, Nōrin-zoku, had close connections with bureaucrats at the Ministry of Agriculture, Forestry and Fisheries. Although the zoku, especially the leaders of the zoku, accumulated expertise and information about a policy area in their division, they did not necessarily confront bureaucrats in policy-making. Rather, they exerted power in the process of budget compilation by cooperating with bureaucrats. The power of the zoku in policy-making increased, and the importance of LDP organizations in the decision-making process of the government was enhanced.

In addition, the separation of the management of the LDP from that of the Cabinet strengthened the independent power of LDP organizations. After Prime Minister Tanaka Kakuei resigned in December 1974, due to the Lockheed Scandal, the Vice President of the LDP, Shiina Etsusaburō, recommended Miki Takeo, the leader of the Miki faction, as the next LDP President, and other leaders of factions agreed to accept this recommendation. They also agreed that the Secretary General of the LDP should not be appointed from the Miki faction. Before the Miki Cabinet, the Secretary General was appointed from a faction to which the LDP President belonged (Sōsaibatsu), except for the third Ikeda reshuffled Cabinet and the First Satō after the third reshuffled Cabinet (in both cabinets, the Chairs of the PARC were appointed from Sōsai batsu). Since the Miki Cabinet, the Secretary General has been appointed from non-Sōsai batsu, except for the First Ōhira Cabinet (established on 7 December 1978). Although the Prime Minister was the LDP President at the same time under LDP dominance, the position of Secretary General was the key one regarding the management of the LDP. As it became a tacit agreement after the Miki Cabinet to appoint the Secretary General from non-Sōsai batsu, control by the LDP President in the management of the LDP has become weaker, and the management of the LDP has become more independent from the management of the Cabinet.

Furthermore, after the Lockheed Scandal, the Tanaka faction – although the largest faction in the LDP – could not put forward a candidate for LDP President. Instead of achieving the position of LDP President, the Tanaka faction obtained executive positions of the LDP, such as Vice LDP President, Secretary General, Chair of the EC, and Chair of the PARC. Table 3.8 shows the important positions of the LDP that the Tanaka (later the Takeshita) faction attained from the Fukuda Cabinet to the Miyazawa Cabinet. It highlights the fact that the Tanaka faction (later the Takeshita faction) almost monopolized the position of Secretary General. When the Tanaka faction did not attain the post of Secretary General, it attained the post of Vice LDP President, the Chair of the EC or the Chair of the PARC instead. Such control by the Tanaka faction in the management of the LDP accelerated the independence of LDP organizations from the Prime Minister and the Cabinet.

Table 3.8 The positions attained by the Tanaka faction from the Fukuda Cabinet to the Miyazawa Cabinet

Name of the Cabinet	Positions attained by the Tanaka (lager Takeshita) faction
Fukuda (Fukuda)	Chair of the EC: Ezaki Masumi (Tanaka)
Fukuda, reshuffled (Fukuda)	Chair of the PARC: Ezaki Masumi (Tanaka)
First Ōhira (Ōhira)	Vice LDP President: Nishimura Eiichi (Tanaka)
Second Ōhira (Ōhira)	Vice LDP President: Nishimura Eiichi (Tanaka)
Suzuki (Suzuki)	Vice LDP President: Nishimura Eiichi (Tanaka)
Suzuki, reshuffled (Suzuki)	Secretary General: Nikaidō Susumu (Tanaka)
First Nakasone (Nakasone)	Secretary General: Nikaidō Susumu (Tanaka)
Second Nakasone (Nakasone)	Vice LDP President: Nikaidō Susumu (Tanaka)
Second Nakasone, reshuffled (Nakasone)	Vice LDP President: Nikaidō Susumu (Tanaka) Secretary General: Kanemaru Shin (Tanaka)
Third Nakasone (Nakasone)	Secretary General: Takeshita Noboru (Tanaka)
Takeshita (Takeshita)	None (the LDP President was Takeshita, the leader of the Takeshita faction)
Uno (Nakasone)	Secretary General: Hashimoto Ryūtarō (Takeshita)
First Kaifu (Kōmoto)	Secretary General: Ozawa Ichirō (Takeshita)
Second Kaifu (Kōmoto)	Secretary General: Ozawa Ichirō (Takeshita)
Miyazawa (Miyazawa)	Vice LDP President: Kanemaru Shin (Takeshita); Secretary General: Watanuki Tamisuke (Takeshita)

Source: Kitaoka 1995: 285–95.

Under LDP dominance, the decision-making process was systematized, and the LDP organization increased its influence on policy-making and its independence from both Prime Minster and Cabinet. Consequently, the system that is called 'Yotō Shinsa' (the scrutinizing of bills by the LDP) became a usual practice. In this system, every bill submitted by the government to the Diet – including the draft budget – was scrutinized and approved by LDP organizations before being discussed in the Cabinet meeting. No substantial change was permitted to the decisions of LDP organizations in the Cabinet meeting. Furthermore, because of the hegemony of the LDP in the Diet, the decisions of LDP organizations were legislated in the Diet, although minor revisions were sometimes made in the process of bargaining with opposition parties. Therefore the government's policies and the legislation in the Diet were actually decided at the level of the PARC and the EC.

Factions

Factions were formed in the process of an LDP Presidential election. Kitaoka Shin'ichi argues that factions were established after the LDP Presidential election of 1956 (Kitaoka 1995: 73–4). During the presidential election of 1956, 11 groups were integrated into 8 factions (Kishi, Kōno, Ishibashi, Ikeda, Satō, Ōno, Miki-Matsumura, Ishii). Out of them, 5 factions (Takeshita (ex-Satō), Miyazawa (ex-Ikeda), Abe (ex-Kishi), Nakasone (ex-Kōno) and Kōmoto (ex-Miki-Matsumura)) remained until the Miyazawa Cabinet in 1993.

Satō Seizaburō and Matsuzaki Tetsuhisa argue that factions have four main functions: supporting an election campaign; giving financial support; dealing with demands from members' constituencies; and allocating the posts of a Cabinet and of LDP organizations (Satō and Matsuzaki 1986: 55–66). Regarding the first function, supporting election campaigns, under the 'multiple seats middle-sized constituencies' election system, more than two LDP candidates stood for election in most constituencies. Since these LDP candidates would be competing against each other, they could not rely on LDP organizations to help with their election campaigns. However, factions also sought new members in order to expand their influence and to win LDP Presidential elections, so factions were constantly recruiting new members as their candidates and supporting their election campaigns.

Second, with regard to financial support, factions collected political funds by receiving donations from business groups or interest groups, and they distributed these to their members.

Third, factions supported their members by dealing with demands from their constituencies. Factions allocated their members to Divisions of the PARC or the Committees of the Diet, and let them negotiate with bureaucrats in order to deal with such demands. For example, the Tanaka faction, which had more than 100 members, was called 'a general hospital' since it could deal with various kinds of demands by allocating its members to almost all Divisions of the PARC and the Committees of the Diet. The prominent ability of the Tanaka faction to sort out demands from constituencies was regarded as the source of its strong power in the LDP (Satō and Matsuzaki 1986: 61–2).

Finally, factions also played a crucial role in allocating the posts in a Cabinet and in LDP organizations. As explained in the previous section, the posts of Ministers and LDP executives were allocated to factions in proportion to the number of factional members. Each faction recommended its members as candidates for the posts, and then the Prime Minister (the President of LDP) appointed Cabinet members and LDP executives according to factions' recommendation. Therefore in order to obtain a post of a Minister or an executive of the LDP, LDP members, in general, had to belong to a faction.

As factions were organized, controls by faction executives over faction members were tightened. When factions were first formed in the 1950s and the 1960s, they were only gatherings of LDP members. However, as factions were integrated into five major factions and the number of their members increased, they gradually strengthened their organizations. Each faction was organized in exactly the same way as the LDP. For example, for Keiseikai (the Takeshita faction), the President of Keiseikai directed the Secretary General, and the Secretary General supervised four bureaux (Secretariat, Policy Affairs, General Affairs, and Public Relations). The Committee of Top Executives decided the line of the administration and activities of Keiseikai (Iseri 1988: 34).

In 1983, the Tanaka faction appointed Ozawa Tatsuo as its first Director General, and other factions also appointed their Directors General one after another (Iseri 1988: 24–5). After the LDP presidential election of 1987, the Directors General decided to form a Committee of Directors General of Factions (Kakuha Jimusōchō Kaigi) and to have regular meetings in order to discuss not only each faction's activity but also important political issues. For example, in August 1988 the Committee agreed that all factions would cooperate with each other to bring about the introduction of the consumption tax system (Ishikawa and Hirose 1989: 210–11), and each faction adopted a resolution that appealed to the members of each faction to unite and devote themselves to getting the Consumption Tax Bill passed. Thus factions were organized, and they established systems to control their members.

Under LDP dominance, the personnel system was systematized. Each faction gathered its members by giving support and benefits, and controlled them through its organization. Accordingly, the LDP's management system, by which LDP members are controlled through their factions, was established under LDP dominance. As for LDP organizations, the decision-making system of the LDP was systematized, and LDP organizations established unshakable positions in the decision-making process of the government and the Diet.

The relationship between politicians and bureaucrats

At the beginning of LDP dominance, the LDP attempted to reform administrative organizations, especially the MOF, in order to expand their power. All attempts failed. The Third Hatoyama Cabinet (from 22 November 1955 to 23 December 1956) presented an administrative reform plan, which included the transfer of the Budget Bureau from the MOF to the Prime Minister's Office. The Third Administrative System Research Council discussed this plan, but it did not pass the Diet. The Second Ikeda Cabinet (from 8 December 1960 to 18 July 1963) created a plan in which the Budget Bureau of the MOF would be transferred to the cabinet as the Fiscal Bureau or the Fiscal Agency. This plan also failed to pass the Diet.

As the Japanese economy rapidly recovered in the 1960s, LDP politicians found that it was more beneficial for them to cooperate with bureaucrats than to confront them. Rapid economic development, for instance in the car manufacturing industry or the electrical appliance industry, resulted in a rapid increase in budget surplus. The LDP distributed this surplus to less competitive industries, such as the agricultural industry, or to rural areas by allocating the surplus as subsidies, public works or grants in return for receiving their support. LDP politicians cooperated with bureaucrats in budget compilation to obtain such subsidies or grants.

As explained in the previous section, the decision-making process of the LDP was systematized and the importance of LDP organizations in the decision-making process of the government increased under LDP dominance. As the importance of deliberation in Divisions of the PARC increased, LDP politicians accumulated information and expertise through their activities in Divisions of the PARC. Such politicians (zoku) represent the benefits of particular interest groups. For example, LDP members of the Agriculture and Forestry division of the PARC are called Nōrin-zoku and they represent the interests of farmers and the Federation of Agricultural Cooperative Associations (Nōkyō). The increase of the power of zoku, however, did not necessarily result in the confrontation between zoku and bureaucrats nor the decline in the influence of bureaucrats. In the process of becoming zoku executives, LDP politicians experienced the positions of Parliamentary Vice Minister or Chair or Vice Chair of a division of the PARC and accumulated expertise and information in a specific policy area. Such a background did not necessarily bring about their independence from bureaucrats in policy-making. An LDP politician, when appointed Parliamentary Vice Minister or executive of a division of the PARC, accumulated expertise and information through contacts with bureaucrats. LDP politicians established close connections with bureaucrats and received information and expertise through those connections.[17]

Bureaucrats established close connections with zoku members, maintaining a position as the only supplier of information and expertise to them. As a result, zoku members shared the same purpose and value as bureaucrats in their policy areas. Consequently, the more LDP politicians accumulated expertise and information as executives of the zoku, the closer became their relationship with bureaucrats, and 'it is unlikely that they have come to a position sharply opposed to bureaucrats' (Katō 1997: 106). For instance, executives of the Tax System Research Council of the LDP (LDP TSRC), such as the Chair, the Vice Chair and the Director General, are regarded as experts in tax matters. They consist of ex-MOF officials, ex-Ministry of Home Affairs (MHA) officials[18] and long-term members of the LDP TSRC. MOF officials have frequent contacts with these executives of the LDP TSRC, and meetings of the executives (chairs and vice-chairs) of the LDP TSRC (Sei-fuku Kaichō Kaigi) have actually made the LDP TSRC decisions. When representatives of business groups requested a 'zero-tax rate' for tax-free transactions in the consumption tax, the MOF strongly opposed it. The MOF submitted its opinion to the LDP TSRC, and the LDP TSRC Subcommittee Vice Chair, Murayama Tatsuo, stated at a press conference that it was not possible to adopt a zero-tax rate system (*Nihon Keizai Shinbun*, 25 May 1988).

While LDP politicians needed bureaucrats to plan policies, it was crucial for bureaucrats to negotiate with LDP organizations in order to implement their policies. Under LDP dominance, without the approval of LDP organizations, drafts of bills could not be submitted to the Cabinet meeting. The decisions of LDP organizations were actually the decisions of the government and their policies were not legislated without the consent of LDP organizations. Therefore bureaucrats vigorously participated in the decision-making process of the LDP. Bureaucrats attended discussions in Divisions of the PARC and cooperated or negotiated with LDP executives. Executives of Divisions of the PARC, leaders of the zoku and bureaucrats informally negotiated with each other and made substantial decisions about important issues (Satō and Matsuzaki 1986: 93). For instance, bureaucrats of the Ministry of Agriculture, Forestry and Fisheries cooperated with Nōrin-zoku (LDP politicians who are members of the Agriculture and Forestry Division of the PARC). Thus LDP politicians and bureaucrats formed close cooperation, and became 'interdependent participants' (Koh 1989: 218) in policy-making processes.

As for the relationship between LDP politicians and bureaucrats, J. Mark Ramseyer and Frances McCall Rosenbluth argue that a principal-agent relationship is observed in the relationship between LDP leaders (principals) and bureaucrats (agents) (Ramseyer and Rosenbluth: 1993: 6). They argue that LDP leaders monitor bureaucrats' behaviour and prevent bureaucrats' deviation from the preferences of LDP leaders by retaining a veto over what bureaucrats do, by controlling bureaucrats' promotion, by obtaining information by encouraging constituents who are dissatisfied with bureaucrats and by encouraging competition among ministries and controlling bureaucrats' post-ministerial posts (Ramseyer and Rosenbluth 1993: 107–9). LDP leaders punish bureaucrats who deviate from their preferences by manipulating the above devices.

The application of the principal-agent model to Japanese politics, however, oversimplifies actual Japanese political processes. Applying the principal-agent model to the Japanese political processes fails to consider the effects of conflicts and cooperation within and between voters, LDP leaders, LDP backbenchers and bureaucrats on policy-making processes. For instance, LDP leaders and LDP backbenchers are divided according to their factions, and factions compete and cooperate with each other. Bureaucrats also compete and cooperate between ministries over their ministry's jurisdiction and authority. LDP zoku and the corresponding ministry's bureaucrats cooperate with each other and compete with other

LDP zoku and ministries. It is not appropriate to understand LDP leaders as principals because they are not coherent actors. The above complicated interactions among and between LDP leaders and bureaucrats cannot be comprehended as a principal-agent relationship.[19] This model also overlooks the effects of third parties, such as interest groups, on the policy-making processes.

The relationship between LDP politicians and bureaucrats is not that the one controls the other, such as that implied by a principal-agent relationship. It is mutual cooperation and dependence. LDP politicians have to rely on bureaucrats regarding policy-making; on the other hand, bureaucrats need party politicians to put their plans into legislation. Such mutual dependence between bureaucrats and politicians brings about close cooperation between them not only in formal processes in LDP organizations, such as the EC and the PARC, but also in informal processes. Bureaucrats' frequent informal consultation with LDP politicians, however, does not mean that the relationship between them is a principal-agent relationship. Rather, it builds a coalition, or constructs 'a broad consensus in which all interests that "need to know" were consulted' (Wright 2002: 370). Sometimes, it is necessary for bureaucrats to compromise with LDP politicians to put their plans into legislation because of such mutual dependence. As a result, the indirect influence of politicians on bureaucrats' policy-making cannot be dismissed, and some policy choices may be precluded. Nevertheless, such a situation does not justify the application of the principal-agent model to the relationship between LDP politicians and bureaucrats. Rather, 'their shared interest, and the mutual dependence of their relationship' (Wright 2002: 373) should be emphasized.

Maurice Wright explores the relationship between bureaucrats and LDP politicians in the process of budget compilation, and rejects 'the polarities of bureaucrats versus politicians' (Wright 2002: 372). Although his analysis is limited to the process of budget compilation, he develops the same argument explained above, mutual dependence based on shared interests between LDP politicians and bureaucrats. Although formal structures and arrangements exist that involve LDP politicians and bureaucrats, such formal procedures are merely ceremonial. Informal procedures, he argues, perform more substantial functions to advance cooperation and coordination between the two (Wright 2002: 372-3).

In addition, he emphasizes that frequent meetings and consultations do not necessarily mean that LDP politicians use such procedures to force their preferences upon bureaucrats. Influence and pressure are exerted by both sides in such informal procedures in order to bring about mutual benefits and expectations.

Indeed, as explained in this section, bureaucrats systematically consulted and negotiated with LDP politicians before and after discussions at LDP organizations. Therefore it cannot be denied that LDP politicians exert indirect and implicit influence through these procedures. By 'knowing the LDP's mind' (Wright 2002: 372), some options may be precluded or foreclosed. It is, however, extremely difficult to distinguish between cases in which bureaucrats' preferences are ruled out due to indirect influence by LDP politicians and those in which some options are ruled out because of the shared interest of bureaucrats and LDP politicians (Wright 2002: 372). As mentioned earlier, LDP politicians achieve expertise by accumulating information from bureaucrats, and this develops 'an identity of interest between bureaucratic and political values' (Wright 2002: 372). The relationship between LDP politicians and bureaucrats is a subtle interdependence in which they exchange information and imply their interests and intentions (Wright 2002: 374).

Katō Junko examines the relationship between LDP politicians and bureaucrats from the viewpoint of their rational behaviour, and in a similar way to Wright and the argument in this book, she rejects the polarities of bureaucrats versus politicians. Although the framework of her analysis (rational behaviour of bureaucrats and politicians) is different from that of this book (historical institutionalism), she also elaborates the same argument developed earlier, the shared interests and cooperation between LDP politicians and bureaucrats (Katō 1997: 37, 101).

Bureaucrats, she argues, create desired policies that are 'consistent with their organizational interests' (Katō 1997: 56). She goes on to argue that they exert their influence through institutional factors, such as decision-making procedures and monopolized policy-information and expertise, to put such policies into practice. They bargain with LDP politicians and make compromises on unimportant factors to achieve their main target (Katō 1997: 87). As for LDP politicians, she emphasizes their 'volunteering cooperation' with bureaucrats. She argues that such cooperation is the result of their rational strategic behaviour in order 'to promote their own influence in policy-making circles' (Katō 1997: 101). She points out that LDP politicians accumulate their expertise by receiving information from bureaucrats. Therefore, she argues, it is unlikely that LDP politicians will sharply oppose bureaucrats. Instead, by supporting bureaucrats' policy plans, LDP politicians demonstrate their understanding of technical matters, which results in an increase in their credibility and influence as policy experts.

Ramseyer and Rosenbluth argue that policy changes during the periods from 1949 to 1954, from 1959 to 1963 and from 1971 to 1976 confirm the principal-agent relationship between bureaucrats and LDP leaders. During the above periods, LDP leaders changed their programmatic aims to boost their electoral performances. They adopted new aims that would move away from growth-oriented goals. In spite of their own preferences, namely economic development, bureaucrats, as the agents of LDP leaders, implemented programmes that would retard economic growth. They implemented policies that gave major benefits to small farmers and small firms (1949–1954), established national health insurance and pension plans

(1959–1963), enhanced welfare and health plans (1971–1976), legislated environmental protection schemes (1971–1976) and gave subsidies to small firms (1971–1976) aiming to promote the electoral success of the LDP (Ramseyer and Rosenbluth 1993: 134–6). Such an argument, however, fails to consider the diversity of preferences pursued by ministries and shared interests between LDP politicians and bureaucrats. Implementing new policies means, for bureaucrats, the expansion of their ministry's jurisdiction, authority, budget and organization. For example, subsidies and aids to farmers result in benefits for the Ministry of Agriculture, Forestry and Fisheries, the enlargement of welfare and health care systems means the expansion of the authority and organizations of the Ministry of Health and Welfare, and subsidies to small businesses are to the benefit of the Ministry of International Trade and Industry (MITI). Policies, therefore, during the above periods were not necessarily against bureaucrats' preferences. Rather, for the ministries in charge of those policies, implementing those policies resulted in benefits for them. During the above periods, the LDP needed policies that would boost support for the LDP, and bureaucrats exploited such needs and presented LDP policies that would also suit their preferences. Policy changes during the above periods were the result of cooperation between the LDP and bureaucrats, and both the LDP and bureaucrats obtained benefits from such policies.

With respect to the relationships between bureaucrats and opposition parties, LDP politicians generally negotiated with opposition parties. LDP members of the Diet Management Committee of the LDP (Giun-zoku) bargained with opposition party executives to pass bills and the budget smoothly. Since the LDP maintained its majority in the Diet until 1993, bureaucrats could concentrate on negotiating with the LDP in order to put their policies into legislation.

Under LDP dominance, based on mutual dependence between LDP politicians and bureaucrats, the issue settling system – in which bureaucrats planned policies, LDP executives, faction leaders and bureaucrats negotiated with each other over those plans, and LDP executives negotiated with opposition parties to legislate them – was established and functioned effectively. Both LDP politicians and bureaucrats obtained benefits from this system. Close cooperation between them enabled bureaucrats to put their plans into law effectively and LDP politicians to maintain themselves in office by distributing subsidies and public works to their supporters. As a result, this system was reinforced under LDP dominance. However, after the general election of 1993, structural changes in the Japanese political system – the end of LDP dominance – reduced the efficacy of such close cooperation.

4   Changes in the Japanese political system since 1993

The background of political changes after 1993

The mature Japanese economy

By the 1980s the Japanese economy had matured, and this damaged the distribution system by which the LDP had obtained constant support. The Japanese economy experienced rapid development in the 1950s and the 1960s. The LDP exploited benefits from such rapid development to obtain support from voters. From the 1950s the LDP had achieved stable support from farmers and small-business owners. Until 1990, about 70 per cent of farmers and 60 per cent of small-business owners had supported the LDP (Richardson 1997: 17).

In the 1980s, however, the Japanese economy had reached a stage of stable development. The average rate of real economic growth from 1981 to 1987 was only 3.71 per cent, compared with that in the 1960s and the 1970s (10.42 per cent and 4.55 per cent respectively). Since the Japanese economy had matured Japanese people could no longer expect benefits from rapid economic development. Increases in benefits were gradually reduced. The growth in the general account revenue gradually declined from 19 per cent in 1970 to 14 per cent in 1979, and significantly dropped from 10.7 per cent in 1980 to 0.7 per cent in 1986. As a result, the LDP's traditional manoeuvre, distributing benefits from economic development and obtaining support in return, was no longer possible, and the LDP therefore had to issue deficit bonds in order to maintain the distribution system and cover the budget deficit.

The budget of the 1974 fiscal year had a deficit of 770 billion yen, and the Minister of Finance, Ōhira Masayoshi, declared in the Diet that Japanese public finance was in crisis. The government issued deficit bonds in the 1975 fiscal year, and after that, deficit bonds were issued every fiscal year. In the budget compilation of the 1982 fiscal year, the MOF decided to adopt an austere budget policy, and it implemented a 'zero-ceiling' in which an estimate of budget requests from each ministry was kept at the same amount as in the initial budget of the preceding fiscal year. Furthermore, in budgets from the 1983 fiscal year to the 1987 fiscal year, the MOF adopted a 'minus-ceiling' in which an estimate of budget requests from each ministry was reduced to be below that of the preceding fiscal year. Conflicts about allocation of shrinking benefits became intense (Satō 1997: 178). For instance, urban areas, which received less benefit than rural areas, complained about their burden. Voters in urban areas began to oppose these LDP policies. In the general election of 18 February 1990, the LDP obtained 36 per cent of votes in the Tōkyō area compared with 51.9 per cent in the Shikoku area. In the general election of 18 July 1993, the LDP suffered a further loss of votes in the Tōkyō area (obtaining only 27 per cent). However, in the Shikoku area, the votes for the LDP increased to 58.7 per cent. As the Japanese economy experienced serious depression in the 1990s, such separation of urban and rural areas became more conspicuous. As for the general election of 20 October 1996, the LDP won 14 seats out of 25 in single-seat constituencies in the Tōkyō area compared with 10 out of 13 seats in those in the Shikoku area. Regarding proportional representation seats, the LDP obtained 27.0 per cent of votes in the Tōkyō bloc, while it obtained 35.97 per cent of votes in the Shikoku bloc. In the general election of 25 June 2000, the LDP significantly lost seats in urban constituencies compared with those in rural areas, while it maintained its support in rural areas. For example, in single-seat constituencies, the LDP won only 9 seats out of 25 in the Tōkyō area, and 7 out of 19 in the Ōsaka area. On the other hand, the LDP won 11 out of 13 seats in constituencies in the Shikoku area. As for proportional representation seats, the LDP obtained only 19.48 per cent of votes in the Tōkyō bloc, while it obtained 35.97 per cent of votes in the Shikoku bloc.

The globalized economy

The globalized economy has promoted both rapid expansion of foreign companies (such as service, finance and retail companies) in Japanese markets and also the expansion of Japanese companies in foreign markets. Severe competition in the globalized economy has widened the differences between winners and losers. Industries that cannot compete with foreign businesses demand more protection in order to retain their profit. On the other hand, competitive industries demand more deregulation in order to compete with foreign companies, and they refuse to cooperate with the government to protect less competitive industries at the cost of their profit. For instance, farmers demanded that the government should protect their business from foreign agricultural businesses by keeping strict restrictions on the import of agricultural products, such as oranges and rice. The car manufacturing industry and the electrical appliance industry made the criticism that such protection caused disadvantage to their industries in foreign markets because they were afraid that the US would impose tough import restrictions on Japanese car manufacturers in retaliation for the Japanese government's import restrictions on American oranges and rice.

The end of the cold war

The end of the cold war made the confrontation between supporters and opponents of the Japan–US Mutual Security Treaty less important. The Japan–US Mutual Security Treaty was concluded in 1951. Based on this treaty the US has deployed military personnel in Japan until now. After the Second World War, the main political theme over which the LDP and opposition parties confronted each other was the question of whether Japan should maintain the Japan–US Mutual Security Treaty. Satō Seizaburō argued that there were two political themes over which political parties confronted each other immediately after the Second World War: support versus revision of the reforms after the Second World War, and support of the Japan–US Mutual Security Treaty versus 'unarmed neutrality'. However, he argued that by the 1960s the first theme had transformed into an interpretation of Article 9 of the Constitution (concerning the security of Japan). As a result, he concluded that only the second theme, which included the interpretation of Article 9 of the Constitution, remained until the 1990s (Satō 1997: 177). The LDP pledged anti-Communism and supported the Japan–US Mutual Security Treaty as an important measure to protect Japan from Communism. On the other hand, opposition parties, such as the Japan Socialist Party (JSP), opposed the treaty and insisted on 'unarmed neutrality'. However, the end of the cold war lessened the anti-Communist characteristic of the treaty. In addition, the Gulf War thrust a difficult issue before Japan: how Japan should contribute to settling regional wars. The response of the Japanese government, 'Japan will send only money not troops', was criticized by foreign countries. Left-wing opposition parties could not present persuasive reasons for their policy of 'unarmed neutrality', whereby they refused to make a commitment to participate in any military activities. All opposition parties, except the Japan Communist Party (JCP), actually accepted the Japan–US Mutual Security Treaty. Consequently, the difference between the LDP and other parties had become less distinct, which made it much easier for the LDP and other parties to form a coalition. Under the Murayama Coalition Cabinet, on 3 September 1994, the JSP approved a new party programme that acknowledged the Self Defence Force and the Japan–US Security Treaty.

Furthermore, because of the disappearance of a distinct ideological confrontation between the LDP and the left-wing parties, it became much easier for LDP supporters who resented the LDP's policies to vote for opposition parties. Kabashima Ikuo examines the loyalty of LDP supporters with respect to the elections of the House of Councillors from 1977 to 1998. He calculates the rate of loyalty, which indicates the correlation between support and voting behaviour of LDP supporters in the elections of the HC since 1977. The more LDP supporters vote for the LDP, the closer the numerical value comes to 1. Before 1986, the value had been relatively stable, at about 0.7. However, in 1989 it dropped sharply to 0.58 and has never recovered to 0.7. The loyalty of LDP supporters plummeted in the election of the HC of 1989. Although it later recovered slightly, it still remained at about 0.62 (Kabashima 1999: 82–3).

T. J. Pempel points out that it was the fragmentation of conservatives that resulted in the demise of LDP dominance (Pempel 1998: 169–205). He argues that, from the 1970s to the 1980s, responding to socioeconomic and electoral challenges, the LDP took a strategy of expanding its supporting groups. With regard to supporting groups for the conservatives, the reduction in the population of farmers and small business owners and urbanization brought about a shrinking supporter base; on the other hand, with regard to supporting groups for the left-wing parties, organized labour abandoned its unmitigated hostile attitude towards the conservatives. Responding to this situation, he argues, the LDP embraced the electorate in urban areas – union members and white-collar workers – by presenting environment and welfare policies, while keeping its core supporting groups, such as farmers, small shopkeepers, small-business owners and business circles. Simultaneously, the supporting bases of the left wing parties (especially the JSP), such as trade unions, were gradually undermined due to economic prosperity under LDP dominance. As a result, conservatives who supported the LDP included not only the core of LDP supporters but also the groups that had been regarded as 'centre-left'. However, this expansion diluted the cohesiveness of the conservatives. In the 1990s, as economic stagnation became chronic, tensions and conflicts within the conservatives emerged, which undermined the supporting bases of the LDP. For instance, a low-price policy, which appealed to urban voters and organized labour, went against the interests of farmers, small business owners and business circles. As Pempel pointed out, it became increasingly difficult to satisfy all segments of conservative supporters because of serious confrontations between them over, for example, 'more protection versus less protection, more pork-barrel policies versus tighter fiscal restraints, high yen versus low yen' (Pempel 1998: 199). His argument supplements the argument examined above to explain conflicts and disintegration within the supporting bases of the LDP. The mature Japanese economy made it difficult for the LDP to maintain its tactics of 'distributing benefits and obtaining votes'. As a result, conflicts between LDP supporting groups were exacerbated.

The globalized economy brought about conflicts among industries that had previously united in supporting the LDP, and the end of the cold war deprived the LDP of its ideological integrity and gave voters alternative choices to voting for the LDP, which also contributed to the fragmentation of conservatives. The bases that had supported LDP dominance changed during the 1980s. The LDP was not able to retain the stable and broad support it had previously maintained, and dissatisfaction with it was accumulating among voters. Such dissatisfaction exploded after a series of political scandals from the end of the 1980s to the beginning of the 1990s, which caused the end of LDP dominance after the general election of July 1993.

Structural changes in the Japanese political system

The end of LDP dominance

From the end of the 1980s to the beginning of the 1990s Japan experienced a series of political scandals. When the 'Recruit Scandal' was revealed over the years 1988 and 1989, the ex-Chief Cabinet Secretary, Fujinami Takao, was arrested for taking bribes.[1] In 1991 two political scandals, the 'Kyōwa Scandal'[2] and the 'Sagawa Kyūbin Scandal'[3] were revealed, and the ex-Director General of Hokkaidō Development Agency, Abe Fumio, was arrested for taking bribes from Kyōwa. Kanemaru Shin admitted he had received 500 million yen from Sagawa Kyūbin and he was forced to resign as Vice President of the LDP. In 1993 the 'Gene-Con Scandal' was revealed, and the mass media reported that many major construction companies allegedly gave illegal political funds to politicians.[4] Public opinion strongly demanded political reform, and junior LDP members reacted to this demand. Immediately after the Recruit Scandal was revealed, junior LDP members formed a study group called 'Utopia' across the factions and requested the revision of the electoral system. When the Kyōwa Scandal and the Sagawa Kyūbin Scandal were revealed, junior LDP members formed another study group on political reforms. In October 1992 junior LDP members formed a study group on 'Regaining Trust in the LDP', and requested that Kanemaru Shin and Takeshita Noboru should leave the LDP and resign as members of the House of Representatives (HR). Some of them, namely Takemura Masayoshi and his group, contacted other parties, such as the Japan New Party (JNP), and they defected from the LDP and formed the New Harbinger Party (NHP) after the dissolution of the HR in July 1993.

However, the main incident that triggered the end of LDP dominance was the struggle within the Keiseikai, the largest faction (the Takeshita faction) in the LDP. In September 1992, Kanemaru Shin, who was the actual leader of the Keiseikai at that time, was involved in the Sagawa Kyūbin Scandal. He was fined for breaking the Political Funds Control Law and resigned from all his political offices. Later, in October 1992, he resigned from his parliamentary seat. The Keiseikai had suddenly lost its influential leader. Over the successor of Kanemaru Shin, the Keiseikai was divided into two groups, the Ozawa Group (led by Ozawa Ichirō, ex-General Secretary under the Kaifu Cabinet and then acting leader of the Keiseikai), and the anti-Ozawa group. The Ozawa group made Hata Tsutomu their leader and pledged political reform. They called themselves 'reformist' and criticized the anti-Ozawa group as being 'anti-reformist'.

However, the Ozawa group could not obtain the leadership of the Keiseikai, and Obuchi Keizō became the leader, supported by the anti-Ozawa group. The Ozawa group split from the Keiseikai and formed 'Forum 21 for Political Reform'. Responding to public demand for political reform, Prime Minister Miyazawa Kiichi pledged political reforms, including the reform of the electoral system. Nevertheless, he abandoned attempts to legislate the package of political reform bills not only because of conflicts with opposition parties but also because of severe confrontation within the LDP. On 18 June, opposition parties called for a no-confidence resolution against the Miyazawa Cabinet. A total of 39 (the members of the Ozawa group) out of the 274 LDP members voted for the resolution, and 18 LDP members (those who were led by Takemura Masayoshi) abstained. LDP members who voted for or abstained from the no-confidence resolution defected from the LDP and formed the Japan Renewal Party (JRP) and the New Harbinger Party (NHP). Prime Minister Miyazawa Kiichi dissolved the HR and a general election was held on 18 July 1993. The LDP could not retain its majority in the HR and lost its position as a ruling party for the first time since its foundation in 1955. Table 4.1 shows the result of the general election of 18 July 1993.

The result of the general election of 1993 caused a significant change in the Japanese poitical structure – from stable LDP dominance to unstable

Table 4.1 The result of the general election of 18 July 1993

Name of party	Number of seats after the election of 18 July 1993	Number of seats after the election of 18 February 1990	Number of seats before the election of 18 July 1993
LDP	223	275	222
JSP	70	136	134
JRP	55	–	36
CGP	51	45	45
JNP	35	–	0
JCP	15	16	16
DSP	15	14	13
NHP	13	–	10
SDL	4	4	4
Others	0	1	2
Independent	30	21	15
Total	511	512	497

LDP: Liberal Democratic Party (Jiyūminshutō)
JSP: Japan Socialist Party (Nihonshakaitō)
JRP: Japan Renewal Party (Shinseitō)
CGP: Clean Government Party (Kōmeitō)
JNP: Japan New Party (Nihonshintō)
JCP: Japan Communist Party (Nihon Kyāsantō)
DSP: Democratic Socialist Party (Minshushakaitō)
NHP: New Harbinger Party (Shintō Sakigake)
SDL: Social Democratic League (Shakai Minshu Rengō)

multiparty coalition politics. Since 1993, three HR general elections (July 1993, October 1996 and June 2000) and three HC elections (July 1995, July 1998, and July 2001) have been held. In each election the LDP has failed to maintain a majority by itself. The LDP obtained 228 seats out of 511 (1993), 239 out of 500 (1996) and 233 out of 480 (2000) in the HR as the results of the respective general elections, and it maintained 111 (1995), 106 (1998) and 109 (2001) seats out of 252 as the result of the elections of the HC. The LDP has therefore been forced to make coalitions with other parties in order to maintain its position as a ruling party.

Consequently, cabinets after the Hosokawa Cabinet have been coalition cabinets (including coalitions in which non-LDP coalition parties do not have ministers' posts). Table 4.2 shows the composition of cabinets after the Hosokawa Cabinet. It shows that all cabinets after the Hosokawa Cabinet were coalition cabinets (except for a short period during the Obuchi Cabinet, July 1998 to December 1998).

The end of LDP dominance brought about significant changes in the factors that were the conditions for the issue settling system based on close cooperation between the LDP and bureaucrats: the decline in the importance of LDP organizations in the decision-making process of the government and the Diet; the loosened management system of the LDP; and the change in politicians' attitudes towards the bureaucrats.

Table 4.2 The composition of cabinets after the Hosokawa Cabinet

Cabinet	Period	Coalition parties
Hosokawa	08.1993 to 04.1994	JNP, JSP, JRP, NHP, CGP, SDL, DSP
Hata	04.1994 to 06.1994	JNP, JRP, NHP, CGP, SDL, DSP
Murayama	06.1994 to 01.1996	LDP, JSP, NHP
1st Hashimoto	01.1996 to 11.1996	LDP, SDPJ,[1] NHP
2nd Hashimoto	11.1996 to 07.1998	LDP, SDPJ, NHP (SDPJ and NHP ended their coalition with LDP in May 1998)
Obuchi	07.1998 to 04.2000	LDP, LP (1.1999–),[2] CGP (4.1999–)[2]
1st Mori	04.2000 to 07.2000	LDP, CP, CGP
2nd Mori	07.2000 to 04.2001	LDP, CP, CGP

LDP: Liberal Democratic Party (Jiyūminshutō)
JSP: Japan Socialist Party (Nihon Shakaitō)
JNP: Japan New Party (Nihonshintō)
JRP: Japan Renewal Party (Shinseitō)
NHP: New Harbinger Party (Shintō Sakigake)
CGP: Clean Government Party (Komeitō, including the new Komeitō formed in 11.1998)
SDL: Social Democratic League (Shakai Minshu Rengō)
DSP: Democratic Socialist Party (Minshatō)

1 On 19 January 1996, the JSP changed its name to the Social Democratic Party of Japan (SDPJ).
2 The Obuchi cabinet formed a coalition with the LP from January 1999 and with the CGP from April 1999.

The decline in the importance of LDP organizations

Under LDP dominance, the decisions of LDP organizations were, in general, approved by the government and they were put into legislation. Although the LDP sometimes revised its decisions in the process of bargaining with opposition parties, the decision-making processes of the government and the Diet were almost always concluded in the LDP. The end of LDP dominance changed these processes.

Figure 4.1 shows the decision-making system under the Hosokawa Coalition Cabinet. The Committee of Representatives of the Coalition Parties (Renritsu Yotō Daihyōsha Kaigi) supervised the Council of Secretaries of the Coalition Parties (Kakuha Kanjikai), which had the Policy Affairs Council (Seisaku Kanjikai) and the Diet Affairs Council (Seimu Kanjikai). The Committee of Leading Members of the Government and Ruling Parties (Seifu Yotō Shunō Kaigi) was formed as the organization in which the coalition cabinet communicated with the ruling coalition parties. The Committee of Representatives of the Coalition Parties, in which Ozawa Ichirō, an actual leader of the JRP, took the leadership, functioned as a supreme decision-making organization. The LDP was excluded from the decision-making process of the government for the first time since its establishment in 1955.

Under the Murayama Coalition Cabinet, the LDP regained the position of ruling party by making a coalition with the NHP and the JSP.

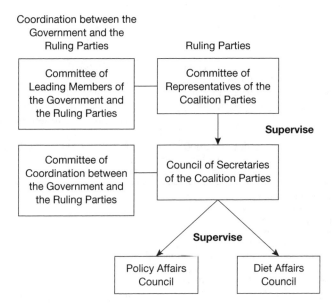

Figure 4.1 The decision-making process of the Hosokawa Coalition Cabinet
Source: Nonaka 1998: 47.

Figure 4.2 shows the decision-making process under the Murayama Coalition Cabinet. Under both coalition cabinets, the Ruling Coalition Parties Representatives Committee (Renritsu Yotō Sekininsha Kaigi, consisting of the Secretary General, the Chief Secretary, the Representative Secretary and other executives) was the supreme decision-making organization in the ruling coalition parties. It supervised the General Committee (Innai Sōmukai), under which the Policy Coordination Committee (Seisaku Chōsei Kaigi) formed 18 different issue-specific project teams and ministry-specific coordination committees (Shōchōbetsu Seisaku Chōsei Kaigi). The project teams and coordination committees made substantial deliberations, and the posts in these organizations were allocated to the LDP, JSP and NHP in the ratio of 3:2:1 in order to prevent the LDP from taking a majority in each organization (Yamaguchi 1997: 43–6, Itō 1997: 166–9). In this decision-making process, the JSP and the NHP obtained power disproportionate to the number of seats they had in the Diet, which caused dissatisfaction among LDP politicians.

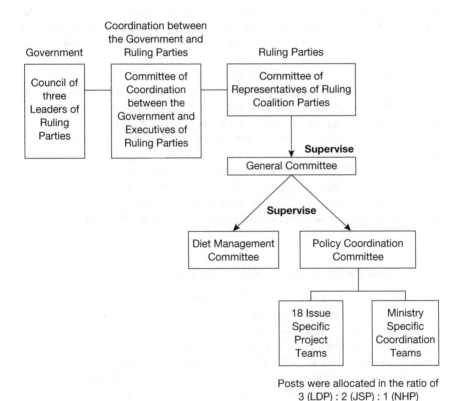

Figure 4.2 The decision-making process of the Murayama Coalition Cabinet

Source: Nonaka 1998: 49.

After the general election of 20 October 1996, both the JSP and the NHP lost many seats (the JSP went from 30 seats to 15; the NHP went from 9 seats to 2) and they did not have enough members of the HR to maintain posts in every project team and committee. Although the importance of coordination among the three parties declined, the LDP had to keep support from them since the LDP did not obtain a majority in the HR by itself.

After the overwhelming defeat in the election of the HC of July 1998, the LDP was forced to make a concession to opposition parties. Since the LDP and other ruling coalition parties could not obtain a majority in the HC, the LDP had to accept opposition parties' demands in order to let bills or the budget pass the Diet. Opposition parties such as the Democratic Party (DP), the Liberal Party (LP) and the Peace and Reform (PR) played a crucial role in the decision-making process of the Diet. As will be explained in Chapter 6, the LDP was forced to accept the plan of three opposition parties (the DP, the LP and the PR) for the revision of the Financial Revitalization Bill. After political confusion about the revision of the Financial Revitalization Bill, the LDP sought to form a coalition with the LP and the Clean Government Party (CGP).[5] The Obuchi Cabinet made a coalition with the LP (in January 1999, the LP split into the LP and the Conservative Party (CP), and the CP maintained its coalition relationship with the LDP) and the CGP (in April 1999). Figure 4.3 shows the decision-making process under the Obuchi Cabinet. Again, the LP and the CGP had disproportionate power in the decision-making process of the government in comparison with the number of seats they had in the HR.

Under the coalition cabinets, agreements between the ruling coalition parties in this decision-making process were given superiority over decisions of the LDP organizations in order to maintain the ruling coalition. The decisions of the government and of the Diet were not the same as those of LDP organizations. Consequently, the importance of the LDP organization in the decision-making process of the government and the Diet had declined.

The weakened management system of the LDP

The end of LDP dominance has affected the management system through factions. LDP factions exerted four functions: allocating cabinet and party posts; distributing political funds; sorting out demands from the constituencies of factional members; and supporting election campaigns. Through these functions, factions gathered and controlled their members. Since 1993 the control power of faction leaders has been weakened for five reasons.

First, as explained in the previous section, the importance of the LDP organization has declined. Under LDP dominance, internal organizations of the LDP, such as the Policy Affairs Research Council (PARC), the Executive Council (EC) and Divisions of the PARC, actually decided

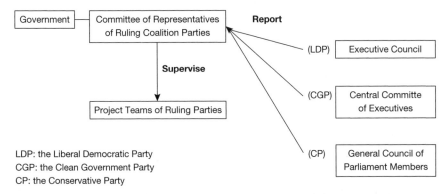

Figure 4.3 The decision-making process of the Obuchi Coalition Cabinet
Source: *Nihon Keizai Shinbun*, 29 December 2000.

government policies. The executive posts of these organizations were allocated to factions' executives according to recommendation by factions. In addition, executives of these organizations held closed-door meetings and made substantial deliberations by themselves (before or after formal meetings of organizations) that actually decided the results of discussion in those organizations. After 1993, under coalition cabinets, decisions between the LDP and other coalition parties have been given priority over the decisions of LDP organizations. As the importance of LDP organizations in the decision-making process of the government has reduced, the power of faction leaders and executives has declined.

Second, one of the functions of factions – allocating posts – faced a difficulty over the strict seniority rule. Under coalition cabinets, the LDP has been forced to share cabinet positions with other coalition parties. Table 4.3 shows allocation of cabinet posts. As this table indicates, important posts such as those of Prime Minister, Minister of Finance and Cabinet Secretary were allocated to non-LDP politicians under the Murayama and the First Hashimoto Cabinet. This reduction in the number of cabinet posts hampered the smooth implementation of the seniority rule in the LDP, and this brought dissatisfaction among LDP members.

Third, the revision of two laws, the Political Funds Control Law and the Public Official Election Law, under the Hosokawa Coalition Cabinets damaged two other functions of factions: collecting and distributing political funds and supporting election campaigns. Eight political parties (the JSP, the JRP, the JNP, the NHP, the DSP, the CGP Kōmeitō and two other minor parties) pledged political reforms and formed the Hosokawa Coalition Cabinet after the general election of July 1993. The Hosokawa Coalition Cabinet made political reform its main political agenda, in response to public demand. The Political Funds Control Law and the Public Official Election Law were revised in 1994. In the revised Political Funds

Table 4.3 Allocation of cabinet posts among parties

	LDP	JSP (SDPJ)	NHP	LP	CGP	Others
Murayama	13	5[1]	2			
Murayama Res.	13	5[2]	1[3]			1
1st Hashimoto	12	6[4]	2			
2nd Hashimoto	20					
Obuchi	20					
Obuchi 1st Res.	18			1		1
Obuchi 2nd Res.	17			1	1	1

Res.:   Reshuffled cabinet
LDP: Liberal Democratic Party
JSP: Japan Socialist Party, The JSP changed its name to the Social Democratic Party of Japan (SDPJ) in January 1996
NHP: New Harbinger Party
LP: Liberal Party
CGP: Clean Government Party
Others: non-Members of Parliament
1 Included the Prime Minister, the Minister of Finance and the Cabinet Secretary
2 Included the Prime Minister and the Cabinet Secretary
3 Included the Minister of Finance
4 Included the Minister of Finance

Control Law, political fund donation is limited in order to prevent corruption associated with political fund donation. Private companies, labour unions and other associations cannot donate political funds, except to political parties, political funds associations or political funds management organizations (each politician is permitted to have only one political funds management organization). As a result, LDP factions have lost their principal means of collecting political funds.[6]

For example, in addition to electoral funds, factions used to distribute political funds to their members. However, the *Asahi Shinbun* reported that four out of the five main factions of the LDP did not distribute political funds to their members in the summer of 1994 because of financial difficulties (*Asahi Shinbun*, 10 August 1994, evening edition). Instead, LDP members themselves have had to collect political funds. They have exploited the LDP's local branches and their political funds management organizations by transferring political funds between these organizations (Yoshida and Yamamoto 1999: 23–4)). The LDP had about 58,000 party branches in August 1998, and the number of branches increased by 935 in three-and-a-half years (Taniguchi 1999: 68).

As for the function of supporting election campaigns, the revised Public Official Election Law adopted a new electoral system based on a combination of single-seat constituencies and proportional representation constituencies instead of multiple-seat medium-sized constituencies. Under this new electoral system, formal recognition by the party as a LDP candidate is crucial for LDP members in order to stand for election as LDP candidates, and there is no possibility that more than two LDP candidates in one constituency will compete with each other. As a result, LDP candidates do not need the factional support for election campaigns they needed under the multiple-seat medium-sized constituencies system.

The fourth reason for the weakened management system of the LDP is the fact that conflicts across factions have weakened faction leaders' control of their members. Factions of the LDP previously competed with each other for the post of Party President. The main LDP factions were formed during the LDP Presidential election campaign in 1956. Eight factions (Kishi, Satō, Ikeda, Ōno, Ishii, Kōno, Miki-Matsumura and Ishibashi) were formed, and five of them remained until the Miyazawa Cabinet in 1993 (Kitaoka 1995: 73–4). A faction to which the LDP President belonged (Sōsaibatsu) and factions that cooperated with Sōsaibatsu formed a power-holding group (Shuryū-ha); factions that competed with Sōsaibatsu in the process of selecting the LDP President formed an anti-power holding group (Han Shuryū-ha). Since the 1990s, the theme of conflicts across factions has emerged: generational conflict (a conflict between junior LDP members and senior LDP members) and conflict over the principle of coalition. Factions have been divided over these issues, and a power-holding group and an anti-power holding group have been formed across factions.

With regard to generational conflict, the dissatisfaction of junior LDP members with the strict seniority rule increased under LDP dominance. After a series of political scandals were revealed from the end of the 1980s to the beginning of the 1990s, they demanded 'a change of generation' within the LDP. Junior LDP members demanded that some senior LDP members should retire and junior members should have more influence on the management of the LDP. In addition, under the Hosokawa Coalition Cabinet and other coalition cabinets, junior members of other parties, who had won elections only once or twice, obtained executive posts within their parties. Compared with such promotion of junior members in other parties, junior LDP politicians were dissatisfied with the strict seniority rule of the LDP.

As for the principle of coalition, the LDP was divided into two groups: the group that supported a coalition with the JSP and the NHP ('Ji-Sha-Sa' group)[7] and the group that preferred a coalition with more conservative parties ('Ho-Ho' group).[8] The former group became a power-holding group under the Murayama and Hashimoto Coalition Cabinets and the latter became an anti-power holding group. The two themes (generational conflict and coalition principle) are related to each other and various groups were formed across factions. The so-called 'YKK' group – Yamazaki Taku (the Chair of the PARC under the first and second Hashimoto Cabinet), Katō Kōichi (the Chair of the PARC under the Murayama Cabinet, and the Secretary General under the First and Second Hashimoto Cabinet), and Koizumi Jun'ichirō (the Minister of Health and Welfare of the Second Hashimoto Cabinet) – were leaders of the power-holding group. They supported the change of generation in the LDP and a coalition with the JSP and the NHP. The YKK group and other junior LDP members formed 'Shinseiki' (New Century) in May 1994. Shinseiki opened its membership to the JSP and the NHP, and attempted to strengthen connections with them. An anti-power holding group, including Kajiyama Seiroku and other senior members, argued for a coalition with more conservative parties, such as the New Frontier Party (NFP). In June 1995 they formed 'Kayūkai'. Junior members who sought coalition with the NFP formed 'a study group on the security of Japan' in May 1997. When Yamazaki Taku (one of the YKK members) and junior LDP members formed 'Kin Mirai Kenkyūkai' across factions in July 1998, the anti-power holding group formed 'Nihon Saiseikaigi' (Committee on the Revitalization of Japan) in August and 'Hazukikai – Nihon Saikōkaigi' (Committee on the Reconstruction of Japan) in September 1998. Table 4.4 shows the groups that were formed across factions.

As conflicts between the two groups became intense, each faction was divided into two groups and the factions' cohesiveness declined. Figure 4.4 illustrates the split in each faction of the LDP under the Second Hashimoto Cabinet. Each faction was divided into two groups.

For example, under the Second Hashimoto Cabinet, within the Obuchi faction, Chief Cabinet Secretary Kajiyama Seiroku was a leader of the Ho-Ho group and Acting Secretary General Nonaka Hiromu belonged to the Ji-Sha-Sa group. As for the Mitsuzuka faction, Minister of Health and Welfare Koizumi Jun'ichirō was a leader of the Ji-Sha-Sa group and Minister of Construction Kamei Shizuka was from the Ho-Ho group. From the Miyazawa faction, Secretary General Katō Kōichi was a leader of the Ji-Sha-Sa group and Director General of Economic Planning Agency Asō Tarō was from the Ho-Ho group. Each faction was divided into these two groups. The faction to which the LDP President belonged (Sōsaibatsu) and

Table 4.4 Groups formed across factions

Ji-Sha-Sa groups

Date of inauguration	Name
May 1994	Shinseiki
July 1998	Kin Mirai Kenkyūkai

Ho-Ho groups

Date of inauguration	Name
June 1995	Kayūkai
May 1997	A Study Group on the Security of Japan
April 1998	Nihon Saisei Kaigi
September 1998	Hazukikai – Nihon Saikōkaigi

	Ji-Sha-Sa Group	Neutrals	Ho-Ho Group
Obuchi faction	Nonaka Hiromu (Acting Secretary General)	Takeshita Noboru Obuchi Keizō (LDP Vice President)	Kajiyama Seiroku (Chief Cabinet Secretary)
Mitsuzuka faction	Koizumi Jun'ichirō (Minister of Health and Welfare) Mori Yoshirō (Chair of Executive Council)	Mitsuzuka Hiroshi (Minister of Finance)	Kamei Shizuka (Minister of Construction)
Miyazawa faction	Katō Kōichi (Secretary General) Miyazawa Ki'ich (Ex-Prime Minister)	Kōno Yōhei (Ex-President of LDP)	Asō Tarō (Director General of Economic Planning Agency)
Ex-Watanabe faction	Yamazaki Taku (Chair of PARC)		Yosano Kaoru (Vice Cabinet Secretariat) Nakasone Yasuhiro (Ex-Prime Minister)

Figure 4.4 Groups within factions under the Second Hashimoto Cabinet
Source: *Asahi Shinbun* 22 August 1997.

factions which supported Sōsaibatsu constituted a power holding group. However, after 1993, the 'Ji-Sha-Sa' group (a power holding group) and the 'Ho-Ho' group (an anti-power holding group) were formed across factions. As a result, factions were divided into these two groups and the cohesiveness of factions was severely damaged, and the power of faction leaders to control their members was significantly weakened. For example, 30 junior members of the Mitsuzuka faction attended the meeting of 'a study group on constructing Japan in the 21st century' (one of the 'Ho-Ho' study groups). The mass media reported a confrontation between faction executives and junior members over attending this study group. The Director of the Mitsuzuka faction, Miyashita Sōhei, asked junior members to refrain from attending them and to notify faction executives beforehand when they wish to attend such study groups. Junior members strongly opposed this and fiercely quarrelled over the issue (*Asahi Shinbun*: 12 August 1997).

The fifth reason for the weakened management system of the LDP relates to the fact that winning the post of the LDP President has not always been the primary target of the factions. As explained above, LDP factions were formed in the process of LDP Presidential elections. Leaders of each faction were candidates for LDP Presidential elections, and factions therefore competed with each other for the post of LDP President. Factions would unite in order to win an LDP Presidential election that maintained their integration and cohesiveness. However, in the 1990s, candidates for the LDP presidential election were not necessarily faction leaders. For instance, Hashimoto Ryūtarō became the LDP President and Prime Minister from 1996 to 1998, although he was not a leader of a faction at that time (he was a member of the Obuchi faction; the leader of the Obuchi faction at that time was Obuchi Keizō). In the LDP Presidential election of July 1998, three factions – the Kōmoto faction, the Watanabe faction and the Miyazawa faction – did not have their own candidate. On the other hand, Koizumi Jun'ichirō stood for election although he was not a leader of the faction to which he belonged (he was a member of the Mori faction). The factions' primary target had been to achieve the post of LDP President for their factional leader since 1955; this had strengthened and maintained the integrity and cohesiveness of the factions. As factions lost such a target, their integrity and cohesiveness weakened.

Weakened control over factional members brought about conflicts within factions, which resulted in splits within factions. Figure 4.5 shows factions of the LDP since 1958. Under LDP dominance, factions integrated into five main factions and, apart for the split of minor groups, the stability of the five factions continued until 1993. The fragmentation of factions after 1993 shows the weakened control power of faction leaders over their members.

The election of the LDP President in 2001 also revealed the weakened power of faction leaders. The Hashimoto faction, the largest in the LDP, decided to support ex-Prime Minister Hashimoto Ryūtarō as a candidate for LDP President. Junior members of the Hashimoto faction openly expressed their dissatisfaction with this decision. Five junior members of the Hashimoto faction absented themselves from the general meeting of the Hashimoto faction on 12 April 2001. Furthermore, 30 junior members of the LDP asked the LDP Presidential Election Administration Committee for permission to have a discussion with each candidate. They united across almost all fations, including the Hashimoto, the Mori and the Horiuchi factions.

Thus since 1993 the control power of faction leaders over their members has been weakened, which has loosened the management system of the LDP.[9]

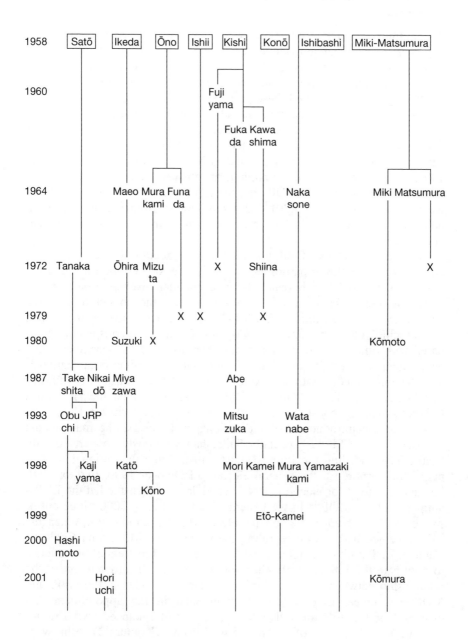

Figure 4.5 Factions of the LDP since 1958

The change in attitudes of politicians towards MOF bureaucrats

The attitude of LDP politicians towards bureaucrats, particularly MOF bureaucrats, has changed. Under LDP dominance, LDP politicians and bureaucrats had established a close partnership. Bureaucrats offered their information and expertise by presenting policies to LDP politicians. LDP politicians, in return, turned these policies into legislation. LDP politicians also received beneficial treatment in budget compilation in the form of subsidies or public works in their constituencies. However, under the Hosokawa Coalition Cabinet, bureaucrats treated the LDP as one of the opposition parties. According to a survey conducted by Nihon Keizai Shinbunsha in 1993, 42 per cent of executive bureaucrats answered that they tried to distance themselves from the LDP after the LDP went into opposition (Nihon Keizai Shinbunsha 1994: 420).[10] Without support from bureaucrats, LDP politicians experienced a lack of information and expertise, and lack of beneficial treatment.[11]

Under the Hosokawa Coalition Cabinet, bureaucrats worked for politicians of ruling coalition parties as they had done for LDP politicians. LDP politicians realized that bureaucrats were not their exclusive partners. In particular, they resented MOF bureaucrats since the cooperation of the Administrative Vice Minister, Saitō Jirō, with the actual leader of the JRP, Ozawa Ichirō, under the Hosokawa Coalition Cabinet was conspicuous compared with other executive bureaucrats. For instance, in December 1993, he voluntarily met representatives of four major economic organizations[12] and the mass media with the Administrative Vice Minister of Industry and International Trade, Kumano Hideaki, and explained the Hosokawa Cabinet's plan to boost the economy. When Prime Minister Hosokawa announced the introduction of the national welfare tax, the mass media reported that the MOF, especially Saitō, had vigorously cooperated with Ozawa in persuading the Prime Minister to institute the national welfare tax.[13] Furthermore, in the general election of October 1996, two ex-MOF bureaucrats stood for election as NFP candidates, which fuelled the LDP's antipathy of the MOF.[14] In the general election of June 2000, three out of five ex-MOF bureaucrats stood for election as DP candidates. When the LDP regained its position as ruling party under the Murayama Coalition Cabinet, LDP politicians intervened in the personnel matters of bureaucrats to eliminate the influence of other political parties. In order to break the relationship between Ozawa Ichirō, an influential leader of the NFP, and MOF executives, LDP executives intervened in the appointment and dismissal of the Administrative Vice Minister of Finance. Two Administrative Vice Ministers of Finance, Saitō Jirō and Komura Takeshi, were forced to take premature retirement since LDP executives believed that they had a close relationship with Ozawa. As a successor to Komura, the MOF attempted to appoint Wakui Yōji. But LDP executives influenced the MOF to appoint Tanami Kōji since they regarded Wakui as one of the

Saitō group having a close relationship with Ozawa. It was the first time that LDP executives had apparently influenced an Administrative Vice Minister of Finance to take premature retirement and had overturned the MOF's decision on the appointment of the Administrative Vice Minister.

As for support – or the lack of it – from bureaucrats, some junior LDP members obtained support from private companies, such as consulting companies or private research institutions, rather than from bureaucrats. As a result, the close relationship between LDP politicians and MOF bureaucrats has changed from that of a close partnership to a more businesslike relationship. Mabuchi Masaru describes the relationship between LDP politicians and MOF bureaucrats since the 1970s as that of 'partners', and that since 1993 as of 'neighbours', a more cool and detached relationship (Mabuchi 1997: 92–131).

The issue of the integration of the Japan Development Bank and the Export-Import Bank of Japan reflected the cool or rather chilly relationship between LDP politicians and MOF bureaucrats. The Murayama Coalition Cabinet pledged administrative reform as its political agenda and pursued the integration and abolition of juridical persons in public law as the main theme of administrative reform. LDP executives, especially the Chair of the PARC Katō Kōichi and Secretary General Mori Yoshirō, advocated the integration of the Japan Development Bank and the Export-Import Bank of Japan in spite of strong opposition from the MOF. Retired MOF executives had occupied the positions of Governor of the Japan Development Bank and Governor of the Export-Import Bank of Japan. Therefore the MOF strongly opposed the integration of the two banks. On the other hand, some LDP members resented the fact that the MOF had cooperated with the JRP, especially Ozawa Ichirō, under the Hosokawa Coalition Cabinet, and they wanted to damage the MOF. The mass media reported a comment made by one LDP executive, 'we will make Administrative Vice Minister Saitō Jirō regret his cooperation with Ozawa Ichirō . . .' (*Asahi Shinbun*, 20 February 1995).

While the deterioration of the relationship with LDP politicians was exacerbated, MOF bureaucrats could not institutionalize a close connection with new political parties as it had with the LDP. New parties mushroomed after 1993, and many of them lacked leadership and party discipline. As for the NFP, two groups, the Ozawa group (led by Ozawa Ichirō) and the anti-Ozawa group, confronted each other in the first NFP Presidential election. Although Kaifu Toshiki, whom the Ozawa group supported, won the election, his leadership was weak because of severe confrontation between the two groups. When the budget of the 1996 fiscal year and a package of bills for the Jūsen were debated in the Diet in January 1996, the NFP was divided into three groups: a group led by Ozawa Ichirō; a group led by Hata Tsutomu; and a group that consisted of ex-members of the Clean Government Party. Finally, in January 1998, the NFP was broken up into six groups. As for the Democratic Party (DP), the first DP (formed in September 1996) started with two leaders, Kan Naoto and Hatoyama Yukio, and was divided with respect to cooperation with the LDP. One of the leaders, Kan Naoto, expressed his view that the DP would consider a coalition with the LDP, while the other leader, Hatoyama Yukio, publicly admitted that his stance towards a coalition with the LDP was different from that of Kan. The second DP (formed in April 1998) consisted of groups whose political principles were significantly different from each other – from ex-JSP members to ex-LDP members. As a result, the DP could not come out with a definite principle with respect to controversial issues such as the revision of the Constitution or the security of Japan. Because of frequent formation and dissolution, and the lack of leadership, bureaucrats could not establish the same connection with the new parties as they had with the LDP.

Conclusion

The result of the general election of July 1993 brought about the end of LDP dominance and the beginning of the era of coalition cabinets. The LDP has had to make coalitions with other political parties in order to maintain its position as a ruling party ever since the Murayama Cabinet. Such a structural change in the Japanese political system has caused institutional changes in the factors that had supported the issue settling system based on close cooperation between LDP executives, faction leaders and bureaucrats.

Under LDP dominance, decisions of LDP organizations were actually decisions of the government and the Diet, and the LDP controlled its members through factions. Therefore bureaucrats participated in LDP organizations, such as the PARC and the EC, and negotiated with faction leaders and LDP executives in order to legislate their policies. Faction leaders and LDP executives controlled LDP members, and bargained with opposition parties to obtain smooth deliberation in the Diet. The negotiation with faction leaders and LDP executives and their consent to plans created by bureaucrats guaranteed support from the LDP as a whole for those plans and their legislation. Thus bureaucrats established and relied on their close relationship with faction leaders and LDP executives under LDP dominance.

Since the end of LDP dominance, the importance of LDP organizations in the decision-making process of the government and the Diet has declined, the faction leaders' control power over their members has been weakened, and the relationship between LDP politicians and bureaucrats, particularly MOF bureaucrats, has grown distant. MOF bureaucrats cannot rely on a close connection with faction leaders and LDP executives to settle political and economic issues. Although MOF bureaucrats obtain consent from faction leaders and LDP executives, such consent does not guarantee that bureaucrats' plans will be put into practice as the government's plan, since under a coalition cabinet, the decision-making process of the government is not concluded in the LDP organization. MOF bureaucrats cannot expect support from the whole of the LDP because the LDP is not integrated under the control of faction leaders.

Thus institutional changes in the Japanese political system caused by the end of LDP dominance seriously reduced the effectiveness of close cooperation between MOF bureaucrats and LDP executives. It seems that the mechanism that had adjusted to political changes until 1993 has not been able to adapt to new political circumstances after 1993. Two factors can be seen as the causes.

One is the rigidity of the relationship between LDP politicians and bureaucrats and its effectiveness under LDP dominance. Under LDP dominance, cooperation between LDP politicians and bureaucrats was firmly institutionalized. Formal cooperation in each LDP organization (from divisions of the PARC to the EC) and informal negotiations before and after the formal meetings in such organizations were solidly organized and functioned effectively, so LDP politicians and MOF bureaucrats did not dare to change such procedures immediately after the General Election of July 1993.

The other cause is the uncertainty of the alignment of parties in the future. As explained before in this chapter, contrary to the expectation of bureaucrats,[15] the Hosokawa Coalition Cabinet did not last one year, and the LDP regained the position of a ruling party in 1994. Nevertheless, the LDP has been forced to cooperate with other parties to keep its majority in the Diet. New parties rapidly mushroomed and disappeared after 1993. The JRP (established in 1993), which was supposed to be a major rival to the LDP, was reorganized as the NFP in December 1994; however, it split into six groups in 1998. The DP, which is supposed to be another major rival to the LDP, has been plagued by internal conflicts since its foundation. Therefore it is difficult for both LDP politicians and MOF bureaucrats to construct strategies to cope with new political circumstances.

When the mechanism, by which bureaucrats planned policies and put them into legislation by cooperating with party politicians, faced the Taishō Democracy and defeat in the Second World War, cooperation between politicians and bureaucrats was not as rigidly institutionalized as under LDP dominance. Regarding the Taishō Democracy, although some MHA bureaucrats became members of the Seiyūkai, the majority of bureaucrats took aloof attitudes towards party politicians to avoid being involved in party politics. During the Second World War, since the activities of political parties were largely limited, cooperation between party politicians and bureaucrats was not so much observed in decision-making processes of the government. As for the uncertainty of political parties' alignment, during the Taishō Democracy bureaucrats' counterparts were two major parties, the Seiyūkai and the Kenseitō, and either of the two parties could obtain the position of a ruling party. Immediately after the Second World

War bureaucrats were in a dominant position in the Japanese political system because of the purge of many party politicians from their public positions, and since 1995 the LDP has monopolized the ruling position of the Diet. Therefore the political circumstances in both these cases were less uncertain compared with those after 1993.

It can be said that since 1993 Japanese politics has been in a period of transition to a new political equilibrium. Politicians and MOF bureaucrats have not been able to establish an effective relationship to settle political and economic issues, which has caused political confusion and delay in taking measures to surmount political and economic problems.

5 Introduction of the consumption tax in 1989

Close cooperation between MOF bureaucrats and the LDP under LDP dominance promoted a high growth in the Japanese economy in the 1960s and 1970s. In July 1960, an ex-MOF executive, Ikeda Hayato, formed the First Ikeda Cabinet, and the Cabinet proposed 'The Income Doubling Programme' in which he pledged to double the national income within ten years. The MOF answered this plan by expanding annual expenditure and a government investment and loans programme (Zaisei Tōyūshi). In the budget of the 1961 fiscal year, while the amount of tax reduction totalled 113 billion yen, the annual expenditure and the government investment and loans programme increased to 19.4 per cent and 30.5 per cent respectively from the previous fiscal year to improve social welfare systems and infrastructure (Ōkurashō Zaiseishishitsu 1998: 209). The average growth rates of the annual expenditure and government investment and loans programme from the 1961 fiscal year to the 1971 fiscal year were 16.76 per cent and 20.8 per cent respectively. The Japanese economy experienced 'the high growth period' (Kōdo Seichōki) during the 1960s and early 1970s.

When the 'oil price shock' attacked the Japanese economy in 1973,[1] the Japanese economy suffered from serious inflation. An ex-MOF executive, Fukuda Takeo, was appointed Finance Minister in 1973. The MOF succeeded in restraining the annual expenditure of the 1974 fiscal year. The growth rate of annual expenditure shrank from 25.7 per cent (in the 1973 fiscal year) to 8.5 per cent. On the other hand, the reduction in income tax amounted to 2 trillion yen, and a supplementary government investment and loans programme (636 billion yen) was put into practice to support small and medium-sized enterprises. Thus the Japanese economy overcame the serious inflation after the 'oil price shock'.

The introduction of the consumption tax, which was enforced in April 1989, illustrates how the issue settling system functioned successfully under LDP dominance. The structure of the Japanese tax system after the Second World War was established following the Shoup Report,[2] which proposed a tax system mainly depending on direct taxes, such as an income tax and a corporate tax. Since then, although there have been minor revisions, there has been no significant change which would bring about a new imposition on Japanese taxpayers as a whole. As will be explained later, the MOF fostered the introduction of a broad-based indirect tax system as a long-term issue in order to cover the shortfall of tax revenue and to stop the issuance of deficit-covering bonds. However, the introduction of a new tax was widely regarded as an unpopular issue. The result of an opinion poll conducted by the *Asahi Shinbun* in March 1987 showed that 82 per cent of respondents opposed the introduction of a new broad-based indirect tax system, while only 7 per cent approved of its introduction (*Asahi Shinbun*, 14 March 1987). After the LDP announced the 'Major Line of Structural Tax Reform' on 15 June 1988, which proposed the introduction of the consumption tax, the *Asahi Shinbun* conducted an opinion poll and found that 60 per cent of respondents still opposed the introduction of the consumption tax (*Asahi Shinbun*, 26 June 1988). Because of strong opposition by the public, opposition parties and even LDP members, the Ōhira Cabinet and the Nakasone Cabinet failed to introduce a new broad-based indirect tax system.

Considering the above situations, it can be said that it seemed most unlikely that the government would legislate a new indirect tax system, such as a consumption tax, which would impose on the Japanese taxpayers as a whole. Nevertheless, the Takeshita Cabinet succeeded in legislating the Consumption Tax Law in 1989.

In the 1980s, organization of and factional control over LDP members was at its height. Not only was the bottom-up structure of the LDP's decision-making process institutionalized (decisions were made in the Divisions of the PARC first and those decisions were passed on to the EC) but also each faction formed an organizational structure similar to LDP organizations. In 1987, the Director General of each faction formed the Committee of Director General of Factions to coordinate the factions. Based on the above circumstances in the LDP, cooperation between bureaucrats, LDP executives and faction leaders was firmly institutionalized in the 1980s. Bureaucrats could grasp the decision-making process of the LDP by participating in its every stage, from the Divisions of the PARC to the EC, and by counting on faction executives' control over their members. As a result, this cooperation, which was the essential component of the issue settling system, became firm and stable by the end of the 1980s. The LDP organizations such as the PARC and the Tax System Research Council (LDP TSRC), kept their important positions in the decision-making process of the government. Therefore their decisions actually determined the government's decisions. LDP members were strictly controlled through factions; as a result, they followed faction leaders' decisions. LDP politicians and bureaucrats formed close relationships. The stability and effectiveness of close cooperation between bureaucrats, LDP executives and faction leaders reached a peak at that time. Consequently, the MOF succeeded in enacting its plan, the introduction of the consumption tax, by making the best use of the issue settling system. It can therefore be said that the success in introducing the consumption tax demonstrates the effectiveness of the issue settling system.

Details of the introduction of the consumption tax

The attempts to introduce a new indirect tax by 1987

After the first oil price shock in 1973, the Japanese economy experienced negative economic growth. As a result, the tax revenue shortfall in the 1975 fiscal year amounted to about 3 trillion yen, which was 22.3 per cent of the initial estimate of tax revenue. The government issued 3 trillion 480 billion yen of national bonds, 2 trillion 290 billion yen of which were deficit-covering bonds.[3] Consequently, the proportion of tax revenue to general account revenue fell to 60 per cent. The bond dependency ratio of the budget sharply increased from 9.4 per cent (the initial budget of the 1975 fiscal year) to 26.3 per cent. Finance Minister Ōhira Masayoshi delivered 'the Declaration of Fiscal Crisis' at the House of Representatives Budget Committee.

The MOF already recognized the need for a broad-based indirect tax and studied the value-added tax (VAT) systems which had already been introduced in European Community countries, and in the autumn of 1970, it formed a research group to study VAT (Kinoshita 1992: 526).

In 1971, the Government Tax System Research Council (GTSRC)[4] emphasized the need for a broad-based tax on consumption in the 'Long Term Proposal on the Tax System'. The large tax revenue shortfall in the budget for fiscal year 1975 put this issue on the political agenda (Mizuno 1993: 19). In October 1977, the GTSRC presented 'A Proposal on the Future Tax System', which suggested that, in order to be freed from dependence on a large issuance of national bonds, it was a reasonable policy to adopt a broad-based tax on consumption, and it advised that the introduction of a system such as the VAT should be considered. Following this proposal, the government began to discuss a new tax on consumption and, in December 1978, both the GTSRC and the Tax System Research Council of the LDP (LDP TSRC) proposed that a general consumption tax should be introduced in the 1980 fiscal year. According to those proposals, the Prime Minister at that time, Ōhira Masayoshi, an ex-MOF official, was determined to implement tax reform in the 1980 fiscal year.

In January 1979 at a Cabinet meeting, the Ōhira Cabinet did decide to introduce a general consumption tax in the 1980 fiscal year. However, LDP members, even the 'zeisei (tax) zoku' took a negative attitude towards the introduction of the general consumption tax. Business circles and public opinion strongly opposed it. Finally, Prime Minister Ōhira was forced to abandon the introduction of the general consumption tax in the 1979 general election campaign. Opposition parties attempted to eliminate the possibility of a future introduction of a general consumption tax by passing a resolution 'to abandon a general consumption tax'. The LDP and the MOF made an effort to preserve the possibility of the future introduction of a general consumption tax. The LDP, especially Finance Minister Takeshita Noboru, and the MOF vigorously negotiated with opposition parties and succeeded in changing the resolution into a resolution 'on fiscal reconstruction'. The resolution admitted that the general consumption tax that the government had attempted to introduce in the 1980 fiscal year had not been supported by the public, and it asked that fiscal reconstruction should be achieved first by administrative reforms and the rectification of tax inequality, and then by fundamental reforms of the current tax system.[5]

After the 1979 general election, the Suzuki Cabinet, which followed the Ōhira Cabinet, announced 'administrative and fiscal reform' and 'fiscal reconstruction without a tax increase'. Although the attempt to introduce the general consumption tax failed, the MOF adopted clever strategies to place the introduction of a value-added tax on the political agenda. Under the label 'administrative and fiscal reform', the expenditure items of each ministry's budget were uniformly curtailed, and the constraint of a 'zero ceiling' – in which the expenditure level of each ministry in the next fiscal year was assessed at the same level as that in the current fiscal year – severely restricted any increase in expenditure, except for defence and official development assistance (ODA). In spite of the restraint of expenditure, deficit-covering bonds were continuously issued. Figures 5.1 and 5.2 show the rates of dependence of revenue on national bonds and the amounts of the issuance of deficit-covering bonds from 1975 to 1985 respectively. The rate and the amount increased from 1975 to 1980, and although both of them slightly decreased after 1980, deficit-covering bonds were issued amounting to more than 6 billion yen every fiscal year from 1980 to 1985. In addition, the restraint of expenditure, especially the expenditure on public works and subsidies, caused dissatisfaction among LDP members.[6]

In the six years after 1978 while expenditure had been curtailed, no reduction of income tax had been put into practice. In the deliberations on the budget of the 1984 fiscal year, the reduction of income tax was heatedly discussed and, as a result, a reduction in income tax was introduced in the 1984 fiscal year. In order to secure a revenue source for this reduction, the rates of corporate tax, commodity tax and liquor tax were raised, and the revision of taxable items of the commodity tax regarding office automation facilities, such as computers and photocopiers, was discussed in the LDP TSRC.[7] Although business leaders had demanded 'fiscal reconstruction without a tax increase', they thought that accepting the introduction of a value-added tax system was inevitable. For example, on 7 January 1985, the Federation of Economic Organizations (Keidanren), one of four major business organizations, decided to create a proposal for the future tax system that would include the introduction of a broad-based indirect tax system (*Asahi Shinbun*, 8 January 1985). Thus the condition for reviving the introduction of a value-added tax on the political agenda was prepared.

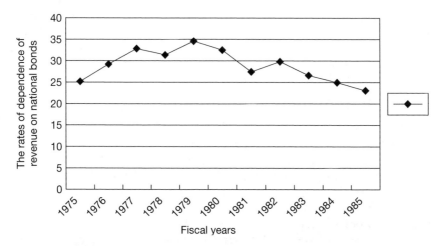

Figure 5.1 The rates of dependence of revenue on national bonds (1975–1985)

Source: *Gendai Yōgo no Kiso Chishiki* 2002: 203.

Note: the rate of dependence of revenue on national bonds (%) = the total amount of revenue by the issuance of national bonds divided by the total amount of general account expenditure x 100 .

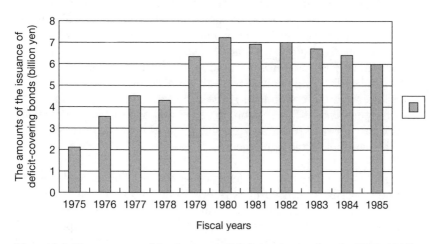

Figure 5.2 The amounts of the issuance of deficit-covering bonds (1975–1985)

Source: *Jiyūkokuminsha* 2002: 203.

After the simultaneous elections of the House of Representatives (HR) and the House of Councillors (HC) in July 1986, the Third Nakasone Cabinet was formed, having gained a record-breaking 300 seats out of 511 in the HR. Prime Minister Nakasone Yasuhiro appealed for tax reform as one of 'final accounts of postwar politics' (*Asahi Shibun*, evening edition, 26 January 1987). In his administrative policy speech of 26 January 1987, he pledged that the tax reform bills that were supposed to be submitted to the Diet would reform the tax system based on the Shoup Proposal of 1949 by revising indirect tax systems. In February 1987, the tax reform bills were endorsed by the Cabinet and submitted to the Diet. Regarding the Sales Tax Bill, opposition parties severely objected, and deliberation in the Budget Committee of the HR was suspended several times because opposition parties refused to attend the Budget Committee. In spite of this, the budget of the 1988 fiscal year passed the Budget Committee of the HR on 15 April. The attitudes of the opposition parties became more confrontational. The LDP began to negotiate with opposition parties with respect to the Sales Tax Bill in order to let the budget of the 1988 fiscal year pass the plenary session of the HR. The LDP presented a plan to the Speaker of the HR and, in accordance with this plan, the Speaker presented a mediation proposal to the LDP and opposition parties. On 23 April 1987, the LDP and opposition parties (except for the Japan Communist Party) agreed to this proposal, and the budget of the 1988 fiscal year passed the plenary session of the HR. The proposal included the following points:

1   The Sales Tax Bill would be left to the Speaker of the HR.[8]
2   All the parties would cooperate and make the maximum effort to put tax reform into practice; this would include the revision of the tax revenue share of direct and indirect tax.
3   A committee on tax reform would be established in the HR.
4   The Sales Tax Bill would be dealt with according to the result of discussion in the committee. If the committee did not present a decision by the end of this session, the LDP and opposition parties would make an effort to reach an agreement and to deal with the Sales Tax Bill according to the agreement.

Although the Sales Tax Bill was finally dropped, the LDP succeeded in preserving the possibility of future tax reform in this proposal. On 13 October 1987, the LDP TSRC decided the 'Principle on Fundamental Reform on Tax System', and on 15 October 1987 the PARC and the EC approved this principle. It was also submitted to and approved by the Cabinet meeting on 16 October 1987. The principle included the following points:

1   Fundamental reform of the present tax system should be implemented according to the mediation proposal presented by the Speaker of the HR on 23 April 1987.

2   Considering the feeling of middle-income-level groups, that the tax was too heavy, a fair income tax system should be implemented.
3   A corporate tax system that would adapt to a globalized economy should be established.
4   The present indirect tax systems should be fundamentally reformed.
5   The inheritance tax and other taxes on properties should be reexamined.

The Takeshita Cabinet, which followed the Nakasone Cabinet in November 1987, tackled tax reform, including the introduction of a new tax on consumption, according to this principle.

Details of the introduction of the consumption tax

In November 1987, the Takeshita Cabinet was formed, and from the beginning, Prime Minister Takeshita Noboru presented structural tax reform as a primary part of the agenda of his cabinet. At the press conference of 31 October 1987, he stated that he would execute tax reform according to the 'Principle on Fundamental Reform on Tax System', and on a television programme he presented the view that: 'The present indirect tax system is too complicated. We should change this system into a more simple tax system. I think conditions for which we have a thorough discussion about this issue have been prepared . . .' (*Asahi Shinbun*, 1 November 1987).

In November 1987, Prime Minister Takeshita submitted an enquiry about structural tax reform to the GTSRC. The enquiry asked the GTSRC to present a concrete proposal with respect to appropriate tax systems on income, corporate, property and consumption considering the 'Principle on Fundamental Reform on Tax System' and the current circumstances. The GTSRC held public hearings on 8 and 9 December 1987, and formed committees on the direct tax system, the indirect tax system and basic issues of tax systems. Concrete issues were discussed in those committees. In February 1988, the GTSRC presented the 'Basic Issues of Tax System Reform', which proposed that the introduction of a broad-based indirect tax should be discussed, and it held public hearings in February and March 1988 regarding the 'Basic Issues of Tax System Reform'. On 28 April, the GTSRC presented an interim report on tax reform. Its outline was to:

1   reduce income tax and residents' tax by decreasing the number of brackets in the tax rate and by increasing the amount of deductions;
2   introduce a new consumption tax;
3   reduce the inheritance tax by raising the lowest taxable limit;
4   reduce the corporate tax by reducing the basic tax rate;
5   revise the existing tax systems in order to ease the public feelings of tax inequality.

As for the LDP, the LDP TSRC, one of the organizations of the PARC, played a main role in dealing with this issue. In December 1987, the LDP TSRC began to discuss structural tax reform. After the budget of the 1989 fiscal year passed the HR on 10 March 1987, the LDP TSRC had an intensive discussion over this issue. In April 1988, it held public hearings with industrial groups and business circles. On 28 May, the LDP TSRC presented an interim report to the EC and the PARC, and it had finished the discussion on the main issues of tax reform by 2 June. On 3 and 4 June 1988, Divisions of the PARC discussed this interim report. Finally, on 14 June the LDP TSRC presented the 'Major Line of Structural Tax Reform' and, on the same day, the PARC and the EC approved it. The outline of the 'Major Line of Structural Tax Reform' was to:

1   introduce a value-added type indirect tax: the consumption tax with the account method;
2   revise existing indirect taxes;
3   reduce income tax and residents' tax by decreasing the number of brackets in the tax rate, reducing the maximum rates and increasing the amount of deductions;
4   reduce the basic rate of the corporate tax from 42 per cent to 37.5 per cent;
5   reduce the inheritance tax by raising the lowest taxable limit and reducing its maximum rate;
6   revise the existing tax system in order to ease the public feelings of tax inequality.

On 15 June, the GTSRC presented the 'Final Report on Structural Tax Reform'. Its content was almost the same as that of its interim report, and it approved the fact that 'the "Major Line of Structural Tax Reform" presented by the LDP TSRC mostly agreed with the basic principle presented in the interim report presented by the GTSRC on 28 April 1987' (*Asahi Shinbun*, 16 June 1987). On 28 June, the Cabinet approved the 'Major Line of Tax Reform', which was created by the MOF based on the 'Major Line of Structural Tax Reform' presented by the LDP TSRC and the final report presented by the GTSRC. On 29 July, the Cabinet submitted a package of bills on tax reform that included the Consumption Tax Bill.

Unlike the sales tax case, opposition parties were divided over the consumption tax.[9] On 15 June, after the 'Major Line of Structural Tax Reform' was approved by the LDP, the leader of the DSP, Tsukamoto Saburō, presented three conditions: the reduction of income tax in the 1989 fiscal year; discussion between the LDP and opposition parties regarding the rectification of tax inequality; and the creation of middle-term plans for administrative reforms and welfare systems. He announced that the DSP would attend the deliberation on the Consumption Tax Bill in the Diet if the LDP promised to implement those conditions. After the package of tax reform bills, which included the Consumption Tax Bill, was submitted to the Diet on 14 September, the Special Committee on Tax System was formed in the HR to deliberate on the package of tax reform bills. Opposition parties demanded that the rectification of tax inequality should be discussed in the Special Committee before the deliberation on the package of tax reform bills. The LDP compromised with opposition parties and first discussed the rectification of tax inequality in the Special Committee; they reached an agreement with respect to taxation on the profit from sales of stocks.[10] In addition, responding to the conditions that the DSP demanded, the 'Plan for the Promotion of Administrative and Fiscal Reforms' and the 'Basic Principles and Targets for Long-Life and Welfare Society' were presented to the DSP and submitted to the Special Committee by the MOF, the Ministry of Health and Welfare and the Ministry of Labour. Although the LDP and opposition parties discussed the rectification of tax inequality as preparation for the deliberation on the package of tax reform bills in the Special Committee on the Tax System, opposition parties still refused to vote on the package of tax reform bills and to deliberate on this in the plenary session of the HR. Finally, on 10 November 1988, the package of tax reform bills passed the Special Committee on the Tax System without the attendance of opposition parties.

Despite such a forced passage in the Special Committee on the Tax System, the LDP wanted to avoid a forced passage of the Consumption Tax Bill in the plenary session of the HR, since this would incur public antipathy. Therefore, although the LDP had a majority in the HR and in the HC, the LDP negotiated with the DSP and the CGP in order to ensure their attendance in the plenary session of the HR. After negotiations between the DSP, the CGP and the LDP, agreements were made between them. These agreements included the addition of an article to the Consumption Tax Bill that provided that the consumption tax law would be applied flexibly mainly through public relations, consultations and administrative guidance for six months from April 1989 and that there would be payment of extra welfare pension to recipients of the old-age welfare pension. The bills passed the HR on 16 November 1988 and the HC on 24 December 1988.

The role of LDP organizations

The LDP TSRC played a key role in introducing the consumption tax. The Special Committee on Tax Reform was formed as an organization of the PARC in 1956, and in 1959 it was renamed the Tax System Research Council (the LDP TSRC). Although it was not particularly active in the first half of the 1960s, in the 1970s it became a more active and influential organization of the PARC. Every year in the process of budget compilation, the current tax systems are re-examined to look at the tax revenue of the fiscal year, and the LDP TSRC creates the 'Major Line of Tax System Reform'. This has actually formed the government's decision on tax reforms in every fiscal year. Satō Seizaburō and Matsuzaki explain that interest groups seeking favourable treatment found that it was necessary to submit requests to the LDP TSRC as it became influential in the 1970s (Satō and Matsuzaki 1986: 112).The number of organizations that submitted requests to the LDP TSRC in connection with the 'Major Line of Tax System Reform' rapidly increased from 95 in 1970 to 84 in 1980s and soared from 198 in 1984 to 358 in 1986 (Satō and Matsuzaki 1986: 113).

Another example showing the influence of the LDP TSRC is its relationship with the GTSRC. Satō and Matsuzaki point out that at first the LDP TSRC decided on the 'Major Line of Tax System Reform' after the GTSRC had presented its own proposal; however, in 1967, regarding the 1968 fiscal year, the LDP TSRC presented the 'Major Line of Tax System Reform' of the 1968 fiscal year on the same day that the GTSRC presented its own proposal. Since then, the LDP TSRC has actually taken the leadership in deciding the contents of tax reform in every fiscal year (Satō and Matsuzaki 1986: 112–13).

Concerning the tax reform of the 1989 fiscal year, which included the consumption tax, the LDP TSRC also took the leadership. The GTSRC tried to keep its proposals of its interim report in line with those of the LDP TSRC.[11] For instance, over the tax rate, which caused a heated discussion, the interim report of the GTSRC only suggested that the same tax rate should be applied to all taxable items.[12] This issue was intensely discussed in the LDP TSRC, and it was finally decided that 3 per cent should be applied to all taxable items. With respect to the method of calculation, the interim report of the GTSRC presented both arguments that supported the invoice method and also arguments that supported the account method.[13] Regarding other issues related to the interests of corporations, such as the tax exemption point, the optional use of the simplified calculation rule and the areas of tax-free transaction, the interim report of the GTSRC did not make a concrete proposal, and the LDP TSRC decided on those issues in the 'Major Line of Structural Tax Reform'. Therefore the details of tax reform, especially on the consumption tax, were decided by the LDP TSRC rather than the GTSRC.

The discussions of LDP organizations such as the LDP TSRC, the PARC and the EC were incorporated into the 'Major Line of Structural Tax Reform'. After the LDP TSRC presented its interim report to the PARC and the EC on 27 May, Divisions of the PARC discussed the report on 3 and 4 June. In each Division of the PARC, details of the discussion in the LDP TSRC were reported. On 6 June, the results of the discussion in 17 Divisions of the PARC were reported to the LDP TSRC, and the LDP TSRC issued the 'Major Line of Structural Tax Reform', based on the discussions in the PARC and the EC.[14]

After the LDP decided the 'Major Line of Structural Tax Reform', the Cabinet meeting approved the 'Major Line of Tax Reform' on 28 June. Table 5.1 shows the main details of the consumption tax in the Interim

Table 5.1 The consumption tax proposals of the GTSRC, the LDP TSRC and the Consumption Tax Bill

	Interim (Final) Report of the GTSRC	'Major Line of Structural Tax Reform' of LDP TSRC	Consumption Tax Bill
Type of tax	value-added tax	value-added tax	value-added tax
Calculation method	invoice method or account method	invoice method	invoice method
Tax rate	single rate is preferable	3%	3%
Date of enforcement	no specific proposal	1 April 1989	1 April 1989
Tax exemption point	no specific proposal	30 million yen of taxable amount sold	30 million yen of taxable amount sold
Tax-free transaction	no specific proposal	transfer or loan of estate interests of loan, insurance contribution transfer of stocks and bonds transfer of stamps commissions of international postal exchange, foreign exchange, services of government (including local government) medical treatments based on medical insurance social welfare service tuition fee of schools founded according to the School Education Law	transfer or loan of estate interests of loan, insurance contribution transfer of stocks and bonds transfer of stamps commissions of international postal exchange, foreign exchange, services of government (including local government) medical treatments based on medical insurance social welfare service tuition fee of schools founded according to the School Education Law
Optional use of simplified calculation rule	no specific proposal	less than 500 million yen of taxable amount sold	less than 500 million yen of taxable amount sold

(Final) Report of the GTSRC (the contents of the final report of the GTSRC were the same as those of its interim report, the 'Major Line of Structural Tax Reform' presented by the LDP TSRC and a Consumption Tax Bill submitted by the Cabinet). As this table shows, the main details of the Consumption Tax Bill were almost the same as the 'Major Line of Structural Tax Reform' approved by the LDP.

In the process of introducing the consumption tax, the LDP TSRC played a main role, and the PARC and the EC also participated in creating the 'Major Line of Structural Tax Reform'. The GTSRC kept its proposals in line with those of the LDP TSRC, and it authorized the proposals of the LDP TSRC in its final report. Furthermore, both the 'Major Line of Tax Reform' approved by the Cabinet meeting and the package of bills of tax reform were based on the 'Major Line of Structural Tax Reform' presented by the LDP TSRC. The results of discussion in LDP organizations such as the LDP TSRC, the PARC and the EC were incorporated in the decision of the Cabinet and the bills submitted by the Cabinet. It can therefore be said that the decisions of LDP organizations were actually the decisions of the government. Thus, with regard to the introduction of the consumption tax, LDP organizations played a crucial role in the decision-making process of the government.

The management of the LDP

When the Nakasone Cabinet attempted to legislate the sales tax, many LDP members, especially junior LDP members or members from closely contested constituencies, were against its introduction. Their supporting groups in their constituencies, kōenkai, were mainly based on local small-sized businesses and shops, which strongly opposed the introduction of the sales tax. LDP members were afraid that they would lose the support of their kōenkai, and they gave priority to their kōenkai's demands over the LDP's decisions. For example, Hatoyama Kunio and Fukaya Ryūji, who were both from the closely contested eigth constituency of Tōkyō, attended an anti-sales tax meeting held by small shopkeepers in their constituency. Prime Minister Takeshita controlled the LDP from the beginning, unlike the situation in the Nakasone sales tax case. He was the leader of the Keiseikai (Takeshita faction), the largest faction of the LDP at that time, and could count on its support. In addition, he was appointed President of the LDP without an LDP Presidential election. Former Prime Minister Nakasone Yasuhiro recommended him as the next Prime Minister, and other factions agreed with Nakasone's recommendation. The Takeshita Cabinet began without severe conflicts between the Keiseikai and other factions.[15]

Prime Minister Takeshita also kept his control over the LDP by appointing his right-hand men to crucial positions in the LDP and the Cabinet. For instance, he appointed Obuchi Keizō (a member of the Keiseikai) as the Cabinet Secretary. He negotiated with the LDP to implement the Prime

Minister's decisions. Vice Cabinet Secretary Ozawa Ichirō (a member of the Keiseikai at that time) handled negotiations with opposition parties.

In addition, Prime Minister Takeshita was well known for his ability to manipulate factional control. He controlled the personnel matters of the LDP, which were based on the balance of factional power, and by managing personnel matters, he had a tight grip on the LDP.[16]

In the process of the introduction of the consumption tax, he made the best use of factions to control LDP members. As the leader of the largest faction, the Keiseikai, he counted on its firm support. Kanemaru Shin, who was an influential executive of the Takeshita faction (Keiseikai) at that time, appealed to members of the Keiseikai at a general meeting that all the members of the Keiseikai should unite together and use all means to ensure that the tax reform bills were enacted.

Prime Minister Takeshita also utilized the management function of factions. On 25 August 1989, at a meeting of the Secretaries General of each faction, the Cabinet Secretary, Obuchi Keizō, asked the Secretaries General to cooperate with the Prime Minister to get the tax reform bills enacted, and they agreed that each faction would do its best to let the Consumption Tax Bill be passed by the Diet. Following this agreement, each faction adopted a resolution to allow the Consumption Tax Bill to be passed by the Diet. On 26 August, the Nakasone faction adopted a resolution: 'We will unite ourselves tightly, devote all our energies, and put the tax reform bills into legislation in this extraordinary session' (*Asahi Shinbun* evening edition, 30 August 1988). On 29 August at the Takeshita faction meeting, Kanemaru Shin, ex-Vice Prime Minister, appealed, 'If the consumption tax is not put into practice, the meaning of the existence of the Keiseikai will be questioned. We must devote ourselves to putting the tax reform bills into legislation' (*Asahi Shinbun* evening edition, 30 August 1988), and members agreed to adopt his appeal as a resolution. On 4 September the Miyazawa faction adopted the following resolution: 'Political circumstances face a crucial moment with regard to the tax reform. We unite ourselves tightly under the leadership of Mr Miyazawa, and put the tax reform bills into practice in this session.' On the same day, the Abe faction also decided, 'We will devote our energies and let the tax reform bills pass the Diet in this extraordinary session.' Furthermore, faction leaders and executives prevented their members from speaking publicly against the consumption tax. The *Asahi Shinbun* reported that executives of the Abe faction told junior members who criticized the procedure of the discussion in the LDP TSRC, 'You should not get the Secretary General [Abe Shintarō, the leader of Abe faction] into trouble' (*Asahi Shinbun*, 18 May 1988).

Faction leaders and executives controlled their members effectively. The LDP was integrated by factional control and supported Prime Minister Takeshita with respect to putting the Consumption Tax Bill into legislation.

Cooperation between the LDP and the MOF

The MOF closely negotiated with executives of the LDP TSRC from the beginning. The decision-making process of the LDP TSRC consists of three stages: the Inner Committee, which consists of ex-Chairs of the LDP TSRC and some influential LDP members; the Chair and Vice Chairs Committee; and the Small Committee in which all members of the LDP TSRC may participate. First, the Inner Committee makes decisions that actually decide a course of discussions in the Chair and Vice Chairs Committee and the Small Committee, then issues are discussed in the Committee of Chair and Vice Chairs, and finally they are discussed in the Small Committee. MOF bureaucrats attend all three stages and hand out materials to them.

With regard to the introduction of the consumption tax, the MOF maintained this close cooperation with executives of the LDP TSRC. When Yamanaka Sadanori was appointed as Chair of the LDP TSRC on 29 July 1986, executives of the Tax Bureau of the MOF 'immediately contacted the Chair of the LDP TSRC, Yamanaka, and discussed how to deal with the tax reform issue' (Mizuno 1993: 82). When the Takeshita Cabinet succeeded the Third Nakasone Cabinet, the MOF created the 'Principles of Structural Tax Reform' and both the LDP and the Cabinet approved them as their own principles. The MOF also consulted the Chair of the LDP TSRC, Yamanaka Sadanori, and created the 'Basic Principles of Structural Tax Reform' (Mizuno 1993: 183). The LDP TSRC agreed it on 13 October, and the PARC and the EC approved it on 15 October as the decision of the LDP. Thus, the plans that the MOF created in consultation with LDP executives were submitted to organizations of the LDP and approved as the decision of the LDP.[17]

When many industries demanded a zero-tax rate system at hearings conducted by the LDP TSRC, the MOF strongly opposed this system. The MOF insisted that a zero-tax rate system would allow 'the tax-exempt corporations reimbursement of the taxes on their purchases' (Katō 1997: 218–19) and submitted the relevant data to the LDP TSRC. The LDP TSRC Subcommittee Vice-Chairman, Murakami Tatsuo, who was an ex-MOF official, implied at a press conference that there was no possibility of conceding a zero-tax rate system in the consumption tax.

As for negotiations with opposition parties, it was the LDP executives who handled negotiations with executives of the opposition parties. The MOF supported the LDP by preparing answers to the demands of the DSP and the CGP. For example, the DSP demanded the postponing of the date of enforcement of the consumption tax until April 1991 as a condition for their attendance at the plenary session of the HR. The government and LDP executives asked the MOF to report to them regarding the following points:

1   the reason why the date of enforcement of the consumption tax could not be postponed; and

2   whether the consumption tax would be applied smoothly although only four and a half months were left until the scheduled date of its enforcement, April 1989 (Mizuno 1993: 328).

The MOF reported to the government and LDP executives:

1   The consumption tax was a part of structural tax reform, which also included the reduction of income tax and residents' tax and the revision of the liquor tax. It was difficult to postpone the reduction of the income tax and the residents' tax, and the postponement of the revision of the liquor tax would cause difficulties with respect to the relationship with the European Community and the UK.
2   The procedure of the consumption tax was substantially simplified and the burden of preparation for its enforcement on corporations was reduced by adopting the account method.
3   Elections for the HC and the Tōkyō Metropolitan Assembly were going to be held in summer 1989, and the general election was going to be held by July 1991. Political confusion would be brought about if these elections were held before the enforcement of the consumption tax (Mizuno 1993: 328–9).

Based on these arguments, 'the MOF strongly requested [LDP executives] that the consumption tax should be enforced on 1 April 1989' (Mizuno 1993: 329). The LDP's answer to the DSP was that the scheduled date of enforcement should not be changed, and consequently the LDP and the DSP agreed a compromise, whereby an article that provided that the consumption tax be applied flexibly through mainly public relations, consultation and administrative guidance by 30 September 1989 was added to the Consumption Tax Bill.

The CGP demanded the payment of an allowance for nursing care of the aged in order to support bedridden aged people. The MOF opposed this request and proposed an alternative plan that would introduce the expansion of tax deductions as a welfare policy for bedridden aged people (Mizuno 1993: 326). Finally, the LDP and the CGP agreed that the deduction amount for dependants would be increased.

The MOF not only maintained cooperation with the LDP but also kept a close connection with Prime Minister Takeshita.[18] He was the Minister of Finance of the Ōhira Cabinet and the Second Nakasone Cabinet. While he was in office, he formed personal contacts with MOF executives. As explained before, after the 1979 general election, opposition parties intended to pass a resolution in which the introduction of a general consumption tax, which was a heated issue during the 1979 general election campaign, would be clearly rejected. The MOF and Finance Minister Takeshita vigorously cooperated and negotiated with opposition parties in order to make the resolution relevant to fiscal reconstruction and to preserve the possibility of future tax reform (Mizuno 1993: 21–3). They succeeded in preserving the possibility of future tax reform in the 'Fiscal Reform Resolution'.

In the process of introducing the consumption tax, the MOF created bills and plans for tax reform, and participated in each stage of the decision-making process of LDP organizations, such as the LDP TSRC, the PARC and the EC, by negotiating with LDP executives, such as the Chair of the LDP TSRC, Yamanaka Sadanori. When LDP executives negotiated with opposition parties, the MOF cooperated with them by creating proposals that answered the demands of opposition parties. The MOF could utilize close connections with LDP executives in order to put into effect their plan for tax reform.

Conclusion

The introduction of a broad-based indirect tax was difficult to put into effect, failing twice – under the Ōhira Cabinet and under the Nakasone Cabinet. The reason why the Takeshita Cabinet succeeded in implementing this unpopular policy was that the issue settling system, which was based on an integrated LDP organization and close cooperation between politicians and bureaucrats, functioned effectively.

As for LDP organizations, the LDP TSRC led the discussion of this issue and played a main role in the decision-making process, not only of the LDP but also of the government. The package of tax reform bills submitted by the government was based on the decisions of the LDP. Through discussion in the decision-making process of the LDP, such as discussions in the LDP TSRC, Divisions of the PARC and the EC, LDP members' opinion was incorporated in the decision not only of the LDP but also of the government.

With respect to factional control, under LDP dominance factions were systematized and they controlled their members by allocating political funds, supporting election campaigns and distributing cabinet and LDP organization posts. When the introduction of the consumption tax became a main part of the political agenda, Secretaries General of each faction had a meeting and agreed to support the Takeshita Cabinet in order to put the package of tax reform bills into legislation. Following this agreement, each faction adopted a resolution to unite to put the tax reform bills into practice. Under such factional control, LDP members obeyed this resolution. With regard to members who still tried to criticize LDP executives, faction leaders suppressed their movements one by one. Thus the LDP maintained its integrity through factional control.

Close cooperation between LDP executives and the MOF also contributed to the success of the introduction of the consumption tax. The MOF made the best use of its close connections with executives of the LDP TSRC and faction leaders. In the process of the discussions in LDP organizations, the MOF participated in every stage of those discussions by negotiating with LDP executives. As for negotiations with opposition parties, LDP executives handled negotiations with executives of opposition parties, and the MOF supported them by presenting answers and proposals. Since the LDP monopolized its position as a ruling party in the Diet and maintained a tight factional control on LDP members, the MOF could concentrate on negotiating with only LDP executives and faction leaders.[19]

Thus in the introduction of the consumption tax, the issue settling system worked effectively. The MOF succeeded in putting a highly unpopular policy into practice by making full use of the issue settling system.

6 The financial crisis in Japan 1994–1998

The MOF has been regarded by the public as the most powerful and competent ministry among Japanese administrative organizations. It has monopolized the jurisdictions of taxation and budget compilation; it has therefore controlled both annual revenue and expenditure. Furthermore, through the budgetary process, it has played the role of arbitrator or coordinator between ministries' policies (Brown Jr 1999: 161). As Peter Hartcher points out, the MOF has been regarded as 'much more than an office of government' and 'In Japan, there is no institution with more power' (Hartcher 1998: 2). In particular, the MOF had strictly controlled financial policies and institutions by monopolizing information, issuing directives (tsūtatsu) and executing administrative guidance. Thus the MOF had effectively dealt with financial institutions that were in difficulties. For example, when the difficulties of the Yamaichi Securities Company were revealed in 1965, the MOF cooperated with the Bank of Japan and city banks that had close business relationships with the Yamaichi Securities Company and succeeded in restoring its business. Until 1993, the MOF had been proud that no financial institution had failed since the Second World War. However, the MOF was severely criticized for financial crises in the latter half of the 1990s. The process of liquidation of the Jūsen and the Long-Term Credit Bank of Japan (LTCBJ) was confused, and such confusion and delay of liquidation worsened the Japanese economy. In this chapter, I explain that such confusion was caused by the decline in the effectiveness of the issue settling system.

The influence of the malfunctioning issue settling system on the process of dealing with financial crises is clearly described by comparing two types of failure. The one is the failure of a financial institution that became a political issue, and the other is a failure that did not become a political issue. Once the failure of a financial institution becomes a political issue, politicians intervene in the process of its resolution, and bureaucrats have to negotiate with them in order to settle it. On the other hand, if the failure of a financial institution does not become a political issue, politicians do not intervene in the process of its resolution and the issue is dealt with by the MOF in its own territory. Therefore the failure of financial institutions in the latter half of the 1990s is examined by classifying them into these two types.

Financial policy after 1945

The MOF had strictly controlled financial policies and institutions and had the initiative in planning policies by monopolizing information and expertise.

Ramseyer and Rosenbluth argue that, in Japanese politics, bureaucrats, as agents of LDP politicians, execute LDP politicians' preferences; therefore LDP politicians, not bureaucrats, have the initiative in planning and implementing policies. As examples supporting their argument, Ramseyer and Rosenbluth cite the abandonment of a new banking law in 1951, the failure of new proposals by the MOF in 1956, the failure of 'the efficiency campaign' from 1965 to 1973, in 1977 and in 1979. They explain that those failures were the result of LDP politicians' veto on those policies. Therefore, they conclude, the MOF could not deviate from the preferences of the LDP (Ramseyer and Rosenbluth 1993: 125–7). However, their argument either overlooks other manoeuvres of the MOF or is based on misunderstanding. As explained in the following paragraphs, the MOF set the target or principles of financial policies and put them into effect using various measures, such as laws, directives and administrative guidance.

From 1946 to 1955, the MOF promoted the following principles for financial policy: the reconstruction of financial systems and the sound management of financial institutions. Responding to fragile economic circumstances immediately after the Second World War, the MOF intended to protect depositors and to maintain the credibility and order of markets by regulating and protecting financial institutions (Ōkurashō Zaiseishishitsu 1991: 80). In order to maintain sound management of financial institutions, the MOF prepared a revision of the Bank Law in 1951. The draft of the new Bank Law included:

1 raising the amount of minimum capital requirement;
2 restricting the amount that could be loaned to a single borrower;
3 restricting the possession of fixed assets for business use; and
4 giving the Minister of Finance authority to order or to direct financial institutions regarding their management.

This draft caused severe opposition from the banking industry, and it failed to be made law. In 1956, following this failure, the MOF created three bills to achieve the above principles: a bill for the introduction of a deposit insurance system; a bill for the introduction of systems to reconstruct financial institutions in financial difficulties; and a bill for the regulation of deposit contracts to prohibit unfair contracts. Of these, only the third bill was made law.

The attempts of the MOF to legislate the above bills failed. Nevertheless, the aims embodied in them were not abandoned by the MOF. The MOF put its intentions into practice through administrative guidance by issuing directives (Ōkurashō Zaiseishishitsu 1991: 167). It executed administrative guidance based on the directives described in the following paragraphs to achieve the sound management of financial institutions (Ōkurashō Zaiseishishitsu 1991: 168).

The directive of 19 March 1953 set the target ratio of current expenses to current income at 78 per cent, and banks whose ratio exceeded the target had to obtain the approval of the Director General of the Banking Bureau, reporting the cause and the measures to deal with such excess.

The directive of 2 November 1957 set the target loan-deposit ratio at less than 80 per cent, and limited the ratio of loans to a single borrower to net worth equity capital at less than 25 per cent.

The directive of 2 March 1959 provided that banks that could not achieve the target loan-deposit ratio (less than 80 per cent) were required to submit the list of the movements of their loan-deposit ratio with data that explained their loans to large-lot debtors and major industries, and that the MOF would then give them concrete directives regarding their business.[1] The directive of 2 March 1959 also set the ratio of the average balance of current assets to total deposit (more than 30 per cent) and the ratio of current expenses to current income (78 per cent).[2]

Following the above directives, banks were required to submit the plan of their business to the MOF and make detailed reports regarding the plan of loans to their major debtors and their demand for funds. Based on the plans and reports, the Banking Bureau made a list of the ranking of banks according to their achievement of the above target ratios, and it used the list as reference material. For instance, the Banking Bureau considered those data when it decided whether it should permit a bank to found a new branch. The Banking Bureau created Gyōmu Keikakuhō (the List of Ranking) bi-annually. With regard to each bank, the list enumerated the ratios of bank-loan deposit, current assets to total deposits, current expenses to current income, necessary expenses to gross revenue, and fixed assets to net worth equity capital, and it ranked the banks according to their ratios (Ōkurashō Zaiseishishitsu 1991: 178–90).

Although the MOF failed to legislate the bills in 1951 and 1956, it succeeded in achieving the same results by issuing directives and executing administrative guidance. Furthermore, by receiving detailed reports of their business from financial institutions, the MOF monopolized information about their business, which was indispensable to planning financial policies.

From 1967, the Banking Bureau set out 'the efficiency campaign', which was intended to promote an efficient financial system (Ōkurashō Zaiseishishitsu 1991: 347). The campaign proposed to re-examine the functional segmentation of financial institutions,[3] to promote competition between financial institutions and to prepare systems that would support such competition by promoting mergers between financial institutions and establishing a saving insurance system. Responding to this proposal, the Merger and Conversion of Business Law (1967) and the Deposit Insurance System Law (1971) were enacted. The Merger and Conversion of Business Law allowed mergers and conversion of business between city banks, mutual saving banks, credit associations and credit unions. As for the effect of this law, the number of mergers from 1965 to 1975 was 108 (13.5 cases per year), compared with 56 from 1956 to 1964 (4.3 cases per year) (Ōkurashō Zaiseishishitsu 1991: 439). Therefore the conclusion of Ramseyer and Rosenbluth about the efficiency campaign (1965–73) – that the efficiency campaign 'went nowhere' (Ramseyer and Rosenbluth 1993: 127) – is not appropriate.

The main theme of the revision of financial systems in 1979 was not the strengthening of the MOF's regulatory powers that Ramseyer and Rosenbluth point out (Ramseyer and Rosenbluth 1993: 127) but the relaxation of the functional segmentation of financial institutions. In June 1979, the Financial Systems Research Council proposed to improve flexibility regarding the business areas of banks. Responding to this proposal, the Long-Term Credit Banks Law and the Foreign Exchange Banks Law were revised. The most heatedly discussed issue was whether banks could sell government bonds 'over the counter' of banks as a business accompanying banking business that was permitted by the Article 5 of the Bank Law (Gotō 1992: 222–40).[4]

On 30 November 1980, the MOF presented the following three principles regarding securities business:

1 The business of public bonds by banks would be put in statutory form in the Bank Law.
2 According to the Securities and Exchange Law, banks were required to obtain approval from the MOF regarding securities business, and the present regulations would be applied to the permitted securities business.
3 This time revision prepared conditions for securities business by banks and the enforcement of securities business by banks would be discussed in future.

Banking business circles pressured LDP politicians to approve banks selling medium-term discount government bonds 'over the counter' as a business accompanying banking business. In April 1981, the Minister of Finance, Watanabe Michio, and the Chair of the PARC, Abe Shintarō, presented the following points to the representatives of banking business:

1 The Minister of Finance, Watanabe Michio, and the Chair of the PARC, Abe Shintarō, reached an agreement that the MOF would

decide whether it would give the approval of securities business to banks according to laws and taking circumstances into account.

2   This time revision of the Bank Law would put the securities business of banks in statutory form through the Bank Law.

3   The Minister of Finance, Watanabe Michio, and the Chair of the PARC, Abe Shintarō, were considering the establishment of a committee, consisting of three experts independent from both banking and securities businesses, to secure fair decisions regarding the enforcement of the approval of banks selling public bonds 'over the counter'.

The above three points were almost the same as the three principles presented by the MOF (Gotō 1992: 233). In May 1981, based on the three principles presented by the MOF, the revised Bank Law passed the Diet, and provided that banks could carry out securities business such as underwriting and distributing associated with the underwriting of public bonds as a business accompanying banking business (Gotō 1992: 235). It can therefore be said that the revision of financial systems in 1979 was put into effect according to the intention of the MOF.

Thus, contrary to the argument of Ramseyer and Rosenbluth that the MOF could not implement its preferences because of LDP politicians' veto, the MOF set forth the principles of financial policies and initiated policies to put them into practice. Although some bills, such as the revision of the Bank Law in 1951 and bills in 1956, were not legislated, the MOF succeeded in legislating some of them later (such as the Deposit Insurance System Law in 1971), and it took other measures, such as administrative guidance based on directives, to fulfil its intention. Formally, administrative guidance is not coercive. Nevertheless, banks followed it since it 'limited competition and protected markets and market shares, and consequently gave them substantial rents and a rather easy life' (Rixtel 2002: 120). If banks were reluctant to follow the directions of the MOF, the MOF could use 'a large array of sanctions' based on its licensing power, particularly licensing new branches, its authority to inspect financial institutions and its influence in tax matters (Rixtel 2002: 120). For instance, the MOF refused to give permission to the Mitsui Bank to open three new branches in 1980 when it transgressed the limit of lending to a single borrower. The Daiwa Bank had difficulties in obtaining approval from the MOF to open new branches after it disobeyed the direction of the MOF to separate banking business and trust business (Rixtel 2002: 120).

The MOF took the lead in planning and implementing financial policies. It set forth principles responding to economic and political circumstances, such as 'the sound management of financial institutions' or 'the efficiency campaign', and created bills and issued directives to achieve the aims of these principles. When bills drafted by the MOF were not legislated in 1951 and 1956, the MOF sought other measures to achieve the same results. It issued directives that regulated the business of financial institutions in detail, and made those institutions follow those directives by manoeuvring administrative guidance. Through those directives and administrative guidance, the MOF tightly controlled financial institutions and monopolized the information of their business. As cited later in this chapter, LDP politicians safely left the matter of financial policies in the hands of the MOF, and, as the case of relaxing the regulation of banks' securities business in 1979 shows, the LDP generally backed up the intentions of the MOF. It therefore seemed highly unlikely that the MOF would lose its control over the financial policy area and cause political confusion.

The failure of two credit unions (Tōkyō Kyōwa and Anzen)

The process of liquidation

The liquidation of two credit unions – the Tōkyō Kyōwa Credit Union and the Anzen Credit Union – was the beginning of the financial crises of the latter half of the 1990s.

On 17 September 1994, the *Nihon Keizai Shinbun*, one of Japan's quality papers, reported the financial difficulties of two credit unions, the Tōkyō Kyōwa Credit Union and the Anzen Credit Union. It revealed that the Tōkyō Metropolitan Government had advised two credit unions to reform their businesses. The MOF knew that financial difficulties had existed since 1993. Although the Governor of a prefecture has the authority to inspect and supervise credit unions, in the case of these two credit unions, it was the MOF and the Tōkyō Metropolitan Government that cooperated in inspecting them in 1993 and 1994. After the inspection of June 1994, the MOF began to plan a liquidation scheme for two credit unions, cooperating with the Bank of Japan and the Tōkyō Metropolitan Government. On 9 December 1994, the liquidation scheme was announced. In this scheme the two credit unions would be liquidated and their business would be transferred to the Tōkyō Kyōdō Bank funded by the Tōkyō Metropolitan Government, financial institutions and the Bank of Japan. Accordingly, the two credit unions were dissolved and their business was transferred to the Tōkyō Kyōdō Bank on 13 February 1995.

MOF's control over these failures

Issues about particular financial institutions have been dealt with by the MOF as administrative issues in which politicians refrained from intervention.[5] Katō Kōichi, the Secretary General of the LDP at that time, explained such behaviour of LDP politicians in an interview with the *Asahi Shinbun*:

> I feel responsibility for financial crises because we (politicians) did not voluntarily collect information about financial institutions or take

the leadership either. But if we intervened in issues of particular financial institutions, we would obtain critical information about financial situations of particular financial institutions, and that might arouse public suspicion of us for insider trading ...

(*Asahi Shinbun*, 22 February 1995)

For example, when the Yamaichi Securities Company faced financial difficulties in 1965, the MOF created a reconstruction plan and executed it, cooperating with the Bank of Japan and other financial institutions. Following this tradition, the planning of the liquidation scheme for the two credit unions was dealt with by the MOF as an administrative issue. Therefore the MOF controlled the whole process of making the liquidation plan, and took the leadership from the beginning. The Director General of the Banking Bureau at that time, Nishimura Yoshimasa, answered at the Budget Committee of the House of Representatives (HR) that the Banking Bureau had begun to prepare for the liquidation of the two credit unions after the inspection of July 1994.

Politicians did not intervene in the process of planning a scheme for liquidation. Even the Minister of Finance was only informed of the detail of the liquidation scheme just before its announcement. The Minister of Finance, Takemura Masayoshi, answered at the Budget Committee of HR that he had been informed of the scheme just before it was announced.[6]

After the scheme was announced, a scandal involving the Chief Executive Officer of the two credit unions and MOF executives about their excessive entertainment was revealed. The newly elected Governor of Tōkyō Metropolitan refused to fund the Tōkyō Kyōdō Bank. However, despite the scandal, the liquidation scheme was implemented, and the two credit unions were dissolved according to the scheme in 1995. The MOF took the lead and controlled the whole process of planning and executing the scheme. There was no political confusion in planning the liquidation scheme, and the liquidation of the two credit unions was carried out according to the scheme.

The failure of two securities companies (Sanyō and Kokusai)

The process of these failures

In 1996 the Japanese economy, which had been stagnant for a few years, seemed to be emerging from recession although its recovery was very fragile. The gross domestic product (GDP) during the January to March and April to June periods of 1996 was 8.4 per cent and –1.1 per cent respectively (annualized). The Second Hashimoto Cabinet set fiscal reform as its main political agenda, and decided that the general expenditure of the 1998 fiscal year would be reduced to less than that of the previous year. In 1997 the Japanese economy was thrown into recession. The GDP during the April to June period of 1997 plunged to –11.2 per cent (annualized). On 1 April 1997, the Hokkaidō Takushoku Bank and the Hokkaidō Bank announced that their merger would take place in April 1998. On the same day, the Nihon Credit Bank (NCB) affiliated non-banks filed for bankruptcy (their bankruptcy was declared on 7 April).

The Securities Bureau of the MOF realized the financial difficulties of the Sanyō Securities Company in advance. In January 1997 one insurance company informed the Securities Bureau that it would be difficult to extend the payment period of Sanyō's subordinate debt. The maturity date of Sanyō's subordinate debt to insurance companies, such as the Japan Insurance Company, was the end of January 1999. A securities company cannot calculate its subordinated debts as its net worth equity capital if their payment period is less than one year. Furthermore, according to the ministerial ordinance about Article 54 Clause 2 of the Securities and Exchange Law, the MOF should order a securities company to form a drastic reconstruction plan, such as a merger plan, when its equity ratio becomes less than 120 per cent. The equity ratio of the Sanyō Securities Company was 164.4 per cent at the end of March 1997. The Sanyō Securities Company was on the verge of failure. The Securities Bureau formed a rescue scheme for the Sanyō in which it would merge with the Kokusai Securities Company and the Sanwa Bank would fund the Kokusai Securities Company and the newly merged company. However, this scheme was revealed by the mass media on 26 September 1997, and the negotiation reached a deadlock. After this, the Securities Bureau prepared a scheme in which the Corporate Rehabilitation Law would be applied to Sanyō. On 3 November 1997 the Sanyō Securities Company, which was a middle-sized securities company in Japanese terms, filed for application of the Corporate Rehabilitation Law at the Tōkyō District Court.

On 12 November 1997, Tōkyō markets marked a triple depreciation (the stock price, the price of the government bonds and the appreciation of the yen against the dollar plunged). Foreign markets immediately reacted to the Japanese financial crisis. As a result the 'Japan premium'[7] in interbank markets of the Euro-dollar was raised to 0.5 per cent in this same week. Financial institutions that were in financial difficulties found it extremely difficult to obtain funds from call markets. The Hokkaidō Takushoku Bank, whose merger plan was actually abandoned on 12 September 1997, announced its failure and the transfer of its business within the Hokkaidō area to the Hokuyō Bank on 17 November. The rating of the Yamaichi Securities Company's bonds was degraded to 'speculative' on 21 November, and it faced severe difficulties in raising funds from markets. Finally, the Yamaichi Securities Company, one of four major securities companies in Japan, announced the closing down of its business on 24 November.

MOF's control over these failures

As in the case of the two credit unions, the Securities Bureau of the MOF knew in advance about the financial difficulties of the Sanyō Securities Company. The Securities Bureau formed a merger plan at first, and then prepared a detailed plan for the application of the Corporate Rehabilitation Law. After its failure, the default of Sanyō in a call market brought about a serious credit crunch in call markets, which caused the failure of the Hokkaidō Takushoku Bank and the Yamaichi Securities Company. It could be said that the MOF and the Bank of Japan (BOJ) underestimated the influence of the default in a call market and the suspicious mood among institutional investors.[8] Although the credit crunch that was caused by the failure of Sanyō was beyond the expectation of the MOF, the process of Sanyō's failure took place according to the plan created by the MOF. As for the failure of the Yamaichi Securities Company, the Securities Bureau decided that it was not appropriate for the Yamaichi to apply for the Corporate Rehabilitation Law because of its large amount of unlisted liability, and the Securities Bureau advised the Yamaichi to close down its business. Both failures were dealt with as administrative issues by the MOF and politicians were not informed of their failure beforehand. Therefore politicians did not intervene in the planning of the schemes for the two securities companies. The MOF controlled the whole process of planning and executing the schemes, and there was no political confusion in that process.

The failure of the Jūsen

The liquidation process

The Jūsen were established in the 1970s with strong support from the MOF. The MOF responded to the increase in public demand for personal housing loans by supporting the establishment of the Jūsen from 1971 to 1976. At that time, corporations demanded loans from city banks in order to expand their businesses, and city banks concentrated on trade with private companies. As a result, individuals found it difficult to obtain loans from city banks. Responding to the demands for personal housing loans, the MOF took an initiative to establish financial institutions specializing in personal housing loans, the Jūsen.

During the first half of the 1980s, the Jūsen steadily expanded their businesses. Table 6.1 shows the amount and the ratio of individual housing loans made by the Jūsen. The Jūsen had increased their ratio during the 1970s. During the second half of the 1980s, however, city banks expanded their business into personal housing loan markets. By the end of the 1980s, private companies had grown rapidly and their demands for loans to expand their businesses had gradually declined. In addition, major private companies tended to raise funds by issuing bonds in markets. As a result, city banks tried to expand their business into personal housing loan markets in order

Table 6.1 Jūsen housing loans to individuals from 1971 to 1994

	Total amount of housing loans to individuals (Billion Yen)	Jūsen housing loans to individuals (Billion Yen)
1971	3,760	27 (0.8)
1975	16,227	610 (3.8)
1980	45,151	3,264 (7.2)
1985	67,605	3,507 (5.2)
1986	72,205	3,057 (4.2)
1987	79,157	2,702 (3.4)
1988	88,013	2,504 (2.6)
1989	99,159	2,643 (2.7)
1990	108,515	3,842 (2.6)
1991	117,434	2,844 (2.4)
1992	123,607	2,699 (2.2)
1993	131,665	2,551 (1.9)
1994	141,824	2,402 (1.7)

Source: Saeki 1997: 30.

to maintain their profits. The Housing Loan Corporation (Jūtaku Kinyū Kōko) also increased its loans to individuals, following the government's housing policy. The Jūsen could not compete with city banks in this market, so they expanded their businesses into another area, loans to speculative real estate business (Saeki 1997: 30). Table 6.2 shows the percentage of Jūsen housing loans to individuals and loans to business. Until the 1980s the Jūsen gave loans mainly to individuals. In the 1990s, however, about 80 per cent of their loans was given to business. The Jūsen had rapidly increased loans to business, mainly speculative real estate business, since the 1980s, which sharply increased the amount of their bad loans. Table 6.3 shows the amount and the percentage of bad loans of the Jūsen in 1991. The bad loans of seven Jūsen totalled more than 4.6 trillion yen and the average ratio of the bad loans of seven Jūsen was 37.8 per cent (Saeki 1997: 55).

Table 6.2 The percentages of Jūsen housing loans to individuals and loans to businesses

	1971	1975	1980	1985	1990	1991	1992	1993	1994
Housing loans to individuals (%)	100	99.5	95.6	67.0	21.4	21.6	21.6	21.4	20.6
Loans to businesses (%)	0	0.5	4.4	33.0	78.6	78.4	78.4	78.6	79.4

Source: Saeki 1997: 28.

Table 6.3 Bad loans of seven Jūsen (1991)

	Amount of bad loans (hundred million yen)	Ratio of bad loans (%)
Nihon Jūtaku Kinyū	6,617	29.1
Jūtaku Loan Service	4,326	26.4
Jūsō	7,465	39.9
Sōgō Jūkin	3,690	39.9
Daiichi Jūtaku Kinyū	5,435	30.7
Chigin Seiho Housing Loan	6,252	59.8
Nihon Housing Loan	12,694	53.7
Total	46,479	39.9

Source: Saeki 1997: 55.

Responding to public demands that the high prices of real estate be slashed, two directives were issued on 27 March 1990. One was issued by the Director General of the Banking Bureau of the MOF to banks and the other was issued by the Director General of the Banking Bureau of the MOF and the Director General of the Economic Bureau of the Ministry of Agriculture, Forestry and Fisheries (MAFF) to the Chief Executive Officer of the National Federation of Agricultural Credit Unions and the Central Agricultural Forestry Bank (Nōrinchūkin). The directive issued by the Director General of the Banking Bureau to banks requested that:

1 the amount of the increase of financial institutions' loans to property business should be reduced to less than that of the total increase in financial institutions' loan (Sōryō Kisei, regulation on the amount of loans to property business); and
2 financial institutions should report to the Banking Bureau about their loans to the real estate business, the construction industry and non-banks (Sangyōshu Kisei, regulation on loans to three industries).

However, the latter directive requested only Sōryō Kisei and lacked Sangyōshu Kisei. As a result, farm-related financial institutions, such as the federation of agricultural credit unions in each prefecture (Shinren), and the Central Agricultural Forestry Bank (Nōrinchūkin), could give loans to the Jūsen (non-banks) without reporting to the Banking Bureau. Furthermore, the first directive was not issued to the Jūsen. Therefore the Jūsen could give loans to property business without regulation of Sōryō Kisei.[9] After the 'bubble economy' collapsed, the prices of real estate plunged and the Japanese economy experienced a severe recession. The number of the Jūsen's bad loans soared and the Jūsen were thrown into financial difficulties.

As explained above, the Jūsen were established under the strong initiative of the MOF responding to an expanding demand for personal housing loans. Some retired MOF executives obtained the top posts of the Jūsen. Six out of the seven presidents of the Jūsen were ex-MOF officials.

Not only the MOF but also the MAFF had a serious interest in the Jūsen problem. When those directives were issued, Jūsen's largest creditors were farm-related financial institutions: Nōrinchūkin (Central Agricultural Forestry Bank), Shinren (Federation of Agricultural Credit Unions in each prefecture) and Kyōsairen (Federation of Mutual Benefit Associations), and the MAFF had the authority over them. Nōkyō (Agricultural Coorporative Associations), Shinren and Nōrinchūkin formed a close financial relationship. The articles of Nōkyō provided that more than two-thirds of idle Nōkyō cash should be deposited in Shinren, and the articles of Shinren provided that more than half of its idle cash should be deposited in Nōrinchūkin. For example, Nōkyō collected 68 trillion yen from their members at the end of the 1994 fiscal year, and 46 trillion yen was deposited in Shinren, and 62 per cent of the deposit of Nōkyō was deposited in Nōrinchūkin through Shinren (Saeki 1997: 186). The MAFF was afraid that the Jūsen problem would cause financial difficulties for Shinren, which would create serious financial damage for Nōkyō. Saeki Yoshimi explains that the financial difficulty of Shinren could have caused the reduction in dividends to Nōkyō or a cut in bonuses to Nōkyō, which could mean serious financial damage to Nōkyō (Saeki 1997: 223–4).

Such serious interest of the MOF and the MAFF in the Jūsen problem caused an intense confrontation between them. In order to solve the Jūsen's bad loans problem, the Director General of the Banking Bureau of the MOF and the Director General of the Economic Bureau of the MAFF wrote a memorandum in February 1993, in which they agreed that the founding financial institutions (financial institutions that funded and kept a close business relationship with the Jūsen) would take responsibility for the Jūsen bad loans following the reconstruction schemes. The memorandum agreed that the MOF would let founding financial institutions confirm that they would take responsibility for restoring the Jūsen following the Jūsen's reconstruction scheme. The memorandum also decided that founding financial institutions, other financial institutions and farm-related financial institutions would reduce the interest rates of their credits to the Jūsen to 0 per cent, 2.5 per cent, and 4.5 per cent respectively. Furthermore, they agreed that the MOF and the MAFF would make adjustments in order that the Bank of Japan would lend any necessary funds to the Central Agricultural Forestry Bank (Nōrinchūkin) as an ordinary loan. Writing a memorandum between ministries was a traditional measure in order to settle an issue in which two or more ministries' interests confronted each other.[10] Usually such a memorandum was kept confidential between the two ministries involved. But this memorandum was revealed later, and it provoked severe criticism that the process of dealing with the Jūsen problem was not transparent but involved closed-door administration.[11]

In spite of the first reconstruction schemes formed in July 1991, the financial difficulties of the Jūsen became worse. The increase in the bad loans of the seven Jūsen after the first investigation (1991–1992) totalled about 3.5 trillion yen in 1995. Table 6.4 shows the amount and percentage of the Jūsen's bad loans at the end of June 1995, by which time the average percentage of bad loans had soared to 75.9 per cent (Saeki 1997: 77). The first Jūsen reconstruction schemes required that financial institutions disclaimed or reduced their interest rates and would not collect the principal of their credit to the Jūsen while the Jūsen made efforts to collect their claims. These schemes assumed early recovery of the price of real estate.[12] However, the price of real estate was still declining, and the MOF took the initiative to plan the second Jūsen reconstruction schemes.

In March 1995 the increase in bad loans caused the insolvency of Sōgō Jūkin and the Jūtaku Loan Service (both Jūsen) in March 1995. The amount of Jūsen bad loans continued to increase. On 14 September 1995, the Nihon Jūtaku Kinyū, the Daiichi Jūtaku Kinyū and the Nihon Housing Loan (all Jūsen) were declared insolvent, and the MOF announced that the total amount of losses of the Jūsen was 7 trillion 700 billion yen.

Foreign governments were aware of the seriousness of the large scale of bad loans of the Jūsen and the negative effect of this on the world economy. At the Annual Conference of Presidents of Central Banks in September 1995, the central bank presidents argued that the issue of bad loans on the part of Japanese financial institutions was serious not only for the Japanese economy but also for the stability of global economy. The House of Representatives of the US had a hearing from experts about the Jūsen problem. The Minister of Finance, Takemura Masayoshi, had to make assurances about the early disposal of the Jūsen's bad loans at the G7 (the summit conference of the finance Ministers and the Presidents of

Table 6.4 Bad loans of seven Jūsen (1995)

	Amount of bad loans (hundred million yen)	Ratio of bad loans (%)
Nihon Jūtaku Kinyū	14,367	74.4
Jūtaku Loan Service	10,833	76.3
Jūsō	12,097	80.2
Sōgō Jūkin	9,606	85.9
Daiichi Jūtaku Kinyū	9,914	65.8
Chigin Sehiho Juūtaku Loan	6,951	79.2
Nihon Housing Loan	16,743	74.2
Total	80,511	76.5

Source: Saeki, 1997: 77.

Central Banks of the seven industrialized nations) on 7 October. His assurances were reported as a pledge to foreign governments to solve the Jūsen problem by the end of 1995.

On 27 September 1995, the Financial Systems Research Council (Kinyū Seido Chōsakai), an advisory council of the Minister of Finance, presented an interim report about the disposal of bad loans of financial institutions. This report did not present a concrete disposal plan for the Jūsen's bad loans. On 31 October 1995, the tripartite ruling parties' study group on financial and securities systems presented an interim report about the Jūsen problem. But it could not decide the concrete ratio of the loss contribution between banks and farm-related financial institutions because of severe conflicts within the LDP. On 1 December 1995 the Committee of Coordination of the Government and Executives of Ruling Parties also presented a guideline. This guideline did not present a plan for the loss contribution. LDP politicians were afraid that the large amount of loss contribution of farm-related financial facilities would create serious financial damage for Nōkyō. Therefore they could not decide on the loss contribution between banks and farm-related financial facilities.

A plan for Jūsen liquidation that the Banking Bureau prepared did not at first include the direct injection of public funds. The negotiations between the MOF and the MAFF reached a deadlock on 15 December; after this the Budget Bureau and the Minister's Secretariat began to make a plan for the injection of public funds into the Jūsen. The Budget Bureau and the Minister's Secretariat were aware that the injection of public funds was necessary to solve the Jūsen problem.

On 16 December the MOF presented a liquidation scheme for the Jūsen. As for loss contribution, which amounted to 6 trillion 300 billion yen, founding banks would disclaim all of their credits (3 trillion 600 billion yen), and farm-related financial institutions would accept a loss contribution of 1.1 trillion yen. In addition, founding banks were supposed to fund a new loan-collecting organization and to share a part of 'the second loss', the loss that would materialize after the Jūsen's liquidation.

On 19 December the Cabinet meeting approved the Jūsen liquidation scheme. The amount of loss contribution of farm-related financial institutions was reduced from 1 trillion 100 billion yen to 530 billion yen. The difference – more than 600 billion yen – would be paid by deficit-covering bonds issued in the initial budget of the 1996 fiscal year. The MOF executives carefully negotiated with LDP politicians about the injection of public funds into the Jūsen. Nevertheless, LDP politicians flinched from the injection of public funds. They were afraid that they would be criticized for rescuing banks by spending public funds. On 18 December 1995, the executives of the ruling coalition parties were so afraid of public criticism that they demanded that the Jūsen's large-lot debtors, funding banks and the MOF should take responsibility. On 19 December, the Committee of Representitives of the Ruling Coalition Parties presented a statement that declared that the responsibility of founding banks and ministries in charge of the Jūsen problem should be investigated, on condition that the liquidation of the Jūsen was enforced. On the same day, at the general meeting of the Executive Council of the LDP, the injection of public funds faced strong objections from its members. In this meeting, LDP politicians expressed their concern that the injection of public funds into the Jūsen would not achieve public support (*Asahi Shinbun*, 19 December 1995, evening edition).

It was a confused and painstaking process to pass the budget of the 1996 fiscal year (685 billion yen was to be injected into the disposal of the Jūsen's bad loans) and a package of six Jūsen liquidation bills. Prime Minister Murayama resigned in the middle of the deliberation of the budget in January 1996, and the Hashimoto Coalition Cabinet followed. One of the opposition parties, the NFP, strongly opposed this package of bills, and formed a picket line in the Diet. As a result, the deliberation in the Diet was suspended from 4 March until 25 March. After an NFP candidate lost the by-election of the House of Councillors in Gifu prefecture on 24 March 1996, the NFP agreed to deliberate on the package of bills for the Jūsen in the Diet. Finally, the budget was approved by the Diet on 10 May 1996, and the package of six bills was approved by the Diet on 18 June 1996.

Analysis of the process of the Jūsen liquidation

The liquidation of the Jūsen became a serious political issue since LDP politicians had a deep interest. It was anticipated that farm-related financial institutions and Nōkyō would suffer from serious financial damage by the liquidation of the Jūsen, and LDP politicians were afraid of the reaction of farmers to this damage.

Farmers have been regarded as a regular support group (kotei hyō) for the LDP. As explained in Chapter 4, the LDP had usually achieved support from more than 70 per cent of farmers. LDP politicians wanted to avoid any decision that would be disadvantageous to farmers before the next general election under a new electoral system. The previous general election had been held on 18 July 1993 (the term of service of a member of the House of Representatives is four years), and the Revised Public Officials Election Law, which introduced a new electoral system, was enforced on 25 December 1994. Politicians expected the next general election under the new electoral system to be just around the corner. Therefore they (especially the Nōrin-zoku) vigorously protected farm-related financial institutions' benefits. In addition, the injection of public funds into the Jūsen required budget allotment. Therefore the deliberation in the Diet was inevitable in order to enforce the liquidation scheme for the Jūsen. Consequently, the liquidation of the Jūsen became a political issue, which was thrown into serious political turmoil.

In the process of Jūsen liquidation, it can be observed that the factors that were conditions for the issue settling system under the LDP dominance had changed; the importance of LDP organizations in the decision-making process of the government and the Diet had declined and the LDP management system through factions had become disintegrated.

The decline in the importance of LDP organizations

Under LDP dominance, the LDP monopolized the Chair of the HR, and members of the LDP Diet Management Committee (Giun-zoku) bargained with opposition parties' executives, exploiting the LDP's predominant position in the Diet. Under the Murayama Coalition Cabinet and the First Hashimoto Cabinet, which dealt with the Jūsen problem, the LDP formed a ruling coalition with the JSP and the NHP. The LDP gave up trying to obtain the speakership of the HR, and the former JSP Chair, Doi Takako, assumed this position. The Giun-zoku could not control the Speaker, Doi Takako, so they were not able to control the deliberation in the Diet at will. The mass media reported the LDP politicians' dissatisfaction with her. In the meeting of LDP executives on 8 March 1996, criticisms against her arose one after another.[13] Under coalition cabinets, the LDP Giun-zoku could not take leadership regarding bargaining with the opposition parties as they used to do under LDP dominance. Furthermore, connections between the LDP Giun-zoku and opposition parties did not function effectively. The NFP also lacked leadership. While the NFP's picketing of the Diet was dragging on in March 1996, there was no influential member who could take the leadership to end the picketing and settle the confusion. In the meeting of the leaders of the LDP and the NFP, it was reported that the leader of NFP Ozawa Ichirō admitted to LDP President Hashimoto Ryūtarō, 'I ordered an end to the picketing. But NFP members do not obey my order . . .' (*Asahi Shinbun*, 23 March 1996). The picketing dragged on until 25 March 1996[14] and the package of the bills for the Jūsen problem passed the Diet on 18 July.

The weakened LDP management system

The weakened LDP management system was reflected in the behaviour of the Nōrin-zoku. There was no influential leader of the Nōrin-zoku who could control its members. Influential members of the Nōrin-zoku, such as Hata Tsutomu, defected from the LDP to establish the Japan Renewal Party. Faction leaders could not control their members of the Nōrin-zoku either.[15] The Nōrin-zoku increased their pressure. The mass media reported that the Nōrin-zoku made the criticism that the ruling coalition parties' study group on financial and securities systems was too favourable to the MOF and founding banks. Responding to this criticism, three executives of the Committee of Coordination of the Government and Executives of

Ruling Parties had to take over this issue from the study group. The Nōrin-zoku applied strong pressure in order to reduce the ratio of farm-related financial institutions' loss contribution, which triggered strong opposition from founding banks. As a result, the committees and the study group that discussed the Jūsen problems could not decide on the concrete loss contribution of the Jūsen's bad loans.

On 27 September 1995 the Financial System Research Council (Kin'yū Seido Chōsa Kai) presented an interim report about the disposal of financial facilities' bad loans; however, it could not decide a principle for the disposal of the Jūsen's bad loans. It only stated:

> It is required that the Jūsen and founding banks should take the leadership to reach an agreement on a basic principle for the future of the Jūsen and the disposal of their bad loans. In the process of reaching an agreement, it is also required for the Jūsen and founding banks to discuss with farm-related and other financial facilities. In this discussion it is required that all the parties should make their best efforts to compromise, considering their responsibility for this problem.
>
> (*Asahi Shinbun*, 28 September 1995)

On 31 October the ruling coalition parties' study group on financial and securities systems presented an interim report, but it did not include a plan for the loss contribution of the Jūsen. On 27 November the Chair of the PARC attempted to settle this issue, but the attempt deadlocked immediately. The Chair of PARC, Yamazaki Taku, listened to an explanation from the Nōrin-zoku and the Ōkura-zoku and attempted to mediate in this conflict. However, he failed to make a compromise. On 1 December the Committee of Coordination of the Government and Executives of Ruling Parties (Seifu Yotō Seisaku Chōsei Kaigi) also could not decide the loss contribution of the Jūsen's bad loans.

Because of such strong pressure from the Nōrin-zoku, the MOF and the MAFF found it difficult to compromise with respect to the loss contribution. The ruling parties asked the MOF and the MAFF to propose a scheme for the disposal of the Jūsen's bad loans by 15 December, but the two ministers failed to reach an agreement.

Strong pressure from the Nōrin-zoku changed the MOF's scheme, and the MOF was forced to formulate a new scheme. Under the MOF's original scheme presented on 16 December, farm-related financial institutions would have had to renounce 1.1 trillion yen of their loans. However, the Nōrin-zoku insisted that this would damage farm-related financial institutions excessively. Finally, on 19 December the government presented a plan in which the farm-related financial facilities would donate 530 billion yen, instead of 1.1 trillion as in the original plan. As for the difference, more than 600 billion yen, it would be paid by deficit-covering bonds issued in the initial budget of the 1996 fiscal year. The MOF had to draw up a budget just before the MOF presented the draft budget of the 1996 fiscal year to the Cabinet on 29 December.

The weakened LDP management system was also reflected in the deliberation of the package of bills for the Jūsen in the Diet. The LDP was divided into the power-holding group and the anti-power-holding group across factions, which caused political conflicts within the LDP and so negotiation with the NFP was confused. The power-holding group, the so-called 'YKK' group (Chair of the PARC Yamazaki Taku, Secretary General Katō Kōichi, Minister of Health and Welfare (the Second Hashimoto Cabinet) Koizumi Jun'ichirō) supported the ruling coalition between the LDP, the JSP and the NHP. On the other hand, the anti-power-holding group, including Kajiyama Seiroku, advocated forming a coalition with a conservative party. The mass media reported serious confrontation between the two groups in the meeting of the Executive Council of the LDP on 5 March 1996. One after another, senior LDP members raised objections against the supplementary scheme for the Jūsen presented by the power-holding group. Yamanaka Sadanori, one of the influential senior LDP members, presented a counter-plan, and the Chair of the Executive Council, Shiokawa Seijūrō, supported this counter-plan. In addition, the ex-Director General of the Management and Coordination Agency, Mizuno Kiyoshi, requested reconsideration of the supplementary scheme. The ex-Cabinet Secretary, Gotōda Masaharu, and the ex-Director General of the Economic Planning Agency, Takashima Osamu, also criticized the supplementary scheme. The LDP was divided and it could not, therefore, take decisive action against the opposition parties.

In the process of planning a liquidation scheme for the Jūsen, there were no influential leaders among the Nōrin-zoku who could control members. Neither could faction leaders control the behaviour of the Nōrin zoku. Therefore, the MOF could not create a liquidation scheme or put into practice its original scheme by negotiating only with LDP executives and faction leaders. The MOF could not decide a scheme for the Jūsen's liquidation until the last moment, and it was forced to change its original scheme. With regard to deliberation in the Diet under LDP dominance, LDP executives and LDP Giun zoku negotiated with other parties, and budgets passed the Diet smoothly. However, in the Jūsen case, LDP Giun zoku and LDP executives could not control the deliberation of the package of bills for the Jūsen, since the Speaker of the HR was not an LDP member. The division within the LDP and the lack of leadership in the NFP made this confusion worse.

As a result, the deliberation of the package of bills for the Jūsen was confused, and the approval of the budget of the 1996 fiscal year was delayed. The legislation for the Jūsen liquidation scheme was also significantly delayed, and the package of bills for the Jūsen liquidation passed the Diet on 18 June 1996.

The failure of the Long-Term Credit Bank of Japan (LTCBJ)

The process of the failure of the LTCBJ

After the failure of three financial institutions (the Sanyō Securities Company, the Hokkaidō Takushoku Bank and the Yamaichi Securities Company) in November 1997, the Hashimoto Cabinet changed its economic policies from fiscal reform to stimulating the Japanese economy. On 16 February 1998 the Immediate Measures for Financial Stabilization Law passed the Diet. According to this new law, public funds – 1 trillion 800 billion yen in total – were injected into 21 banks. On 26 March 1998, the government and the LDP decided to revise the Financial Structural Reform Law and to enforce a tax increase. However, the financial situation was not improved, and the LDP was badly defeated in the election for the House of Councillors (HC) held on 12 July 1998. LDP seats decreased from 119 to 102, while the number of seats held by the opposition parties increased substantially; for instance, the Democratic Party (DP) improved from 38 to 47. After the election, the ruling coalition parties (the LDP, the SDPJ and the NHP) had 118 out of 252, which meant they could not keep the majority in the HC. In spite of the overwhelming defeat, the LDP still kept the largest number of seats in the Diet, so the Obuchi Cabinet succeeded the Second Hashimoto Cabinet on 30 July.

On 5 June 1998, *Gendai*, a monthly magazine, reported that the Long-Term Credit Bank of Japan (LTCBJ) was on the verge of failure. Institutional investors sold stocks of the LTCBJ one after another. The LTCBJ negotiated with the Sumitomo Trust Bank about a merger in order to escape financial difficulties. The LTCBJ and the Sumitomo Trust Bank formed a committee for their merger on 2 July 1998, and negotiated to reach an agreement about the merger. On 21 August 1998 the LTCBJ announced the disposal of its bad loans – 750 billion yen – and a reconstruction plan that included a complete withdrawal from overseas business. It requested the injection of public funds of more than 500 billion yen.

Responding to the successive failures of financial institutions, the government and the LDP re-examined the policy of injecting public funds into failed financial institutions. On 2 July 1998 the LDP agreed on the 'Comprehensive Plan for Financial Revitalization', and submitted the package of bills for financial Rehabilitation to the Diet. This plan adopted a 'bridge bank' system. A failed financial institution was to be managed by supervisors appointed by the Financial Supervisory Agency (FSA), its bad loans were transferred to the Resolution and Collection Bank (RCB), and other loans were bought by private financial institutions. If no private financial institutions bought its loans, a bridge bank was to be established, funded by the Deposit Insurance Corporation, and the failed financial institution's business would be transferred to this bridge bank. On the other hand, three opposition parties (the DP, Peace and Reform (PR), and the Liberal Party (LP)) drew up a counter-plan; they demanded the abolition of the Immediate Measures for Financial Stabilization Law, which provided for the injection of public funds to financial institutions before their failure.

The opposition parties' counter-plan did not include the injection of public funds into financial institutions before their failure, and this issue became a serious political topic between the LDP and opposition parties. It was related to the LTCB's rescue scheme: the LDP insisted that the LTCBJ was not insolvent and it should be rescued by the injection of public funds according to the Immediate Measures for Financial System Stabilization Law; on the other hand, three opposition parties demanded abolition of this law and insisted that the LTCBJ should be dealt with as a failed financial institution without the injection of public funds.

At first the DP announced that it would attend the deliberation of the revision of the Financial Revitalization Bill in the Diet, although the LDP decided to settle the LTCBJ case by adopting the injection of public funds. The leader of the DP, Kan Naoto, announced that the DP would not relate the LCBJ issue to the deliberation of the revision of the Financial Revitalization Bill in the Diet. However, the DP suddenly changed its attitude and insisted that the LTCBJ should be dealt with as a failed financial institution and that the new system for failed financial institutions must be applied to the LTCBJ case.[16] The LTCBJ case was related to the deliberation of the revision of the Financial Revitalization Bill in the Diet, and became a serious political issue.

The LDP was forced to compromise with opposition parties in order to pass the package of bills because of its overwhelming defeat in the most recent HC election. On 15 September 1998, the LDP presented a compromise plan in which liquidation-like measures would be applied to the LTCBJ. In this plan, a financial institution would reduce its capital when its capital ratio became less than 2 per cent, and then the government would buy its stocks and temporarily nationalize it. The LDP proposed that this new system be applied to the LTCBJ. However, negotiations between the LDP and opposition parties were deadlocked with respect to the split of divisions of financial policies from the MOF (this issue is the main theme of MOF reform, which will be explained in the next chapter), and the LDP was also forced to compromise on this issue. On 18 September 1998, leaders of the LDP and three opposition parties reached an agreement. Prime Minister Obuchi and leaders of the DP, LP and PR agreed that:

1 Regarding the system for failed financial institutions, the new law would include not only the bridge bank system, which the LDP insisted upon but also a temporary nationalization, which opposition parties insisted upon.

2   Regarding the injection of public funds, the present system of injecting public funds into financial institutions before their failure would be abolished, and a new system would be founded in which a financial institution whose equity ratio was extremely low would be temporarily nationalized.

3   A Financial Reconstruction Commission would be established according to Article 3 of the National Administrative Organization Law. Integration of jurisdiction over financial policies into one organization would be legislated by the ordinary session in the next year.

4   The LTCJB case would be settled by the application of the new system, a temporary nationalization, etc., which would be legislated in this session according to the agreement between executives of the LDP and the three opposition parties.

This agreement was deliberately ambiguous with respect to the LTCBJ case, which caused confusion between the LDP and the three opposition parties. In the agreement, the LTCBJ case would be settled by 'the application of a new system, a temporary nationalization system, etc., which would be legislated in this session according to the agreement between the executives of the LDP and the three opposition parties.' The ambiguous 'etc.' left the possibility of applying the injection of public funds to the LTCBJ. Some LDP members stated that the LTCBJ case could be settled by the injection of public funds and the merger with the Sumitomo Trust Bank. The Chair of the PARC, Ikeda Yukihiko, insisted, 'the system of the injection of public funds into financial facilities before their failure will remain in the revised bill . . .' (*Asahi Shinbun*, 19 September 1998). The LDP Secretary General, Mori Yoshirō, emphasized on a TV programme, 'we will not make the LTCBJ fail, and we prepare the condition for a merger with the Sumitomo Trust Bank . . .' (*Asahi Shinbun*, 21 September 1998). The LDP and the three opposition parties continued negotiations concerning the deal with the LTCBJ, and the LDP was forced to abandon the injection of public funds into the LTCBJ.

On 26 September the LDP and the three opposition parties finally reached an agreement. They agreed that the LTCBJ would be temporarily under state control and would then become a subsidiary of a private financial facility by transferring its shares to it.

Analysis of the process of the LTCBJ liquidation

The decline in the importance of LDP organizations

After the election of the HC of July 1998, the ruling coalition parties – the LDP, the SDPJ and the NHP – lacked a majority. Therefore the LDP was forced to compromise with the three opposition parties in order to pass the Financial Revitalization Bill. At first, the LDP decided to introduce a bridge bank system to deal with a failed financial institution and to rescue the LTCBJ by the injection of public funds and a merger with the Sumitomo Trust Bank according to its original scheme. However, the LDP was forced to accept the demands of the three opposition parties and to revise the Bill according to their demands. The LDP therefore accepted the temporary nationalization system for failed financial institutions, and it abandoned the plan to merge the LTCBJ with the Sumitomo Trust Bank by injecting public funds to the LTCBJ.

Such one-sided concessions triggered strong objection and criticism from senior LDP politicians, which considerably delayed the whole process. Although leaders of the LDP and the three opposition parties reached an agreement on 18 September, they had to continue the negotiation (which dragged on until 26 September) because of the strong dissatisfaction among senior LDP politicians. The fact that the LDP was forced to change the bills that had been based on LDP organizations' decisions and to accept the opposition parties' plan clearly shows the decline of importance of LDP organizations in the decision-making process of the Diet.

The weakened management system of the LDP

The LDP was divided over the LTCBJ case into two groups across factions: the so-called 'new policy-oriented politician' (Seisaku Shinjinrui) group and a group of senior members. Members of the first group, such as Ishihara Nobuteru and Shiozaki Yasuhisa, who were actually in charge of revising the Financial Revitalization Bill, showed a positive attitude towards the counter-plan of the three opposition parties, and cooperated with DP members. They united across factions and resisted pressure from faction leaders with respect to revising the Financial Revitalization Bill. On the other hand, the latter group resisted accepting the opposition parties' draft of the Financial Revitalization Bill, and they attempted to rescue the LTCBJ by a merger with the Sumitomo Trust Bank. They pressured junior LDP members of the 'new policy-oriented politician' group.

Nevertheless, the 'new policy-oriented politicians' resisted control by faction leaders and senior LDP politicians. In addition, there was no influential mediator to settle this confrontation. The *Asahi Shinbun* reported the complaints of one DP executive: 'We cannot find who is taking the leadership in the LDP and the government' (*Asahi Shinbun*, 17 September 1995). Negotiations between the LDP and the three opposition parties was confused and delayed until just before the Prime Minister left Japan to meet the US President. Although the leaders of the LDP and the three opposition parties reached an agreement on 18 September 1998, the agreement triggered severe objections from senior LDP politicians. The meeting of the Executive Council of the LDP on 18 September fell into turmoil because of strong objections from senior LDP members.

In spite of the agreement, senior LDP members, who constituted anti-power holding groups and were dissatisfied with the concessions made by the Cabinet to the opposition parties, attempted to rescue the LTCBJ by a merger with the Sumitomo Trust Bank expressed their favour for a merger plan, which broke off the negotiation between the LDP and opposition parties concerning revision of the Financial Revitalization Bill. However, LDP exectutives who constituted a power-holding group restored the negotiations between the LDP and three opposition parties despite the dispproval of senior members of the anti-power holding group. The negotiation was confused because of the split in the LDP and was prolonged until 26 September.

The change in the attitude of politicians towards MOF bureaucrats

Under LDP dominance, bureaucrats exerted influence on LDP politicians by presenting information and drafts of bills. The 'new policy-oriented politicians', who were in charge of the revision of the Financial Revitalization Bill, rejected the MOF's support. They revised the draft, cooperating with DP members. Usually the MOF participated in the whole process of legislation by planning drafts of bills, attending discussions in LDP organizations and negotiating with LDP executives before and after those discussions. But in this case, the 'new policy-oriented politicians' did not seek support from the MOF regarding creating the revised draft. The main venues of this revising process were not LDP organizations but negotiations between the LDP, the DP, the LP and the CGP, and the MOF was excluded from these. The MOF could negotiate only with the senior members' group, which included, for example, the Minister of Finance, Miyazawa Kiichi, and the Chair of the PARC, Ikeda Yukihiko. These senior members could not impose their preferences on junior LDP members of the 'new policy-oriented politicians'. DP members also took a negative attitude towards support from the MOF and the MOF therefore failed to have an influence on the revision of the Financial Revitalization Bill.[17]

In the LTCBJ case, like the Jūsen case, the institutional factors that supported the issue settling system under LDP dominance had changed. First, the decision-making process did not conclude in the LDP organizations. Since the LDP and ruling coalition parties had lost their majority in the HC, the LDP had to compromise with opposition parties. In spite of strong objection from LDP members, the LDP was forced to negotiate with opposition parties and to accept their plan for the LTCBJ. Second, the management system of the LDP through factions did not work effectively. The LDP was divided over the LTCBJ issue, and there was no influential member who could integrate LDP politicians. Third, some LDP politicians refused the MOF's support for revising the Bill, and they excluded the MOF from negotiation with the three opposition parties and the process of the revision of the Bill. In order to settle the LTCBJ case, MOF bureaucrats were not able to rely on the close connections with LDP executives and faction leaders that were established under LDP dominance. As a result, the process of planning a scheme for the LTCBJ was seriously confused and the scheme was considerably delayed.

Conclusion

With regard to the financial crisis in the latter half of the 1990s, the effects of foreign markets and the decline of the control by the MOF over financial markets have been pointed out. Indeed, the trend of foreign financial markets and foreign investors entering the domestic financial markets exacerbated the difficulties of those institutions that had already fallen into difficulties. While Japanese financial institutions expanded their business into foreign markets, foreign investors increased their business in Japanese financial markets. As a result, the control by the MOF over domestic financial markets became weakened and Japanese financial institutions became vulnerable to the trend of foreign markets. For instance, the Yamaichi Securities Company experienced severe difficulties in raising funds from markets after a foreign grading institution downgraded the rating of the bonds of the Yamaichi to 'speculative' on 21 November 1997. The Yamaichi Securities Company was forced to announce the closing of its business on 24 November 1997.

What is investigated in this case study, however, is not the causes of the financial crisis but the reasons for political confusion and the delay in taking countermeasures. And the trend of foreign markets and foreign investors entering the domestic market did not necessarily affect the MOF's process of making liquidation plans. The venue for creating a liquidation plan was concluded in domestic political settings that were not generally affected by the movements of foreign markets and investors. For example, in the cases of the two credit unions and the two securities companies examined in this chapter, it is true that trends in foreign markets and the actions of foreign investors exacerbated the financial difficulties of those credit unions and securities companies, finally causing their failure. Nevertheless, the processes of making liquidation plans for them were controlled by the MOF.

It can therefore be said that malfunctioning in the issue settling system was the principal cause for political confusion and the delay of measures regarding the failure of the Jūsen and the LTCBJ.

First, the importance of LDP organizations in the decision-making process of the government and the Diet declined. The decisions of the government and the Diet were not the same as the decisions of LDP organizations since the LDP had to compromise with other ruling coalition parties or opposition parties. As a result, consent from faction leaders and LDP executives did not guarantee that plans created by bureaucrats would be submitted to the Diet as the government's bills or legislated in the Diet. In the Jūsen case, LDP Giun-zoku could not control the deliberations on the budget of the 1996 fiscal year and a package of bills for the Jūsen in the Diet. As a result, the legislation was significantly delayed. In the LTCBJ case, the LDP and the government were forced to abandon their plan for the LTCBJ and the Financial Revitalization Bill and to accept the opposition parties' plan, which caused political confusion and the delay of legislation.

Second, the management system of the LDP through factions disintegrated. LDP executives and faction leaders found it difficult to make LDP members obey their orders, and therefore consent from faction leaders and LDP executives did not guarantee support from LDP members as a whole. In the Jūsen case, faction leaders and LDP executives could not control the Nōrin-zoku, and the LDP was divided into a power-holding group and an anti-power-holding group. The MOF had to abandon its original scheme. In the LTCBJ case, the LDP was divided into 'new policy-oriented politicians' and senior members. 'New policy-oriented politicians' cooperated with DP politicians in the process of revising the Financial Revitalization Bill, and faction leaders could not control them.

Third, the relationship between LDP politicians and MOF bureaucrats became more detached compared with that under LDP dominance. Some LDP politicians did not rely on MOF bureaucrats for creating a bill. In the LTCBJ case, 'new policy-oriented politicians' refused the MOF's support and they created the draft of the revision of the Financial Revitalization Bill by cooperating with the DP.

Because of such changes in institutions and institutional relationships caused by the end of LDP dominance, the efficacy of the issue settling system based on close cooperation between LDP executives, faction leaders and bureaucrats considerably declined. The negotiation and consent from LDP executives and faction leaders did not guarantee the expectation of the MOF that the plans that the MOF created would be submitted to the Diet as the government's bills and legislated in the Diet. The issue settling system, on which the MOF had relied in order to settle the failure of the Jūsen and the LTCBJ, did not work in either case. Consequently, the process of dealing with the failure of the Jūsen and the LTCBJ was thrown into political turmoil, and their liquidation was significantly delayed, which brought about serious damage to the Japanese economy. For instance, the movement of the 'Japan premium' illustrates how foreign financial markets evaluate the Japanese financial systems. The 'Japan premium', which had soared from 0 per cent in October 1997 to more than 0.7 per cent in January 1998, had declined to less than 0.2 per cent by June 1998. But, as the deliberation of the Financial Revitalization Bill in the Diet (from August 1998) was thrown into political turmoil and the rescue plan for the LTCBJ was delayed, the 'Japan premium' began to soar, reaching almost 0.7 per cent in November 1998.

7   The reform of the Ministry of Finance

The MOF protected its organization from the attempts of party politicians to reorganize it. From the 1950s to the beginning of the 1960s, LDP politicians had attempted to reorganize the MOF. Under the Third Hatoyama Cabinet (from November 1955 to December 1956), the Director General of Administrative Management Agency, Kōno Ichirō, presented a plan for administrative reforms which proposed reorganization of central ministries and agencies. The crucial point of this plan was that jurisdiction over budget compilation, which belonged to the Budget Bureau of the MOF, would be transferred to the Prime Minister's Office (PMO). Although this plan was discussed in the Third Research Council on the Administrative System (established in December 1955) it was not put into practice. The Second Ikeda Cabinet (from December 1960 to July 1963) established the Provisional Research Council on the Administrative System in 1962. This Council attempted to transfer the jurisdiction of the Budget Bureau of the MOF to the Cabinet. However, this attempt also failed. Since then, the LDP had preferred to form close connections with the MOF rather than reorganize it. LDP politicians obtained beneficial treatment regarding public works and subsidies in return for cooperating with MOF bureaucrats, and they secured their seats in the Diet by distributing those public works and subsidies to their supporting groups, i.e. LDP politicians found it profitable to maintain this cosy cooperation, which reinforced the issue settling system. Intervening in the personnel and organizational matters of the MOF was supposed to harm this profitable cooperation because such intervention would directly affect MOF bureaucrats' interests. Accordingly, LDP politicians refrained from intervening in the personnel matters of MOF bureaucrats and putting MOF reform on the political agenda to avoid harming such a beneficial relationship with MOF bureaucrats, and therefore reorganizing the MOF, especially dividing its jurisdiction, was regarded as very unlikely.

Nevertheless, in 1998 a part of MOF jurisdiction was divided from the MOF and transferred to two newly established organizations, the Financial Supervisory Agency (FSA) and the Financial Reconstruction Commission (FRC). In the processes of legislation related to MOF reform, such as the

Foundation Law of the Financial Supervisory Agency, the Foundation Law of the Financial Reconstruction Commission, the Financial Revitalization Law and the Basic Law on the Reform of Central Ministries and Agencies, the MOF attempted to take the lead and influence the legislation by drafting bills and negotiating with LDP executives and faction leaders as it had done under LDP dominance through the issue settling system. Under LDP dominance it had drafted bills, attended each stage of discussion in LDP organizations from Divisions of the PARC to the EC, and negotiated with LDP executives and faction leaders before and after those discussions, and thus legislation that agreed with the intentions of the MOF had been enacted. However, the processes of the legislation of the laws referred to at the beginning of this paragraph were different from that under LDP dominance. As examined later in this chapter, three institutional changes transformed the decision-making process under LDP dominance, which was based on the issue settling system. The main venues for this legislation process shifted from LDP organizations to organizations that consisted of ruling coalition parties or negotiation meetings with opposition parties. The LDP was forced to change its decisions, compromising with other ruling coalition parties or making concessions to opposition parties. Regarding the Financial Revitalization Bill, the MOF was excluded from its revising process. The MOF could not control the legislation processes of the above laws through the issue settling system, and as a result of this, it failed to prevent its reorganization. Therefore MOF reform in the latter half of the 1990s highlights the point that the issue settling system did not function in the Japanese political processes after 1993.

The target of the attempts at MOF reform from the 1950s to the beginning of the 1960s was to transfer the jurisdiction of budget compilation away from the MOF. However, the aim of MOF reform in the latter half of the 1990s was to split the jurisdiction of financial policies away from the MOF, in response to the following political circumstances.

In June 1991, it was revealed that four major securities companies (Nomura, Nikkō, Yamaichi and Daiwa) had compensated institutional investors for the losses suffered in stock prices, which went against a direction issued by the MOF that forbade securities companies to make such compensation. The MOF was criticized on the ground that it could not detect or prevent such compensation through the inspection of the four major security companies. As a result, in 1992, the Securities and Exchange Surveillance Commission (SESC) was established as an organization that would inspect financial institutions regarding illegal transactions in securities and financial futures markets. The establishment of the SESC entailed the reorganization of the MOF because parts of the divisions of the MOF were transferred to the SESC. However, the SESC was established as an organization that was supposed to be supervised by the MOF, so the establishment of the SESC actually enlarged MOF organization.

After the massive bad loans of the Jūsen were revealed and a package of bills for the liquidation of the Jūsen was submitted to the Diet in December 1995, criticism against the MOF regarding its inspection and supervision surged again. The MOF was criticized on the ground that it could neither detect the large-scale bad loans of the Jūsen nor prevent the failure of the Jūsen. The necessity for an independent organization from the MOF that would execute the inspection and supervision of financial institutions was discussed in the mass media. For instance, a leading article in the *Asahi Shinbun* argued that:

> it is time to settle structural problems of the MOF. . . . we should discuss the reorganization of the MOF which includes splitting the Banking Bureau, the Securities Bureau, and the Foreign Finance Bureau from the MOF and transferring them to a new organization which would inspect and oversee financial transactions.
>
> (*Asahi Shinbun*, 31 December 1995)

As a result, removing from the MOF the jurisdiction of financial policies, especially the inspection and supervision of financial institutions, was on the political agenda. The movement for MOF reform in the 1990s emerged in the above political circumstances. Therefore it focused on the transfer of the financial policy divisions, especially inspections and supervision of financial institutions, away from the MOF.

The first wave of MOF reform: the establishment of the Financial Supervisory Agency

The injection of public funds into the Jūsen brought about severe public criticism of the government, including the LDP and the MOF. The LDP and other ruling coalition parties were afraid that such criticism would damage the approval rating of the Murayama Coalition Cabinet. When the government's scheme for the Jūsen was presented, the LDP and other ruling coalition parties' politicians demanded that the MOF should take responsibility for the injection of public funds. On 19 December 1995, the Committee of Representatives of Ruling Coalition Parties presented a statement that demanded that the responsibility of the ministries in charge of the Jūsen problem should be investigated. The deliberation of the budget of the 1996 fiscal year and the package of bills for the Jūsen liquidation in the Diet was seriously confused. In January 1996 Prime Minister Murayama Tomi'ichi suddenly resigned in the middle of this deliberation, and the Hashimoto Coalition Cabinet was formed. As a result, criticism of the MOF arose among LDP politicians.[1]

Thus the reform of the MOF suddenly appeared on the Cabinet's political agenda. On 6 February 1996, the government and tripartite ruling coalition agreed to reorganize and to re-examine MOF's jurisdiction. The

Tripartite Ruling Camp's Committee on MOF Reform (chaired by the Secretary General of the LDP, Katō Kōichi) was established on 17 February 1996 and, under this committee, a study group (chaired by Itō Shigeru, a member of the Social Democratic Party of Japan (SDPJ)) was formed.

On 2 March 1996, the study group decided that the revision of the Bank of Japan Law should be discussed first in order to strengthen the independence of the Bank of Japan (BOJ) from the MOF. The main points of the discussion were strengthening the authority of the Policy Board of the BOJ and providing the inspection conducted by the BOJ in the Bank of Japan Law.

While the study group was discussing the revision of the Bank of Japan Law in June and July 1996, it became a serious issue as to whether the study group should discuss splitting the divisions of inspection and supervision of financial institutions away from the MOF. On 2 June, the *Asahi Shinbun* scooped the 'basic policy' of the study group on MOF reform. It reported that the basic policy would not include a split of the divisions of inspection and supervision of financial institutions away from the MOF. The mass media criticized this basic policy and demanded that these divisions should be split away from the MOF. For example, the *Asahi Shinbun* demanded in its article of 5 June 1996 that the study group should undertake intense discussion and accomplish MOF reform. The article argued: '[the study group] should clearly present the split of jurisdiction over financial policies from the MOF, and this issue should be thoroughly discussed in public . . . (*Asahi Shinbun*, 5 June 1996). On 13 June 1996, the study group formally presented its basic policy, 'The Construction of New Financial Policies and Administration'. The study group agreed the following points:

1   The Bank of Japan Law would be revised to strengthen its independence from the MOF and to clarify its responsibility for financial policies.
2   The study group would continue to discuss the reorganization of the MOF including the split of the divisions of inspection and supervision on financial institutions, and a plan would be presented by September 1996.

When Chair Itō presented a memorandum on 6 August 1996, the LDP members of the study group opposed this draft proposal and refused to receive it. The draft proposed that the divisions of inspection and supervision of financial institutions should be split away from the MOF and transferred to a new committee. The draft also proposed that a complete split of jurisdiction on financial policies away from the MOF should be discussed in the study group. LDP members of the study group opposed the memorandum. They argued that discussion in the study group was not enough, and that some of the contents of the memorandum were unacceptable. On the next day, the LDP Secretary General and executives of ruling coalition parties discussed how to settle this conflict. The LDP compromised with the SDPJ and the NHP, and they agreed that Itō's draft proposal should be a springboard for discussion in the study group. On 21 August 1996, the study group reopened discussion.

As for the stance of the LDP about the type of new organization, by 11 September 1996, LDP executives had agreed to establish an Article 8 type committee[2] supervised by the MOF, and the study group was supposed to follow this agreement. Nevertheless, the LDP suddenly changed its stance and took more of a positive attitude towards MOF reform. On 18 September 1996, the Committee of Top Eight Executives of the LDP agreed that the divisions of inspection and supervision of financial institutions should be split away from the MOF and transferred to a new FTC-like organization (an Article 3 type).

On 25 September 1996, the study group on MOF reform agreed on a final report, and the LDP Secretary General and executives of other ruling parties approved it. They agreed that the Banking Bureau and the Securities Bureau would be integrated into one bureau and the divisions of inspection and supervision of financial institutions would be split away from the MOF and transferred to a new FTC-like (Article 3 type) organization. This report proposed that:

1   The Banking Bureau and the Securities Bureau would be integrated into one bureau (Financial Bureau). The International Financial Bureau would keep its current organization for the time being.
2   The divisions of inspection and supervision of financial institutions would be split away from the MOF and transferred to a new committee, an FTC-like organization. This new committee would fulfil the following requirements:
    i   high independence from the MOF, especially with respect to its personnel system;
    ii   immediate, appropriate and responsible administration;
    iii   precise and objective understanding of the business of financial institutions;
    iv   employment of those with expertise in financial issues.
3   The integration of the jurisdiction over financial policies would be discussed without delay.
4   The system of budget compilation would be discussed later.
5   With respect to public financial institutions, the transparency and efficiency of government investment and loans (Zaisei Tōyūshi) would be maintained and drastic reforms of their management would be required.
6   A drastic revision of the 'amakudari' system would be made. (The 'amakudari' system is a custom among bureaucrats and private companies after 1945 in which many retired bureaucrats obtain executive positions of private companies or public-service corporations. For instance,

retired MOF bureacrats obtain executive positions of financial institutions, or public-service corporations which are subject to regulation by the MOF.)

7   The separation of the jurisdiction between revenue and expenditure would be discussed in future.

A general election was held on 20 October 1996; this was the first general election under the new electoral system. The LDP won 239 seats out of 500 (the number of LDP's seats before the election was 211). Although the SDPJ (which had split shortly before the election) and the NHP found their numbers in the HR had decreased from 30 to 15 and from 9 to 2, respectively, the LDP retained the support of the SDPJ and the NHP in order to keep a majority in the Diet.

On 21 November, the LDP decided that the new organization should be an Article 3 type (an FTC-like) organization. However, the LDP proposed to the NHP and the SDPJ that only the divisions of inspection would be transferred to this new organization at first, and the divisions of supervision would be discussed later in the process of creating an administrative reform plan that would be implemented in 2001. The NHP and the SDPJ strongly opposed this proposal. At this stage, the LDP and the other ruling coalition parties (the NHP and the SDPJ) disagreed with each other on three points:

1   to which organization (the MOF or the PMO) the new organization would belong;
2   what form (a council committee or an agency) the new organization would take; and
3   whether the jurisdiction of the new organization would include both inspection and supervision of financial institutions or whether only inspection would be included.

While negotiation between the LDP, the SDPJ and the NHP over the three points was prolonged, on 1 December 1996 Prime Minister Hashimoto directed Secretary General Katō Kōichi to form a plan in which both divisions of inspection and supervision would be separated from the MOF. On 4 December the government and the LDP decided to split both divisions away from the MOF and transfer them to an Article 3 type agency supervised by the Prime Minister's Office. Finally, on 25 December 1996, the tripartite ruling coalition agreed on a final plan of MOF reforms. They agreed in this final plan that:

1   The Banking Bureau and the Securities Bureau would be integrated into the Financial Bureau. The International Financial Bureau would maintain the current jurisdiction for the time being, except that a part of its jurisdiction would be transferred to the Financial Bureau.

2   With respect to a new agency:
   i   a new organization, the Financial Supervisory Agency (FSA), would be established according to Article 3 of the National Administrative Organization Law;
   ii the FSA would belong to the PMO and the Director General of the FSA would be appointed by the Prime Minister;
   iii the FSA and the MOF would have regular discussions in order to keep order in market systems;
   iv the FSA would consult the MOF when the measures for failed financial institutions adopted by the FSA brought about change in the current systems;
   v when the FSA inspected financial institutions in provincial areas, the FSA would use the MOF's current organization in those areas.
3   In the discussion of drastic reform of the central ministries and agencies, the separation of jurisdiction over financial policies from the MOF would be clarified.

After this agreement, the main organization to discuss MOF reform was transferred from the study group to the Committee of Representatives of Ruling Coalition Parties[3] and the Council on Administrative Reform (CAR). After the general election of 20 October 1996, the second Hashimoto Cabinet presented administrative reform as its political agenda, and the CAR was established as a Prime Minister's advisory council. The CAR had its first meeting on 28 November 1996, and MOF reform was discussed in the CAR as a part of administrative reform.

From 18 to 21 August 1997, the CAR held an intensive discussion of its interim report. With regard to MOF reform, three issues were discussed: the complete split of jurisdiction over financial policies from the MOF; the separation of the National Tax Administration Agency from MOF organization; and the allocation of jurisdiction between the FSA and the MOF.

On 3 September 1997, the CAR agreed on its interim report. This report did not present a clear proposal about the complete separation of jurisdiction over financial policies from the MOF, and it decided that removing the National Tax Administration Agency from MOF organization was to be discussed after the interim report was presented.[4] As for the allocation of jurisdictions between the MOF and the FSA, the MOF's jurisdiction over planning of financial policies was limited to the planning of financial policies for maintaining order in market systems. The SDPJ and the NHP criticized this interim report on the grounds that it did not decide on the complete split of the jurisdiction over financial policies away from the MOF.

Because of the NHP's and the SDPJ's firm attitudes, the negotiation between the LDP, the NHP and the SDPJ was prolonged, and executives of the ruling coalition parties agreed to continue negotiating over this issue and to make a final decision by January 1998. Finally, on 20 January 1998, the tripartite ruling coalition reached an agreement. The MOF would maintain its jurisdiction over the planning of financial policies for the time being, and the date of transfer of this jurisdiction to the FSA was not clearly stated in this agreement. The agreement included the following points:

1   The jurisdiction over overseas monetary policies would remain with the MOF for the time being.
2   The establishment of the FSA and the revision of the Bank of Japan Law should be regarded as a part of the division of jurisdiction over financial policies away from the MOF.
3   The jurisdiction over the management of failed financial institutions and financial crises would remain in the MOF for the time being.
4   The following issues would be legislated by the time the administrative reform of central ministries was completed:
  i   the FSA would be reorganized as the Financial Agency (FA);
  ii   the jurisdiction over planning of domestic financial policies (except the management of failed financial institutions and financial crises) would be transferred to the FA.

According to this agreement, the FSA was established on 22 June 1998.

Analysis of the first wave of MOF reform

The decline in the importance of LDP organizations

In the process of the first wave of MOF reform, the decline in the importance of LDP organizations was observed in two ways: the change of organizations that controlled the government's decisions; and successive concessions of the LDP to the SDPJ and the NHP.

First, it was not LDP organizations but the organizations of the ruling coalition parties that played a main role in the decision-making processes of the government. The study group of ruling coalition parties under the Tripartite Ruling Camp's Committee on MOF Reform and the Committee of Representatives of Ruling Coalition Parties led the discussion in the coalition government. In these organizations, the SDPJ and the NHP obtained disproportionate influence considering the number of their seats in the Diet. The study group consisted of 21 members: 10 were LDP members, 7 were SDPJ members and 4 were NHP members. Under the Murayama and the Hashimoto Coalition Cabinets, the ruling coalition parties formed several organizations in the decision-making process of the government. In order to maintain the ruling coalition, these organizations were carefully constituted so that the LDP would not obtain a majority in each organization. As a result, the NHP and the SDPJ obtained excessive power in the decision-making process of the government compared with the number of seats that they had won in the Diet. In addition, the Chair of the study group, Itō Shigeru, was a member of the SDPJ; therefore, it was difficult for the LDP to control the discussion at will in the study group. For example, while the revision of the Bank of Japan Law was being discussed in the study group, the Chair, Itō, in an interview with the *Asahi Shinbun*, suddenly emphasized the importance of the separation of the divisions of inspection and supervision of financial institutions from the MOF, and tried to lead the discussion in the study group to this issue. In an interview with the *Asahi Shinbun*, he stated:

> It is crucial for MOF reform whether the divisions of inspection and supervision of financial institutions should be split from the MOF and transferred to an organization which will be established according to Article 3 of the National Administrative Organization Law.
>
> *(Asahi Shinbun, 18 April 1996)*

LDP members, especially LDP executives, took a negative attitude towards Itō's proposal for the split of the MOF.[5] Nevertheless, after this interview, the LDP had to discuss in the study group the removal of divisions of the inspection and supervision of financial institutions from the MOF.

Second, to maintain a ruling coalition, the LDP had to compromise with the SDPJ and the NHP by changing the decisions of LDP organizations. Although the LDP and other ruling parties (the SDPJ and the NHP) agreed to establish a study group of the tripartite ruling parties, their attitudes towards MOF reforms were different from each other. The mass media reported that the real intention of many LDP members was to soothe public anger against the injection of public funds into the Jūsen and to pass the budget of the 1996 fiscal year smoothly (*Asahi Shinbun*, 8 February 1996). The NHP took the most aggressive attitude. The NHP presented its idea of MOF reform, in which the MOF would be divided into three agencies – finance, public finance and revenue – and a budget agency of the PMO would be established that would be directly supervised by the Prime Minister.

In the study group, the LDP had to make concessions to the SDPJ and the NHP successively. After presenting a basic policy on 13 June 1996, the study group continued discussion to create a plan for MOF reform. Whereas the LDP took a negative attitude towards splitting the divisions of inspection and supervision of financial institutions away from the MOF, the NHP insisted that they would not compromise with respect to the reorganizing of the MOF. The NHP implied that if reorganizing of the MOF was not put into practice, it would break out of the ruling coalition. As a result, the study group had to continue discussions on splitting the MOF and postponed presenting a plan about this issue until September 1996. When LDP members refused to receive Chair Itō's memorandum on 6 August 1996, on the next day the LDP negotiated with the NHP and the SDPJ. They agreed to discuss Chair Itō's draft in the study group. By 11 September 1996, the LDP decided to adopt an Article 8 type organization (less independent from the MOF than Article 3 type) as the new organization. Nevertheless, the LDP changed this decision and decided to adopt an Article 3 type, which was what the NHP and the SDPJ were pressuring for. On 21 November, the LDP presented its plan in which only the division of inspection would be split away from the MOF; however, responding to the strong opposition of the NHP, on 4 December 1996, the LDP finally agreed to separate both divisions of inspection and supervision from the MOF at the same time.

While the CAR discussed administrative reforms, the LDP continue to compromise with the SDPJ and the NHP. In its interim report, the CAR proposed that the MOF's jurisdiction over planning of financial policies should be limited to the planning of financial policies for the purpose of maintaining order in market systems. The NHP and the SDPJ opposed this decision and insisted on a complete split of jurisdiction over financial policies away from the MOF. Some NHP hard-liners insisted that the NHP should dissolve its coalition with the LDP if a complete separation were not accomplished. The LDP was forced to reduce the MOF's jurisdiction over planning of financial policies from maintaining order in market systems to managing failures of financial institutions.[6]

In the first wave of MOF reform, therefore, LDP organizations were deprived of a leading position in the decision-making process of the government and replaced by organizations of ruling coalition parties.

The weakened management system of the LDP

LDP politicians were not united with regard to what extent the reorganization of the MOF should be put into practice.[7]

Under coalition cabinets, the issue of the coalition principle, i.e. whether the LDP should continue the current coalition with the SDPJ and the NHP or form a new coalition with more conservative parties, emerged. A confrontation over the reorganisation of the MOF within the LDP was related to the principle of coalition because the NHP took a strong attitude towards MOF reform and the negotiation with the NHP was prolonged. A power-holding group, which consisted of LDP members who supported the current coalition with the NHP and the SDPJ, such as Katō Kōichi (the Secretary General of the LDP), Yamazaki Taku (the Chair of the PARC), and Koizumi Jun'ichirō, tried to compromise with them by adopting the demands of the NHP about MOF reform. On the other hand, an anti-power-holding group, which consisted of LDP members who preferred a coalition with more conservative parties, including Kajiyama Seiroku and many senior LDP members, criticized the attitude of the power-holding group in that they made too many concessions. The confrontation between the two groups was intensified across factions. At a general meeting of the Executive Council on 20 November 1997, the power-holding group asked members of the EC to delegate this issue to LDP executives consisting of members of the power-holding group, but the anti-power-holding group strongly opposed making a further concession to the NHP and refused to make such a delegation. The mass media reported fierce confrontation between these two groups at this meeting. One member of the anti-power-holding group stated: 'we need not make a coalition with the NHP', and the Chair of the EC, Mori Yoshirō, angrily answered, 'What are we supposed to do if we dissolve the coalition with the NHP?' (*Asahi Shinbun*, 21 November 1997). Ultimately, the power-holding group failed to obtain the delegation of this issue to them from members of the EC at this meeting. The conflict over the principle of coalition divided factions, and faction leaders could not, therefore, control this conflict. In addition, there was no influential leader who could mediate it.

Thus in the process of the first wave of MOF reform, factional control did not functioned effectively because of intense confrontation across factions. As a result, it was difficult for the MOF to obtain the unanimous support of the LDP by negotiating with faction leaders.

The change in politicians' attitudes towards MOF bureaucrats

Under the Hosokawa Coalition Cabinet, LDP politicians realized that MOF bureaucrats would cooperate with other political parties, and that MOF bureaucrats were not their own exclusive partners. Furthermore, many LDP politicians resented the detached attitudes on the part of bureaucrats, particularly MOF bureaucrats, towards LDP politicians under the Hosokawa Coalition Cabinet. Therefore, when the LDP regained the position of ruling party under the Murayama Coalition Cabinet, LDP politicians had lost their strong motivation for protecting the MOF at all costs.

Furthermore, LDP politicians were anxious about the effects on the electorate of their attitude towards MOF reform. When the study group discussed MOF reform, a general election under a new electoral system was close at hand. On 19 September 1996, while executives of the ruling coalition parties were negotiating with respect to the separation of the divisions of inspection and supervision on financial institutions from the MOF, Prime Minister Hashimoto informed the leaders of the SDPJ and the NHP that the next general election would be held on 20 October 1996. In addition, LDP politicians were concerned about the threat of new political parties, which pledged administrative reform. The founding committee of the DP was formed on 17 September 1996, and the DP attracted considerable attention from the mass media. On 19 September, the *Asahi Shinbun* reported the result of an opinion poll in which 34 per cent of respondents showed a favourable attitude towards the establishment of the DP, so LDP politicians were very sensitive to public opinion.[8]

Although by 12 September 1996 LDP executives had agreed to adopt an Article 8 type as the new organization, they suddenly changed this decision and decided to adopt an Article 3 type (more independent from the MOF than an Article 8 type) on 18 September. It can be said that this sudden change reflected the severe political circumstances facing the LDP at that time.[9]

After 1993, LDP politicians lost their strong motivation to take the risk of protecting the MOF at the cost of public support. To win the next general election and secure the position of ruling party, LDP politicians dared to implement MOF reform.

The second wave of MOF reform

The reform of the MOF temporarily died down after the establishment of the FSA; however, the serious defeat of the LDP in the House of Councillors election of 12 July 1998 changed the political circumstances of MOF reform.

Responding to the financial crisis that had existed since November 1997, the LDP formed the 'Comprehensive Plan for Financial Revitalization' on 2 July 1998. Following this plan, the Obuchi Cabinet submitted a Financial Revitalization Bill and a package of bills for financial crises to the Diet. On 13 August, three opposition parties (the DP, the Liberal Party (LP) and the Peace and Reform (PR)) presented a counter-plan that included the complete separation of jurisdiction over financial policies from the MOF.

In the Financial Revitalization Bill presented by the government and the LDP, the MOF, the Bank of Japan (BOJ) and the FSA would cooperate to deal with the financial crises caused by the failure of major financial institutions. On the other hand, in the opposition parties' counter-plan, an Article 3 type committee would be established in order to deal with financial crises and supervise the FSA. In this counter-plan, the MOF was eliminated from the procedure of planning and managing of financial crises, which meant a complete split of jurisdiction over financial policies away from the MOF.

The LDP and other ruling coalition parties did not win a majority in the HC (the number of LDP seats in the HC was 102 (out of 252), the SDPJ held 13 seats, and the NHP 3). Therefore, to pass the Financial Revitalization Bill, the LDP had to compromise with opposition parties by accepting their demands. At first, the LDP attempted to reach an agreement with the three opposition parties by presenting a revised bill. In this revised bill, the Committee would be established according to Article 3 of the National Administrative Organization Law. A Minister would be appointed Chair of the Committee, and the authority of the Committee would be strictly limited to declaring the failure of financial institutions. The majority of LDP members took a negative attitude towards the reorganization of the MOF. The three opposition parties criticized the proposal in that it did not change the current MOF organization, and they refused to accept it. The LDP was forced to make a further concession to the three opposition parties.

On 18 September 1998, the LDP President and Prime Minister, Obuchi Keizō, and the leaders of the three opposition parties reached an agreement. In the split of the MOF organization, they agreed that the Financial Reconstruction Commission would be established according to Article 3 of the National Administrative Organization Law, and that the Commission would have authority to declare the failure of financial institutions and the temporary nationalization of failed financial institutions. They also agreed that the integration of the jurisdiction over financial policies would be legislated by the end of the ordinary session in the following year. Although leaders of the LDP and the three opposition parties reached this agreement, it was ambiguous with respect to the MOF's jurisdiction over financial policies for financial crises and the date of operation of the separation of MOF organization. Such ambiguity caused confusion between the LDP and the three opposition parties. As for the split of the MOF, the LDP explained that the jurisdiction over the managing of financial crises would remain with the MOF, and the division of the MOF would operate from 2001 at the earliest. On the other hand, the three opposition parties explained that all jurisdictions over financial policies would be split from the MOF and transferred to a new agency, which would begin to operate during the ordinary session in the next year. As a result, negotiation between the LDP and the three opposition parties was confused. Finally, on 26 September 1998, the LDP and the three opposition parties reached an agreement. With respect to the removal of jurisdiction over financial policies from the MOF, they agreed that the authority of the Financial Reconstruction Commission would be legislated by the end of the current session and the removal of jurisdiction over financial policies from the MOF would be legislated in the ordinary session of the next year.

Additionally, the LDP, the DP and the PR wrote a memorandum when they presented the revised Financial Revitalization Bill to the Diet. In this memorandum, they agreed that a complete split of jurisdiction over financial policies away from the MOF and the integration of jurisdiction over financial policies into a new organization, the Financial Agency, would be legislated by the end of the next ordinary session and enforced by 1 January 2000.

Such a considerable concession to opposition parties provoked strong dissatisfaction among LDP politicians. After submitting the revised Financial Revitalization Bill to the Diet, the LDP sought to form a coalition with other political parties, such as the LP and the PR (the PR merged with Kōmei and reconstituted the Clean Government Party (CGP) on 7 November 1998).[10] The Obuchi Coalition Cabinet began negotiation with the LP to form a ruling coalition on 14 January 1999. On 26 January, the coalition government and the LDP Headquarters' Office on Reforms of Central Ministries and Agencies decided the 'Basic Outline of Reforms of Central Ministries and Agencies'. With respect to the removal of jurisdiction over financial policies from the MOF, they decided that the jurisdiction of planning and managing of the failure of financial institutions and financial crises would remain with the MOF.

On 15 April 1999 the LDP also reached an agreement with the CGP on MOF reform. In this agreement the planning or managing of financial crises would be a joint jurisdiction of the MOF and the new financial agency, and authority over public financial institutions and overseas monetary policies would remain in the MOF's jurisdiction.

Analysis of the second wave of MOF reform

The decline in the importance of LDP organizations

LDP organizations suffered further damage after the election of the HC in July 1998. The LDP was forced to compromise with not only the other ruling coalition parties but also the three opposition parties (the DP, the LP and the PR) in the decision-making process of the Diet, because the LDP and the other ruling coalition parties could not achieve a majority in the HC. At first, the government and the LDP submitted to the Diet the Financial Revitalization Bill, which was based on the 'Comprehensive Plan for Financial Revitalization' decided by the LDP. However, the LDP had to abandon the attempt to legislate this bill. It had no choice but to accept the plan presented by the three opposition parties, which included reorganization of the MOF. The Financial Revitalization Bill put forward by the LDP was substantially changed, which highlighted the decline of the importance of LDP organizations.

The weakened management system of the LDP

After 1993, as well as the issue of a coalition principle, the issue of the change of generation in the LDP emerged. In the process of the second wave of MOF reform, the LDP was divided into two groups: a 'new policy-oriented politician' group and a group of senior LDP members. The new policy-oriented politician group consisted of junior LDP members who had won elections only once or twice and who advocated that politicians should take the lead in policy-making. They supported reorganization of the MOF and cooperated with the DP on the revision of the Financial Revitalization Bill.

On the other hand, senior LDP members opposed the reorganization of the MOF.[11] Nevertheless, a new policy-oriented politician group resisted the pressure from senior LDP members and created the revised draft of the Financial Revitalization Bill which included reorganization of the MOF.

In the process of the second wave of MOF reform, faction leaders could not control junior LDP members who criticized LDP executives' decision and cooperated with opposition parties.

The change in the attitudes of politicians towards MOF bureaucrats

Under LDP dominance, bureaucrats monopolized the presentation of expertise and information on policy-making to LDP politicians. Bureaucrats formed close connections with LDP politicians and exerted influence on them by giving them information and expertise. On the other hand, LDP politicians accumulated expertise through such connections. However, the new policy-oriented politician group, which was actually in charge of revising the Financial Revitalization Bill, refused the support of the MOF, and the MOF was excluded from the decision-making process of the Diet. As a result, the MOF was unable to participate in revising the Financial Revitalization Bill and could not influence its process.

Conclusion

MOF reform in the latter half of the 1990s was the first significant reorganization of the MOF. The reasons why this time MOF reform succeeded has been explained by presenting three institutional changes in the Japanese political system caused by the end of LDP dominance: the change of LDP politicians' attitudes towards MOF bureaucrats; the weakened LDP management system; and the decline of the importance of LDP organizations.

Regarding the decline in the importance of LDP organizations, under the coalition cabinets organizations of the ruling coalition parties (such as the study group and the Committee of Representatives of Ruling Coalition Parties) decided the government's policies instead of LDP organizations (such as the PARC or the EC). Furthermore, in the process of negotiation in the study group and the Committee of Representatives of Ruling Coalition Parties, the LDP had to compromise with other ruling coalition parties, the NHP and the SDPJ, in order to maintain a coalition cabinet. Although the MOF persuaded LDP executives and faction leaders to agree with plans created by the MOF, it was no longer guaranteed that the government's decisions would be the same as the decisions of LDP organizations. In addition, after the defeat in the election of the HC of July 1998, the LDP had to make concessions to opposition parties in the Diet by accepting their demands, which included reorganization of the MOF. Nor were the decisions of LDP organizations necessarily the same as those of the Diet. Although the MOF negotiated with LDP executives and faction leaders and obtained their consent, it was no longer guaranteed that their decisions would be legislated in the Diet.

With regard to the control over LDP members by factional executives, conflicts between LDP members over the coalition principle and the change of generation in the LDP were intensified in the processes of the first and second wave of MOF reform. The issue of MOF reform had been related to the principle of coalition since the NHP took a firm attitude towards the reorganization of the MOF. The LDP was divided as to how far it should compromise with the NHP. In the first wave of MOF reform, the anti-power-holding group, which included Kajiyama Seiroku, which was against the current coalition with the NHP and the SDPJ, criticized the power-holding group, which included Katō Kōichi (the Secretary General of the LDP) and Yamazaki Taku (the Chair of the PARC), on the grounds that it made too many concessions to the NHP. Confrontation between the two groups was intensified across factions. Another cross-factional issue, the change of generation in the LDP, affected the process of the second wave of MOF reform. The LDP was divided into a 'new policy-oriented politician' group, which consisted of junior LDP members, and a senior LDP politicians' group. The new policy-oriented politician group resisted senior LDP members' control and cooperated with DP members. In both cases the LDP was divided across factions, therefore faction leaders could not control their members. As a result, the MOF could not obtain support from LDP members as a whole, although it negotiated with faction leaders and obtained their consent.

In addition, because of a change in the attitude of LDP politicians the MOF faced difficulties in persuading LDP politicians to protect its organization. LDP politicians resented the attitude of the MOF towards them under the Hosokawa Coalition Cabinet. Furthermore, when the first wave of MOF reform was in progress, the next general election was close at hand. LDP politicians were afraid of the negative effects of their attitude towards MOF reform and the positive effects of opposition parties, which pledged fundamental administrative reform to the electorate. In order to obtain support from public opinion and to maintain their position as a ruling party, LDP politicians promoted MOF reform. With regard to some LDP politicians, the MOF lost its ability to exert influence on them. Expertise in policy planning had been a powerful means by which the MOF bargained with LDP politicians. However, in the process of the second wave of MOF reform, new policy-oriented generation politicians refused such support from the MOF, and planned reorganization of the MOF in cooperation with DP members.

Thus, three institutional changes were observed in the first and second wave of MOF reform. The MOF attempted to protect its organization, influencing the decision-making processes of the LDP and the government through the issue settling system. However, the decision-making processes that were based on the issue settling system were transformed under the coalition cabinets. The main venues of the government's decision-making shifted from LDP organizations to organizations that consisted of ruling coalition parties. Additionally, in those organizations the LDP had to change its decisions, compromising with other ruling coalition parties. Cooperation between MOF bureaucrats and LDP executives and faction leaders no longer resulted in the decisions being taken up by the government and the Diet. Under LDP dominance, the MOF drafted bills and negotiated with LDP executives over those bills. In the revising process of the Financial Revitalization Bill, the 'new policy-oriented politicians' created the revised draft cooperating with the DP and the LDP politicians, and the MOF was excluded from this process. Consequently, the MOF could not control the decision-making process of the government and the Diet through the issue settling system and failed to prevent the splitting of its jurisdiction.

8 Conclusion

Under LDP dominance, there was an effective issue settling system, in which bureaucrats planned policies and negotiated with LDP executives and faction leaders in order to submit those plans as bills to the Diet, while LDP executives negotiated with opposition parties to obtain smooth deliberation in the Diet. This was a result of an incremental adjustment of the mechanism consolidated in the Meiji era. The efficacy of this issue settling system considerably declined, particularly regarding the MOF, as the result of institutional changes caused by a fundamental political change after 1993, the end of LDP dominance.

We have explored the above argument from a historical institutional approach, clarifying the structure of contemporary Japanese politics. The analysis of Japanese politics, in terms of institutions and institutional relationships, elucidated the existence of the mechanism that consisted of an autonomous bureaucracy and cooperation between bureaucrats and party politicians. Our historical investigation, examining the original political settings of institutions and the process of their incremental adjustment, clarified that, despite political changes, the Japanese bureaucracy and party politicians preserved their structure and characteristics. As a result, the mechanism has been maintained since the Meiji era. In spite of structural changes in Japanese social and political circumstances, such as defeat in the Second World War, the relationship between the Japanese bureaucracy and party politicians remained more or less intact. Adopting a historical institutional approach, the book has highlighted the formidable resilience of the Japanese bureaucracy and the chronic dependence of party politicians on bureaucrats with respect to policy-making.

The path dependent process of institutions and institutional relationships is divided into three stages: initial critical juncture, the stage of reproduction and the end of the path.

The initial critical juncture of the mechanism The initial critical juncture of the mechanism is the Meiji era. The Japanese bureaucracy and political parties were established and the mechanism was consolidated during this period. The original setting in which a particular institutional configuration is selected decides its reproduction mechanism. Therefore the political settings of the Japanese bureaucracy and political parties during the Meiji era affected the structure and characteristics of the Japanese bureaucracy, political parties and the relationship between them.

Hanbatsu politicians who dominated the political processes of the Meiji government faced strong demands for participation in the political process and dissatisfaction with the government of those who were excluded from the government. Hanbatsu politicians required administrative organizations that would protect the vulnerable government from such political movements. Therefore the structure of the Japanese bureaucracy was elaborated to secure the vulnerable position of the government by centralizing information and expertise of policy-making with the bureaucracy and by ensuring the independence of administrative organizations. As a result, the Japanese bureaucracy achieved a high ability to plan and implement policies and an autonomous organization from the beginning. On the other hand, those who were dissatisfied with the government formed political parties as opponents to the government. Therefore political parties were excluded from the decision-making process of the government when they were formed, and they could not obtain opportunities to accumulate the information and expertise necessary for policy-making.

The above political setting affected the relationship between bureaucrats and party politicians and decided the structure of the mechanism: highly autonomous bureaucracy; bureaucrats' superiority to party politicians in policy-making; and cooperation between bureaucrats and party politicians in the legislative process. This structure brought about the reproduction pattern of the mechanism. Bureaucrats' superiority in policy-making was reinforced by the reproduction of the monopoly of information and expertise through the structure of the Japanese bureaucracy (the closed career system, the on-the-job training system, the promotion system). Both bureaucrats and party politicians found the mechanism was beneficial, which reinforced it. Bureaucrats found that cooperating with party politicians was an effective way to put their plans into effect. Party politicians could secure their positions in the Imperial Diet because they could concentrate on their election campaign.

The long-lasting equilibrium known as the Edo Shogunate was disrupted by the Meiji Restoration, and a new institutional arrangement – the mechanism explained above – was consolidated under the Meiji government. Political circumstances at the beginning of the Meiji era determined the structures of the Japanese bureaucracy, political parties and the relationship between them. Thus the circumstances formed the reproduction pattern of the mechanism – the monopoly of expertise in policy-making by bureaucrats and the effectiveness of cooperation between bureaucrats and party politicians.

The reproduction stage of the mechanism In its reproduction stage, the mechanism evolved through incremental adjustments to the changes of

Japanese political circumstances, such as the Taishō Democracy, defeat in the Second World War and LDP dominance after 1955. During the Taishō Democracy (from the 1910s to the beginning of the 1930s), the areas in which party politicians intervened were limited to functions such as public works and police activities related to the regulation of election campaigns. Therefore the reproduction pattern of the mechanism, namely the monopolizing of expertise of policy-making by bureaucrats and the effectiveness of the cooperation between bureaucrats and party politicians, did not change during this period. After the Second World War, political reforms executed by the GHQ brought about a significant change in Japanese politics – namely, the rejection of the sovereignty of the Emperor. However, the reproduction pattern of the mechanism was not damaged by the political reforms. The structure of the Japanese bureaucracy that had reproduced the monopoly of expertise and information by bureaucrats did not change despite the reforms because the Japanese bureaucracy succeeded in preserving its employment and personnel system. Since many party politicians were purged by the GHQ from their public positions, newly elected party politicians lacked expertise and experience of policy-making. Therefore, in order to keep their seats in the Diet, it was highly profitable and effective for party politicians to cooperate with bureaucrats relying on the mechanism. Thus, the mechanism survived after defeat in the Second World War. After the LDP monopolized the position of ruling party in the Diet in 1955, bureaucrats immediately established close connections with LDP politicians. For bureaucrats, concentrating on maintaining connections with the LDP was the most effective way of putting their plans into legislation. For LDP politicians, maintaining close cooperation with bureaucrats in the legislative process was profitable and the most effective way of securing their positions because they could concentrate on election campaigns and obtain votes by distributing public works and subsidies among their supporters. Under LDP dominance, the mechanism evolved as the issue settling system by establishing close cooperation between LDP executives, faction leaders and bureaucrats.

It can be argued that the period from the end of the Meiji era to 1993 was that of the reproduction of the mechanism. Despite political changes, such as party cabinets during the Taishō Democracy, political reforms after the Second World War and LDP dominance after 1955, the reproduction pattern of the mechanism – the monopoly of expertise by bureaucrats and the effectiveness of cooperation between bureaucrats and party politicians (LDP politicians under LDP dominance) – was not fundamentally disrupted.

The end of the mechanism Since the general election of 1993, it can be said that the mechanism has been at the third stage, the end of the path. After the general election of 1993, the single party dominance of the LDP in the Diet collapsed and the era of coalition cabinets began. The reproduction pattern of the mechanism – namely, the effectiveness of close cooperation between LDP executive, faction leaders and bureaucrats – declined, particularly with regard to the MOF, because of this fundamental change. Close cooperation between LDP executives, faction leaders and MOF bureaucrats could not solve issues efficiently because of the three institutional changes caused by the end of LDP dominance (decline in the importance of LDP organizations, the weakened management system of the LDP and the detached attitudes of LDP politicians towards MOF bureaucrats). Therefore, for MOF bureaucrats, the mechanism was not an effective measure to use to put their plans into effect. For LDP politicians the mechanism was not profitable since it could not solve political and economic issues efficiently, which might jeopardize their positions in the Diet.

The mechanism was not able to overcome this breakdown of the reproduction pattern by adjusting itself incrementally. Under LDP dominance bureaucrats and the LDP elaborated formal and informal connections between them from divisions of the PARC to the EC, and such connections were solidly institutionalized. The cooperation between them was so institutionalized and rigid that it was difficult for both MOF bureaucrats and LDP politicians to change their way of cooperation immediately after the general election of July 1993. After 1993, coalition parties such as the JSP (later the SDPJ), the NHP and the CGP participated in the decision-making process of the government. Nevertheless, coalition partnerships with the LDP were not stable. Under the Murayama and Hashimoto Cabinets, the LDP aligned itself with the JSP (later the SDPJ) and the NHP, and under the Obuchi Cabinet it cooperated with the CGP and the LP. The LDP itself was divided over the principle of coalition. Furthermore, new political parties mushroomed and disappeared, which increased the uncertainty and unpredictability of political situations under the era of coalition cabinets. Accordingly, both MOF bureaucrats and party politicians could not comprehend the alignment of political parties in the future.

Compared with the above situation, political situations during the Taishō Democracy, after the Second World War and during LDP dominance were either more comprehensible or more flexible. During the Taishō Democracy, there were only two major parties, the Seiyūkai and the Minseitō, and one or other of them was able to obtain the position of ruling party in the Imperial Diet. Immediately after the Second World War, major party politicians were purged from their public positions. As a result bureaucrats were dominant over party politicians in the political processes. Furthermore, there was no institutionalized tie between bureaucrats and political parties immediately after the Second World War. During the Taishō Democracy, bureaucrats took an aloof attitude towards party politicians although some MHA bureaucrats became members of the Seiyūkai. When the Imperial Rule Assistance Association was formed in 1940, all political parties were dissolved, and after the Second World War all political parties were newly formed. Therefore bureaucrats and party politicians could construct connections between them flexibly. Once the LDP dominated the position of ruling party in the Diet, bureaucrats could concentrate on establishing connections with the LDP.

Contrary to those situations, political circumstances after 1993 were inflexible for bureaucrats and LDP politicians because of rigidly institutionalized ties between them and also uncertain because of the unpredictability of the alignment of political parties in the future. Consequently, the mechanism was not able to cope with the end of LDP dominance by making an incremental adjustment.

Therefore, since 1993, the mechanism has been at the third stage, the end of the path. Its reproduction pattern was interrupted since the effectiveness of the cooperation between LDP politicians and bureaucrats, especially MOF bureaucrats, significantly declined because of the three institutional changes caused by the end of LDP dominance. The long-lasting political equilibrium of the mechanism was disrupted.

The three case studies in this thesis support the above argument. The process of the introduction of the consumption tax shows the effectiveness of the issue settling system under LDP dominance. Decisions made by LDP organizations were almost all put into practice as decisions of the government and the Diet. The LDP TSRC and the PARC played a main role in the decision-making process of the government, and their decisions were embodied in legislation as the Consumption Tax Bill and the Consumption Tax Law. LDP executives and faction leaders controlled their members. LDP members obeyed their factions' resolution, which appealed to them to unite to pass the Consumption Tax Bill. Therefore MOF bureaucrats mainly concentrated on negotiating with LDP executives (such as the Chair of the LDP TSRC) and faction leaders to obtain support from the LDP for their consumption tax plan. As a result, the introduction of the consumption tax, which had been regarded as highly unlikely to be put into practice, was legislated. The issue settling system worked effectively under LDP dominance.

Contrary to the consumption tax case, the case studies of Chapters 6 and 7 – the financial crises and MOF reform in the latter half of the 1990s – show the inefficacy of the issue settling system. The three institutional changes after 1993 were observed in both cases. The management system of the LDP through factions did not function effectively. There was no influential leader who could control the behaviour of the Nōrin zoku, who strongly opposed the Jūsen liquidation plan that had been created by the MOF. As a result, the plan created by the MOF was overturned and measures to solve the Jūsen problem were delayed. With respect to the LTCBJ case, the LDP was divided over the liquidation of the LTCBJ across factions, and LDP executives and faction leaders could not control junior LDP members who advocated the liquidation of the LTCBJ and cooperated with opposition parties (the DP and the LP) in revising the Financial

Revitalization Bill. Furthermore, the importance of LDP organizations in the decision-making process of the Diet declined. The LDP was forced to make a concession to opposition parties in order to let the Financial Revitalization Bill pass the Diet. As a result, the Financial Revitalization Bill submitted by the LDP to the Diet was entirely revised to incorporate most demands of the opposition parties. The MOF failed to put into practice its liquidation plans for the Jūsen and the LTCBJ although it relied on the issue settling system.

With regard to MOF reform, organizations consisting of ruling coalition parties – such as the study group of ruling coalition parties and the Committee of Representitives of the Ruling Coalition Parties – played the main role in the decision-making process of the coalition government. The LDP had to compromise with other coalition parties, the SDPJ and the NHP, which demanded fundamental MOF reform. Additionally, the LDP was divided across factions over the coalition principle – whether the LDP should continue with the coalition with the SDPJ and the NHP. Such confrontation escalated in connection with MOF reform. LDP members who did not support the current coalition with the SDPJ and the NHP opposed making further concessions to them with regard to MOF reform. On the other hand, LDP members who supported the current coalition sought to make further concessions with respect to MOF reform in order to maintain the current coalition. The MOF attempted to protect its organization by negotiating to influence the decision-making process of the government. It attempted to control the process through the issue settling system by drafting bills, attending discussion in LDP organizations and negotiating with LDP executives and faction leaders. However, LDP organizations were replaced in their important position in the decision-making process of the government by organizations of ruling coalition parties. The consent of LDP executives and faction leaders did not result in decisions of the LDP – or the coalition government either. In addition, some LDP politicians resented the attitudes of MOF bureaucrats under the Hosokawa Cabinet, and many LDP politicians were concerned about the influence of new parties, such as the DP, which appealed to the electorate for fundamental MOF reform. Therefore LDP politicians did not have a strong motivation to protect the MOF from reorganization. Consequently, the MOF failed to prevent the splitting of its jurisdiction by influencing the decision-making processes of the LDP and the government through the issue settling system.

The institutional changes in the three factors that supported the issue settling system significantly reduced its effectiveness. Consequently, its reproduction pattern was interrupted, and the long-lasting equilibrium of the issue settling system was disrupted, which brought about political confusion in the cases of the financial crises and MOF reform in the 1990s. It can be argued that the effectiveness of the issue settling system would not have declined as much as it actually did if any one of the three factors had not changed.

If LDP faction leaders' control of their members had remained strict after 1993, LDP members would have obeyed faction leaders' decisions about MOF reform and the liquidation schemes for the Jūsen and the LTCBJ. The LDP could have taken a more decisive attitude when it negotiated with other ruling coalition parties and opposition parties. Deliberation in the Diet would not have been thrown into political turmoil and the liquidation schemes would have been put into practice without significant delay. Under LDP dominance, the LDP sometimes made a concession to opposition parties. For instance, the LDP compromised with the CGP and the DSP to obtain smooth deliberation of the Consumption Tax Bill in the Diet. Nevertheless, the LDP took a decisive attitude in the negotiation process, and the Consumption Tax Bill passed the Diet without significant delay.

Supposing LDP organizations had maintained the same influence on the decision-making processes of the government and the Diet as they had under LDP dominance, the decisions of the LDP would have been adopted by the government as its own decisions and put into legislation. Although the LDP was divided over MOF reform and the liquidation schemes for the Jūsen and the LTCBJ, it would not have compromised with other parties in the Diet. Therefore the deliberation of a package of bills for the Jūsen and the Financial Revitalization Bill would not have been thrown into serious confusion. As for MOF reform, the LDP would not have changed its decision and made compromises with other ruling coalition parties and opposition parties that strongly demanded the complete split of the MOF organization.

If the relationship between MOF bureaucrats and LDP politicians had been still as close as it was under LDP dominance, the MOF would not have been excluded from the revising process of the Financial Revitalization Bill. MOF bureaucrats and LDP politicians would have closely cooperated with each other, and the Financial Revitalization Bill and the liquidation scheme for the LTCBJ created by the MOF would have been put into practice even if they might have been modified. Both the revised bill and the liquidation scheme would not have faced strong opposition from senior LDP politicians, which in practice caused serious political confusion. About MOF reform, LDP politicians would have given priority to close cooperation with MOF bureaucrats as they did under LDP dominance, and, even though some junior LDP politicians might have supported MOF reform, the LDP as a whole would not have promoted the complete split of the MOF organization.

It can therefore be argued that if any one of the three factors had not changed after 1993, the effectiveness of the issue settling system would not have declined so much and the political processes of the financial crises and MOF reform would not have taken the same confused processes as described in Chapters 6 and 7.

After 1993, as two case studies illustrate, cooperation with LDP executives and faction leaders has not guaranteed that plans created by MOF bureaucrats will either be transformed into LDP plans or confirmed as the decision of the government. While the mechanism has not been able to adapt itself to new political circumstances, the decision-making system under coalition cabinets has not been clearly established. Rather, MOF bureaucrats are forced to take the role of coordinators between ruling coalition parties.

There are two types of response by MOF bureaucrats and politicians to this structural change in the Japanese political system. One is an incremental adjustment of the mechanism, and the other is a fundamental change of the mechanism, reshaping the relationship between politicians and bureaucrats in policy-making.

Regarding an incremental adjustment, MOF bureaucrats are trying to form the same connections with other political parties as the ones they had with the LDP. Some ex-MOF bureaucrats have stood for election as candidates for other political parties. For example, in the general election of October 1996, two ex-MOF bureaucrats stood as NFP candidates, and in the general election of June 2000, three out of five candidates who were ex-MOF bureaucrats stood as DP candidates. Some junior MOF bureaucrats have sought to make contact with other political parties. LDP organizations are losing their crucial position in the decision-making process of the government. Although the LDP has kept its position as a ruling party, it has been forced to form a ruling coalition with other parties. Considering such circumstances, in order to legislate their policies smoothly, MOF bureaucrats are trying to form with other political parties the same connections as those with the LDP under LDP dominance. It could be said that their strategy is just the expansion to other political parties of the connections that they formed with the LDP under LDP dominance.

Concerning the fundamental reshaping of this mechanism, there are signs of change among politicians. Some junior LDP members, the so-called 'new policy-oriented politician', insisted that party politicians should take the lead in policy-making, and they created the revised Financial Revitalization Bill without the support of the MOF. In 2000, a vice-minister system was introduced, the main aim of which is that junior politicians can accumulate expertise while they are serving as vice ministers. In March 2002, the LDP Headquarters' Office on National Vision presented a 'Plan for the Reform of the Policy-Making System', which proposed that the ability of the Cabinet to solve political and economic problems should be enhanced and politicians' leadership with regard to policy-making should be strengthened. The plan presented three principles: strengthening the leadership of the Prime Minister and the cabinet; strengthening the leadership of politicians in policy-making; and the abolition of the zoku system. As for strengthening the leadership of the Prime Minister and the cabinet, the plan proposed that:

1   The meeting of Administrative Vice Ministers, which in practice has settled issues before the Cabinet meeting, should be abolished, and the meeting of Ministers should deal with issues that require coordination between ministries.
2   The Prime Minister and Ministers should be allowed to employ experts from administrative organizations and private companies as political advisers at their disposal.
3   The function of the intelligence service of the Cabinet Secretariat should be enhanced.
4   A political appointee system should be introduced with regard to senior positions of ministries.

To strengthen the role of politicians in policy-making, the plan proposed the introduction of a system of political advisers and the enhancement of the Legislation Bureaux of the House of Representatives and the House of Councillors. However, this plan also proposed the abolition of the so-called Yotō Shinsa (prior screening by the LDP). Yotō Shinsa was established under LDP dominance, and in it, LDP organizations screened the government's policies, such as bills and budgets, before a Cabinet meeting. The aim of this proposal was to change the balance of power between the Cabinet and the LDP in the decision-making process of the government and to strengthen the leadership of the Prime Minister and Ministers in policy-making by preventing intervention by LDP members, especially the zoku. This proposal is likely to provoke severe objection among LDP members, and it is therefore not clear whether the proposals of this plan will be put into practice.

  Although the pace of reshaping is slow, the new direction in policy-making, strengthening the ability of the Cabinet, has been gradually put into practice since 1993. The Central Ministries and Agencies Reform Law, promulgated in July 1998, provides the basic principles of the reform of central ministries and agencies in Article 4: 'the function of the cabinet should be strengthened, the leadership of the Prime Minister with regard to implementing national policies should be more clarified, and the systems which support the cabinet and the Prime Minister should be reorganized' (Article 4 of the Central Ministries and Agencies Reform Law). In addition, Article 9 of this law paves the way for the introduction of political appointees in the Cabinet Secretariat by providing that 'officials of the Cabinet Secretariat should consist of those who are personally appointed by the Prime Minister, and necessary systems to employ officials of the Cabinet Secretariat from and outside of administrative organizations should be established' (Article 4 of the Central Ministries and Agencies Reform Law). Following those principles, planning and making bills with respect to the Cabinet's important policies were added to the jurisdiction of the Cabinet Secretariat. The number of officials in the Cabinet Secretariat was also increased, and new positions were included, such as that of Assistant

Vice-Cabinet Secretary. Furthermore, in order to assist the Cabinet Secretariat, the Cabinet Office (Naikakufu) was established in 2001.

The following situations, which weakened the power of MOF bureaucrats, propelled this movement. One was a number of scandals concerning MOF bureaucrats, which damaged their credibility and integrity. During the first half of 1998, the Japanese mass media, especially weekly magazines, reported scandalously excessive entertainment of MOF bureaucrats by financial institutions. On 26 April 1998, two MOF officials who were in charge of the inspection of security companies were arrested for bribery. On 27 April 1998, 112 MOF officials were reprimanded, and this included one official who was suspended from office and 17 who had their pay cut, and resulted in two resignations and five demotions of career officials. On 5 March 1998, the Assistant Chief of the Coordination Division of the Security Bureau was arrested for bribery. This apprehension significantly damaged the reputation of the MOF since no career MOF officials in active service had been arrested before. As a result of the above scandals, the reputation of MOF bureaucrats was tarnished. Japanese people had trusted the morals and competence of MOF bureaucrats since the Meiji era, but now they became doubtful about the morals and integrity of MOF bureaucrats. According to a survey conducted by the *Asahi Shinbun*, 71 per cent of respondents answered that they did not trust bureaucrats (*Asahi Shinbun*, 4 November 1998).

The other situation that has weakened the bureaucrats' power is the trend toward deregulation and globalization. Since the 1990s, deregulation of the Japanese economy has been strongly demanded by foreign countries, especially the US, and deregulation has been on the political agenda. The financial crisis in 1997 pushed forward the movement toward deregulation since it was pointed out that excessive control by the MOF of financial institutions had weakened the institutions' independence and capability. On 8 June 1998, the MOF abolished 400 directions (tsūtatsu) to financial institutions and 243 circulations (jimurenraku) issued by the Directors of Bureaux, which were the basis for the detailed regulation of financial institutions. Deregulation meant that bureaucrats lost measures, such as administrative guidance based on directions and circulations, through which they had tightly controlled financial institutions. In addition, the above revelations about the excessive entertainment of MOF bureaucrats by financial institutions caused severe criticism of the excessively close connections between them. Many financial institutions announced the abolishment of the MOF-tan system.[1] The MOF had accumulated information through measures such as administrative guidance and the MOF-tan system, so the ability of MOF bureaucrats to collect information became seriously weakened.

Furthermore, the globalized economy introduced many foreign institutions, which were not under the tight control of the MOF, to Japanese markets. It also brought about a flood of information that was highly technical and rapidly became obsolete. It is difficult for MOF bureaucrats, who are transferred from one position to another every two to three years, to understand highly technical and rapidly changing information and to grasp Japanese markets flooded with such information and new foreign actors.

Thus, through these two situations, MOF bureaucrats lost the trust of the Japanese people and the close control of Japanese financial institutions, which weakened their political power.

The recent political situations, however, have also not necessarily been favourable to politicians. Successive scandals involving politicians have damaged their reputation. On 9 April 2002, Katō Kōichi, who was regarded as one of the future candidates for Prime Minister, resigned as a member of the HR when one of his secretaries was arrested for the violation of Income Tax Law. On 19 June, a member of the HR, Suzuki Muneo (an LDP member), was arrested for bribery, and his improper use of close connections with the Ministry of Foreign Affairs was reported as a scandal by the mass media. During the first half of 2002, newspapers and weekly magazines were flooded with scandals not only of LDP politicians but also of SDP politicians, reporting that they had illegally received or misappropriated the salaries of their government-paid secretaries. On 9 August 2002, the former Foreign Minister, Tanaka Makiko, resigned a member of the HR due to an allegation of the misappropriation of the salaries of her government-paid secretaries. On 18 July 2003, a member of the HR, Tsujimoto Kiyomi (an SDP member) and one of the secretaries of the ex-SDP Leader, Doi Takako, were arrested for the illegal receipt of the salaries of her government-paid secretaries. It was alleged that the SDP systematically supported illegal receipts of government-paid secretaries of its members. From April to May 2004, in the process of the deliberation of pension reform bills, pension scandals were revealed that related not only to the LDP but also to other political parties. In April 2004, it was revealed that seven out of eighteen ministers of the Koizumi Cabinet had failed to pay national pension premiums. On 7 May 2004, the Cabinet Secretary, Fukuda Yasuo, resigned his office because of his failure to make the payment. On 10 May, the Leader of the DP, Kan Naoto, also resigned his position because of his failure to pay. On 12 May 2004, the leader of the CGP, Kanzaki Takenori, and the Secretary General of the CGP, Fuyushiba Tetsuzō, admitted their failure to make the payments. On 13 May, five DP members resigned their positions as the Chairs of the Committees of the HR and the HC because of their failure to pay. On 14 May, Prime Minister Koizumi and the ex-Leader of the SDP, Doi Takako, admitted they had failed to pay national pension premiums.

Despite the above succession of scandals, the majority of the Japanese people seem to be in favour of shifting the balance towards party politicians with regard to policy-making. When the most recent general election was held on 9 November 2003, both the LDP and the DP announced packages of policy plans as their 'manifestos', and according to the survey conducted by the *Asahi Shinbun*, 69 per cent of respondents considered those manifestos when they cast their votes (*Asahi Shinbun*, 12 November 2003).

The relationship between politicians and bureaucrats under such new political circumstances is not yet clearly defined. Nevertheless, it can be said that politicians and public opinion share a common goal, namely, that politicians should take more initiative with regard to policy-making. This trend may contribute to bring about more democratically controlled administration.

Unless, however, the balance between politicians and bureaucrats of the ability to plan policy innovation is reshaped, this goal will be hard to achieve. In order to take the lead in policy-making processes, it is necessary for party politicians to obtain the ability to plan policies. Sufficient staff to support politicians, especially Ministers, is required for achieving such ability. Considering the broad range of jurisdiction of a ministry and the increasing amount of information, it is unrealistic to presuppose that a Minister can grasp every issue in his or her ministry's jurisdiction. The LDP Headquarters' Office on National Vision proposed in a 'Plan for the Reform of the Policy-Making System' that the Prime Minister and Ministers should be allowed to employ experts from administrative organizations or private companies as political advisers at their disposal. Such a personal political adviser system has been adopted in the UK. The Blair Cabinet strengthened the ability of the Cabinet by making the most of task forces and by increasing the number of personal advisers. Task forces, which are set up to deal with specific issues, include a large number of non-civil servants and are less reliant on civil servants for advice (Smith 1999: 171). Under the Blair Cabinet, the number of political advisers significantly increased to more than 50. 'Ministers now draw on several sources of policy advice: political advisors, think-tanks, consultants' (Rhodes 2001: 107). Nevertheless, it is also pointed out that 'the senior civil service is not bypassed, nor is their influence reduced to that of second stringers to political advisers. Rather, they put together packages of advice from many sources' (Rhodes 2001: 107). However, the negative sides of a political appointee system are also pointed out. It is argued that the value of a politically neutral civil service, evaluating all factors objectively, would be lost and policies could become biased towards the short term. The deterioration of civil service morale is also noted, and it is argued that competent young candidates will not enter administrative organizations (Drewry and Butcher 1991: 166–7). If a personal political adviser system were to be introduced in Japan, it would have significant effects on bureaucratic organizations. The introduction of a political appointee system and personal political adviser system would cause significant changes in the employment and personnel systems of bureaucrats, which constitute the structure of autonomous organizations. A closed career system and a seniority rule would be re-examined, which would damage bureaucrats' homogeneity and monopoly of expertise. Their loyalty to their ministry might be also damaged. As a result, the organizational factors of bureaucratic autonomy – organizational integrity and organizational ability

– which have been the source of the overwhelming power of bureaucrats, would be significantly affected. Not only for administrative organization but also for private companies, comprehensive reforms of employment and payment systems based on life-time employment and a seniority rule would be required, and recruitment, payment, promotion and pension systems would have to be reformed in order to promote personnel interchange between private and public sectors.

Another serious problem is politicians' intervention in the personnel matters of bureaucrats. Preventing the politicization of bureaucrats' personnel matters is a prerequisite for protecting the core characteristics of bureaucracy, the continuity and the political neutrality. In the UK, although the Labour Party obtained the position of ruling party after 18 years, it is said that 'so far, however, there has been no overt politicization of appointments to the senior civil service' (Rhodes 2001: 106). In Japan, excessive intervention by politicians in the personnel matters of bureaucrats during the Taishō Democracy (from the beginning of the 1910s to the beginning of the 1930s) brought about severe criticism and strong antipathy to political parties among bureaucrats, and this was one of the factors which resulted in criticism and distrust of party politics not only from bureaucrats but also from public opinion.

After the general election of July 1993, it was argued that the political circumstances in which the LDP would be replaced by other political parties had finally come. The Hosokawa Coalition Cabinet was formed in August 1993 with unusually high support from public opinion, but the Cabinet lasted only a short period. From 1994 the LDP returned to the position of ruling party and, superficially, there seems to be no change in Japanese political circumstances. Nevertheless, the position of the LDP as a ruling party has become more vulnerable. The LDP has been forced to make a ruling coalition, which has gradually weakened its integrity.

The decision-making system in such political circumstances has not been established. What is apparent is that, especially regarding the MOF, the issue settling system now does not work effectively. It is also clear that an incremental adjustment of the mechanism consolidated in the Meiji era by expanding close relationships between LDP politicians and MOF bureaucrats to those between other political parties and MOF bureaucrats is not attainable. This is because a political party that could substitute for the LDP has not yet appeared in Japanese politics.

It could be said that it has become a common aim among the public that the leadership of the Cabinet and the Prime Minister should be strengthened and politicians should take more initiative in policy-making. In order to implement this aim, the Cabinet Law was revised, and new political systems such as the Cabinet Office and the Junior Minister system were introduced. The Koizumi Cabinet (26 April 2001–) put structural economic and political reforms at the top of its political agenda. Japanese politics has been in a transition period since 1993, and it seems that no conspicuous result of political and economic reform has been achieved so far. Nevertheless, it is clear that the decision-making system under LDP dominance, whereby informal negotiations between LDP executives and bureaucrats made substantial decisions, is no longer operative. For instance, under LDP dominance, every bill submitted by the Cabinet to the Diet was scrutinized and approved by the LDP before being discussed in the Cabinet meeting. In April 2002, the Koizumi Cabinet submitted a package of bills for the deregulation of postal services to the Diet without the approval of the LDP, which showed the significant change in the decision-making process of Japanese politics. Although it takes time for the new systems referred to above to fulfil their functions, they pave the way for an empowered Prime Minister, Cabinet and politicians to take the lead in policy-making.

On the other hand, MOF bureaucrats have not coped well with the new political circumstances under coalition cabinets. The Japanese bureaucracy has protected its structure and preserved its characteristics in spite of political changes. Such resilience and path dependency prevent the Japanese bureaucracy from implementing fundamental changes in its structure. MOF bureaucrats tried to cope with the new circumstances by expanding their close connections with the LDP to encompass other political parties as well. Nevertheless, as mentioned above, such a tactic has not worked effectively. Until now, MOF bureaucrats have not been able to redefine their role following the end of LDP dominance.

Since the collapse of single-party dominance by the LDP in 1993, Japanese politics has been in a transition period. Although some movements seem to go in the direction of more democratically controlled administration, a new decision-making system that can substitute for the issue settling system under the LDP dominance has not yet been established. In addition, it is not clear to what extent MOF bureaucrats would develop new roles under new political circumstances. So long as MOF bureaucrats, who have exerted overwhelming power in policy-making, fail to construct new roles for themselves, the confusion of Japanese politics will continue.

Appendix
Chronology of Japanese politics

1978

7 December   The First Ōhira Cabinet is formed.

1979

19 January   The cabinet presents the 'Major Line of the Tax System Revision' for the fiscal year 1979, including the introduction of the general consumption tax in 1980.

7 October   General election is held.

9 November   The Second Ōhira Cabinet is formed.

21 December   The Diet issues a resolution on 'fiscal reconstruction'.

1980

17 July   The Suzuki Cabinet is formed.

1982

27 November   The First Nakasone Cabinet is formed.

1983

27 December   The Second Nakasone Cabinet is formed.

1986

6 July   Simultaneous elections of the House of Representatives and the House of Councillors are held.

22 July   The Third Nakasone Cabinet is formed.

28 October   The GTSRC issues its final report on structural tax reform, including the introduction of a new consumption tax.

| 23 December | The LDP TSRC proposes the introduction of the sales tax in the 'Major Line of the Tax Reform'. |

1987

10 February	The tax bills, including the sales tax bill, are submitted to the Diet.
27 May	The 108th session of the Diet ends. The tax bills are dropped.
16 October	The LDP and the government decide on the introduction of a structural tax reform in the future.
6 November	The Takeshita Cabinet is formed.
12 November	The GTSRC receives an inquiry from Prime Minister Takeshita about a structural tax reform.

1988

28 April	The GTSRC presents an interim report on tax reform.
14 June	The LDP TSRC presents the 'Major Line of Structural Tax Reform', including the introduction of the consumption tax.
15 June	The GTSRC presents the 'Final Report on Structural Tax Reform'.
28 June	The 'Major Line of Tax Reform' is approved by the Cabinet.
29 June	The tax bills are submitted to the Diet.
16 November	The tax bills are passed by the House of Representatives.
24 December	The tax bills are passed by the House of Councillors.

1989

| 3 June | The Uno Cabinet is formed. |
| 10 August | The First Kaifu Cabinet is formed. |

1990

18 February	General election is held.
28 February	The Second Kaifu Cabinet is formed.
27 March	The Director General of the Banking Bureau of the MOF issues a directive, in which the MOF is to regulate financial institutions' total amount of loan on real property business.

1991

January	Seven Jūsen get into financial difficulties. First schemes for their reconstruction are formed.
5 November	The Miyazawa Cabinet is formed.

1992

26 July	Election for the House of Councillors is held.
October	The MOF announces that the total amount of non-performing loans (loans to failing companies or those delayed more than six months) of 21 major banks is 12 trillion 300 billion yen.

1993

3 February	The Director General of the Banking Bureau of the MOF and the Director General of the Economic Bureau of the MAFF make a memorandum in which the founding financial institutions take responsibility for the Jūsen's bad loans according to the reconstruction schemes.
26 February	The founding banks of Nihon Jūtaku Kin'yū (one of the Jūsen) make the second reconstruction scheme. Based on this scheme, other Jūsen make their second reconstruction schemes.
18 June	The Diet passes a vote of no-confidence in the Miyazawa Cabinet.
21 June	The NHP is formed.
23 June	The JRP is formed.
18 July	The general election is held.
9 August	The Hosokawa Cabinet is formed.

1994

29 January	A package of four bills for political reforms is approved by the Diet.
8 February	The government announces the 'Administrative Guideline for Disposal of Financial Institutions' Non-performing Loans'.
March	The Chigin Seiho Housing Loan Company and the Jūso (two Jūsen) are declared insolvent.
28 April	The Hata Cabinet is formed.

25 June	The Hata Cabinet resigns en masse.
30 June	The Murayama Cabinet is formed.
9 December	The liquidation plans for the two credit unions (the Tōkyō Kyōwa Credit Union and the Anzen Credit Union) are announced.
10 December	The NFP is formed.

1995

March	The Sōgō Jūkin and the Housing Loan Corporation (two Jūsen) are declared insolvent.
8 June	The MOF announces that the total amount of non-performing loans of financial institutions is 40 trillion yen, and publicizes the guideline for the disposal of its bad loans in the 'Principle for the Reconstruction of Financial Systems'.
4 July	The Financial Systems Research Council forms the Committee on Stabilizing the Financial System. The Committee starts to examine the injection of public funds for the disposal of financial institutions' bad loans.
23 July	Election for the House of Councillors is held.
1 August	The Tokyo Metropolitan Government announces the suspension order to the Cosmo Credit Union.
13 August	The MOF announces a liquidation plan for the Hyōgo Bank.
16 August	The MOF makes on-the-spot inspections of the Jūsen.
29 August	The liquidation plan for the Cosmo Credit Union is announced.
30 August	The MOF and the Ōsaka Metropolitan Prefectual Office announce suspension orders to the Hyōgo Bank and the Kizu Credit Union.
2 September	The MOF publicizes a liquidation plan for the Hyōgo Bank.
14 September	The MOF announces that the total loss of the Jūsen is 7 trillion 700 billion yen. The Nihon Jūtaku Kin'yū, the Daiichi Jūtaku Kin'yū and the Nihon Housing Loan are declared insolvent.
27 September	The Financial System Research Council presents an interim report, in which it proposes an injection of public funds into financial institutions. Finance Minister Takemura announces the 'Principle of Early Disposal of Bad Loans of Financial Institutions'.

7 October	Finance Minister Takemura assures the early disposal of bad loans at the conference of G7.
31 October	The tripartite ruling parties' study group on financial and security systems presents an interim report on the Jūsen problem.
1 December	The Committee of Coordination of the Government and Executives of Ruling Parties presents guidelines to the disposal of bad loans of the Jūsen.
16 December	The MOF presents the liquidation scheme for the Jūsen.
19 December	The Cabinet approves the Jūsen liquidation scheme.
	The Committee of Representatives of Ruling Coalition Parties presents a statement about the responsibility of founding banks and ministries for the Jūsen problem.

1996

5 January	Prime Minister Murayama announces his resignation.
11 January	The First Hashimoto Cabinet is formed.
6 February	Ruling coalition parties and the government agree to form a study group on the reform of the MOF.
17 February	Ruling coalition parties and the government establish the Committee on MOF Reform, under which a study group (chaired by Itō Shigeru) is formed.
4 March	The deliberation of the Diet is suspended until 25 March because of picketing by the NFP.
10 May	The budget of the 1996 fiscal year, which includes the injection of 685 billion yen for the disposal of the bad loans of the Jūsen, is approved by the Diet.
13 June	The study group on MOF reform presents the 'Construction of New Financial Policies and Administration', which includes the splitting of the divisions of financial policies away from the MOF.
18 June	A package of six Jūsen liquidation bills is approved by the Diet.
6 August	LDP members of the study group on MOF reform refuse to receive a draft proposal prepared by the Chair, Itō.
7 August	The Secretaries General and executives of the ruling coalition parties agree that discussion in the study group should be based on the draft proposal prepared by the Chair, Itō.
20 August	The study group on MOF reform restarts discussion.

18 September	The Committee of eight LDP executives reaches an agreement in which the divisions of inspection and regulation of financial institutions should be split away from the MOF and transferred to a new organization based on Article 3 of the National Administrative Organization Law.
25 September	The study group on MOF reform presents its final report, and Secretaries General and executives of ruling coalition parties approve it.
27 September	The House of Representatives is dissolved.
28 September	The DP is formed.
20 October	A general election is held under the new election system.
7 November	The Second Hashimoto Cabinet is formed.
11 November	Prime Minister Hashimoto presents a comprehensive plan for fiscal reform.
19 November	The Cabinet approves a package of Cabinet orders for establishing the Council on Administrative Reforms.
21 November	The MOF announces a suspension order to the Hanwa Bank.
28 November	The first meeting of the Council on Administrative Reforms is held.
2 December	The government and the LDP decide to split the divisions of inspection and regulation of financial institutions from the MOF and to transfer them to a new agency by April 1999.
25 December	Ruling coalition parties agree on the final plan for MOF reform.

1997

21 January	The first meeting of the Council on Fiscal Structural Reform is held.
11 March	The Cabinet submits a package of MOF reform bills to the Diet.
1 April	The Hokkaidō Takushoku Bank and the Hokkaidō Bank announce their merger, to take place in April 1998.
	The Nippon Credit Bank-affiliated non-banks file for bankruptcy, and the bankruptcy is declared on 7 April.
25 April	The MOF announces a suspension order to the Nissan Health Insurance Company.
28 May	A package of MOF reform bills is approved by the Diet.

11 June	The revised Bank of Japan Law is approved by the Diet.
16 June	A package of bills for the Financial Supervisory Agency is approved by the Diet.
20 August	The Council on Administrative Reforms decides a plan for the reorganization of central ministries and agencies.
12 September	The Hokkaidō Takushoku Bank and the Hokkaidō Bank announce the postponement of their merger.
6 October	The Council on Administrative Reforms presents a draft proposal for MOF reform.
3 November	The Sanyō Securities Company files for application of the Corporate Rehabilitation Law at the Tōkyō District Court.
12 November	'Japan premium' at the inter-bank market of the Euro-dollar is raised to 0.15 per cent. The Tōkyō markets mark triple depreciation (the stock price, the price of government bonds and the appreciation of the yen against the dollar plunge in the market).
14 November	The LDP announces 'A Package of Emergent Policies to Stimulate Economy'. The Nikkei Stock Average marks less than 15 thousand yen.
17 November	The Hokkaidō Takushoku Bank announces its failure and the transfer of its business within the Hokkaidō area to the Hokuyō Bank.
	The Council on Administrative Reforms has intensive deliberations from 17 to 20 November to prepare for its final report.
18 November	The LDP Committee on Urgent Countermeasures to Economic Crises presents a plan to rescue financial institutions.
24 November	The Yamaichi Securities Company announces the closing down of its business. The Bank of Japan announces extraordinary funding to the Yamaichi Securities Company.
26 November	The Tokuyō City Bank announces its failure and transfer of its business to the Sendai Bank.
28 November	The Financial Structural Reform Law is approved by the Diet.
3 December	The Council on Administrative Reforms agrees on a final report.
12 December	The Revised Deposit Insurance Law is approved by the Diet.

23 December	The Marushō Securities Company files for bankruptcy to the Tōkyō District Court.
24 December	LDP Extraordinary Headquarters' Office on Stabilization of Financial System presents 'Urgent Countermeasures for Stabilization of the Financial System'.

1998

20 January	The cabinet approves a package of six bills for financial stabilization.
21 January	The House of Representatives starts to deliberate the Law on Urgent Measures for Financial Stabilization and the Revised Deposit Insurance Law.
15 February	The Revised Deposit Insurance Law and the Law on Urgent Measures for Financial Stabilization are approved by the Diet.
5 March	Nine city banks, three long-term credit banks, six credit banks and three regional banks request the injection of public funds to the Deposit Insurance Corporation.
31 March	The Examination Committee on Financial Crises under the Deposit Insurance Corporation decides to inject 1 trillion 815 billion 600 million yen of public funds into 21 banks.
24 April	The cabinet decides an additional economic stimulus package (total amount 16 trillion yen).
27 April	The DP (new) is formed.
1 May	The SDP decides to leave the ruling coalition.
20 May	The Nippon Credit Bank requests 22 insurance companies to postpone the maturity date of its subordinate debt.
28 May	The Special Committee on a Comprehensive Plan for Financial Rehabitalization presents its interim report.
29 May	The Revised Financial Structural Reform Law and a package of three bills of tax reduction are approved by the Diet.
1 June	The NHP leaves the ruling coalition.
5 June	A package of bills for the Financial System Reform Law is approved by the Diet.
8 June	The MOF announces that its 400 directives regarding financial institutions will be disestablished.
9 June	The Basic Law on Central Ministries and Agencies Reform is approved by the Diet.
19 June	The Bank of Japan funds the Long-Term Credit Bank of Japan (LTCBJ).

22 June	The Financial Supervisory Agency starts.
28 June	The Special Committee on a Comprehensive Plan for Financial Rehabitalization starts extensive deliberation for a final plan.
2 July	The Special Committee on a Comprehensive Plan for Financial Rehabitalization decides to introduce the 'Bridge Bank System' for failed financial institutions.
12 July	The election for the House of Councillors is held.
24 July	Obuchi Keizō, Koizumi Jun'ichirō and Kajiyama Seiroku stand for election for the LDP Presidency.
30 July	The Obuchi Cabinet is formed.
5 August	The Cabinet submits a package of six bills for financial revitalization to the Diet.
21 August	The LTCBJ announces the disposal of its bad loan, 750 billion yen, and the reconstruction plan including requesting the injection of public funds of more than 500 billion yen.
25 August	Three opposition parties (the DP, the LP and the Peace and Reform Party) reach an agreement about a plan for financial revitalization.
7 September	The Director General of the DP, Kan Naoto, announces that the DP will attend deliberations regarding the revision of the package of bills for financial revitalization presented by the cabinet, although the cabinet decides on an injection of public funds to the LTCBJ.
10 September	The Director General of the DP, Kan Naoto, announces that the liquidation of the LTCBJ is a condition for deliberation of the package of bills for financial revitalization.
17 September	The LDP accepts a plan that includes the complete splitting of financial divisions away from the MOF and the establishment of the Financial Services Agency in 2001.
18 September	The leaders of the LDP and the three opposition parties reach an agreement on a compromise plan for the LTCBJ and the splitting of financial divisions away from the MOF.
20 September	Prime Minister Obuchi leaves Japan for a meeting with the President of the US.
26 September	The LDP and the three opposition parties reach an agreement regarding the LTCBJ and the splitting of financial divisions from the MOF.

27 September	LTCBJ-affiliated non-bank Nippon Lease files for application of the Corporate Rehabilitation Law at the Tōkyō District Court.
28 September	The LDP and the three opposition parties agree to submit the joint revised Financial Revitalization Bill.
1 October	The LDP, the DP, and the Peace and Reforms agree on the splitting of the financial divisions away from the MOF.
2 October	The LDP, the LP and the SDPJ agree on the revised bill of the National Railway's Debt Law.
7 October	The Cabinet submits the Urgent Measures for Early Improvement of the Financial System Bill to the Diet.
12 October	The LDP, the LP and the Peace and Reform submit the joint revised bill of the Urgent Measures for Early Improvement of the Financial System to the Diet.
	A package of bills for financial revitalization is approved by the Diet.
	The LDP, the SDP and the LP agree on the revised bill of the National Railway's Debt Law.
16 October	A package of four bills for financial revitalization and the joint revised bill of the Urgent Measures for Early Improvement of the Financial System are approved by the Diet.
23 October	Prime Minister Obuchi decides to put the LTCBJ under temporary state control. The government declares the insolvency of the LTCBJ and decides on its liquidation.
19 November	The LDP and the LP agree to form a ruling coalition.
24 November	The major 15 banks announce that they are requesting an injection of public funds.
13 December	The government announces the failure of the Nippon Credit Bank (NCB) under Article 36 of the Financial Revitalization Law, and decides to put the NCB under temporary state control.
15 December	The Financial Revitalization Committee starts.

1999

| 14 January | The Obuchi Coalition Cabinet (the LDP and the LP) is formed. |
| 26 January | The Cabinet and the LDP Headquarters' Office on Reforms of Central Ministries and Agencies decide on the 'Basic Outline of Reforms of Central Ministries and Agencies'. |

15 April	The LDP and the CGP reach an agreement on MOF reform.
28 April	The Cabinet approves a package of bills for reform of central ministries and agencies.
8 July	A package of bills for reforms of central ministries and agencies is approved by the Diet.

Notes

1 Introduction

1 The eight parties were the Japan Renewal Party (Shinseitō), the New Harbinger Party (Shintō Sakigake, NHP), the Democratic Socialist Party (Minshatō, DSP), the Clean Government Party (Kōmeitō, CGP), the Japan Socialist Party (Nihonshakaitō, JSP), the Japan New Party (Nihonshintō, JNP), the Social Democratic League (Shakai Minshu Rengō, SDL), and the Democratic Reform League (Minshu Kaikaku Rengō, DRL).

2 After the Second World War, in 1949, the Japanese tax system was fundamentally reformed according to a recommendation presented by the Shoup Mission, lead by Carl Sumner Shoup.

2 The Japanese political system: a historical institutional approach

1 'Bokuminkan' is a concept that originated from 'Shi-ki', a classic Chinese book that describes ancient Chinese history.

3 The Japanese political system from the Meiji era to 1993

1 Hanbatsu mainly consisted of four *han* (fiefs) – Satsuma, Chōshū, Kōchi and Hizen – that played crucial roles in the Meiji Restoration. Many politicians who played an important part in the early stage of the Meiji era originated from these four *han*.

2 Young Navy officials had felt strong resentment against party politicians since the London Navy Disarmament Treaty, which limited the military power of the Japanese Navy, was concluded under party cabinets. A group of junior military officials assassinated Prime Minister Inukai Tsuyoshi on 15 May 1932.

3 Sasaki Suguru names bureaucrats in the early stage of the Meiji era (from 1968 to 1871) as 'Ishin Kanryō' (bureaucrats of the Restoration era). He argues that Ishin Kanryō had the characteristics both of influential politicians who participated in the decision-making process on national policies and of bureaucrats who were engaged in practical administration.

4 Ex-Administrative Vice Minister of Finance Matsukuma Hideo explained the seniority rule in the MOF: '[Concerning promotion in the MOF] we were waiting in line with the year [we were employed]. Unless those who were employed before us moved to a new position, we could not get promotion. On the other hand, it was highly unlikely that those who were employed after us would get a higher position than us' (Naiseishikenkyūkai 1971: 6).

5 An ex-MOF executive, Hoshino Naoki, explained in an interview: 'the MOF had relatively little connection with political parties. Party politicians thought

that the MOF had no interest in party politics and party politicians themselves did not expect the MOF to do party politics' (Naiseishikenkyūkai 1964a: 6).

6 The ex-Administrative Vice Minister of Commerce and Industry, Yoshino Shinji, answered in an interview in his memoirs: 'I did not have serious difficulties with political parties. Neither I nor my senior colleagues were forced to resign or were sacked because of intervention by political parties . . .' (Yoshino 1962: 249).

7 The ex-Administrative Vice Minister of Commerce and Industry, Yoshino Shinji, recalled the attitude of bureaucrats towards party politicians in his memoirs: 'Although it was the era of party politics, we did not respect party politicians . . . they were absorbed in taking care of their constituencies . . .' (Yoshino 1962: 114).

8 Yoshino Shinji also stated in his memoirs: 'Party politicians rarely intervened in our work. It was highly unlikely that party politicians would interfere with our budget compilation. . . . Although political parties had committees on policy research, I hardly ever went to those committees to explain our plans . . .' (Yoshino 1962: 114–15).

9 On 26 February 1936, about 20 junior army officers attempted to carry out a coup d'état, leading more than 1,300 army soldiers. They attacked the residences of high government officials, such as the residences of the Prime Minister and the Finance Minister, and killed some Ministers, such as Finance Minister Takahashi Korekiyo. Martial law was proclaimed and, on 29 February 1936, the revolt was repressed.

10 Twelve Ordinances (Ordinance of Employment Control, Ordinance of Labour Management, Ordinance of National Recruitment, Ordinance of Reporting Professional Abilities, Provisional Ordinance of Wages Control, Provisional Ordinance of Office Workers' Salary Control, Ordinance of Employees Movements Control, Ordinance of Labour Management in Key Industries, Ordinance of Mariners Recruitment, Ordinance of Working Hours in Factories Control, Ordinance of Wages Control, and Ordinance of Technicians in Factories Training) regulated human resources. Thirteen Ordinances (Ordinance of Agricultural Production Control, Ordinance of Commodities Control, Ordinance of Price Control, Provisional Ordinance of Agricultural Land Prices Control, Ordinance of Electric Power Management, Ordinance of National Mobilization Commodities Expropriation, Ordinance of Metal Goods Collection, Ordinance of Living Necessities Control, Ordinance of Rent Control, Ordinance of Agricultural Lands Control, Provisional Ordinance of Agricultural Land Management Control, Ordinance of Electric Power Distribution Control, and Ordinance of Buildings Management and Expropriation) controlled material resources. Four ordinances (Ordinance of Dividends and Funding, Ordinance of Accounting Control, Ordinance of Banks' Fund Management, and Ordinance of Stock Prices Control) regulated the flow of funds. Eleven Ordinances (Ordinance of Organizations of Key Industries, Ordinance of Business Licenses, Ordinance of Land Transportation Control, Ordinance of Wartime Marine Transportation Control, Ordinance of Financial Organizations, Ordinance of Business Management, Ordinance of Marine Transportation Control, Ordinance of Factories Management, Ordinance of Munitions Factories Inspection, Ordinance of Factories Expropriation, and Ordinance of Trade Control) regulated business activities. Two ordinances (Ordinance of Newspaper Business and Ordinance of Publishing in Newspapers Control) inspected the mass media.

11 The six cabinets were the Hirota, Hayashi (February 1937 to May 1937), First Konoe (May 1937 to January 1939), Hiranuma (January 1939 to August 1939), Abe (August 1939 to January 1940), and Yonai (January 1940 to July 1940) Cabinets.

12 After the 26th February Uprising in 1936, some bureaucrats who were called 'revisionist bureaucrats' (Kakushin Kanryō) advocated reform of the Japanese economic, social and political systems. They proposed a change in the existing order – political, social, and economic – to 'increase the nation's spiritual and military strength'. In a word, they advocated changing the *status quo*. (Spaulding Jr 1974: 70).

13 The Army was divided into two factions, the Imperial Way (Kōdō) faction and the Control (Tōsei) faction, and they fiercely confronted each other. In August 1935, General Nagata Tetsuzan, one of leaders of the Control faction, was assassinated by an Army officer of the Imperial Way faction. The leaders of the 26th February Event were members of the Imperial Way faction.

14 The total number of seats that both groups won in the general elections of 1952, 1953 and 1955 were 111, 138 and 156 respectively.

15 Kawato Sadafumi argues that a seniority rule was being constantly applied to the personnel matters of the LDP by the end of the 1970s because the number of LDP politicians who won elections a sufficient number of times to be appointed Minister (five or six times) became stable in the 1970s (Kawato 1996: 118).

16 Kawato Sadafumi argues that this rule was also established in the LDP by the end of the 1970s. By the end of the 1970s, factions were integrated into five major factions (Tanaka, Ōhira, Fukuda, Nakasone and Miki), and the secession of one faction from the LDP would have resulted in the loss of its position as a ruling party. Therefore power-holding factions (factions to which the President of the LDP belonged (Sōsaibatsu) and factions which cooperated with Sōsaibatsu) had to make concessions to the anti-power holding factions (factions that competed with Sōsaibatsu in a LDP presidential election) by allocating posts of ministers and LDP executives in order to prevent such a result (Kawato 1996: 126).

17 The ex-Prime Minister Takeshita Noboru referred to such a relationship in his memoirs: 'When we hold the office of Parliamentary Vice Minister, although there are some exceptions, bureaucrats make a judgment on our capability. . . . Bureaucrats, once they regard a politician who holds office of the Parliamentary Vice Minister as competent, give him thorough lectures including expertise and information regarding the policy area of their ministry. . . . I studied very hard. [When I was the Parliamentary Vice Minister of the International Trade and Industry] I eagerly received lectures from bureaucrats' (Takeshita 2001: 109–10).

18 The jurisdiction of the Ministry of Home Affairs includes taxation on residents by local governments, such as a residents' tax.

19 After 1993, as will be explained in Chapter 4, the power of factions declined. The weakened factions, however, did not bring about coherent LDP leaders. Several groups were formed across factions, and those groups both cooperated with each other and confronted each other. In addition, zoku did not suffer significant changes after 1993. Therefore it is still not appropriate to apply a principal-agent model to the relationship between LDP leaders and bureaucrats after 1993.

4 Changes in the Japanese political system since 1993

1 The Recruit Company, a major personnel placement agency, transferred its affiliated company's unlisted shares to many politicians, ex-bureaucrats and executives of private companies. Prime Minister Takeshita Noboru was forced to resign since he received a 50 million yen loan from the Recruit Company.

2 The Kyōwa Co., a major steel frame industry company, gave bribes to politicians, and ex-Prime Minister Suzuki Zenkō allegedly received 230 million yen from Kyōwa.

3 The Sagawa Kyūbin, a major road delivery company, contributed political funds illegally to many politicians. The Vice President of the LDP, Kanemaru Shin, admitted that he had received 500 million yen and he was forced to resign as Vice President and member of the House of Representatives. In 1993 Kanemaru Shin was arrested for tax evasion.

4 The Mayor of Sendai City, Ishii Tōru, the Governor of Ibaraki Prefecture Takeuchi Fujio, the Governor of Miyagi Prefecture Honma Toshitarō and the ex-Minister of Construction, Nakamura Kishirō, were arrested for taking bribes from construction companies.

5 The Peace and Reform and other ex-Clean Government Party members re-established the Clean Government Party in November 1998.

6 One LDP politician admitted in an interview that his faction had asked him to donate money to it (interview with an LDP politician on 19 March 2001).

7 In Japanese, the LDP is (Jiyūminshutō), the JSP is Shakaitō and the NHP is Shintō Sakigake. The group that supported a coalition between these three parties was called 'Ji-Sha-Sa' in abbreviation.

8 In Japanese, conservative is 'Hoshu'. The group that advocated a coalition with more conservative parties was called the 'Ho-Ho' group in abbreviation.

9 An MOF executive admitted in an interview: 'When we negotiate with faction executives, they say, "I agree with you. But I cannot guarantee that other faction members will also agree with you" ' (interview with a MOF executive, 13 April 2002).

10 One LDP politician recalled that when he had asked the MOF about tax issues, the Director General of the Tax Bureau sent a junior official to him although the Director General himself had used to come to see him (interview with an LDP politician, 19 March 2001).

11 One ex-LDP politician explained that LDP politicians were deeply shocked and seriously afraid that they would lose political power forever (interview with a member of the HR (member of the CP), 3 August 2001).

12 The four major economic organizations were: the Federation of Economic Organizations; the Japan Committee for Economic Development; the Japan Federation of Employers' Associations; and the Japan Chamber of Commerce and Industry.

13 The *Asahi Shinbun* reported a comment of an executive of the Japan Trade Union Confederation (Rengō, one of supporting groups of the Hosokawa Coalition Cabinet): 'the attempt of the introduction of the national welfare tax was played by the MOF as the scriptwriter, Ozawa and Ichikawa [the Secretary General of the CGP] as the directors, and Hosokawa as the leading ō(*Asahi Shinbun*, 4 February 1994).

14 Interview with an ex-MOF executive, 22 December 2000.

15 According to a survey conducted by Nihon Keizai Shinbunsha in 1993, 30 per cent of executive bureaucrats answered that the current coalition of the Hosokawa Coalition Cabinet would exist in 1994; 35 per cent of them answered that the parties of ruling coalition might change while the LDP would remain one of opposition parties (Nihon Keizai Shinbunsha 1994: 422).

5 Introduction of the consumption tax in 1989

1 After the fourth Middle East War broke out, the six member nations of OPEC regarded Japan as a hostile country and announced a reduction in the amount of oil exports to Japan and an increase in oil prices.

2 After the Second World War, the Japanese tax system was fundamentally reformed according to a recommendation by the Shoup Mission, led by Carl Sumner Shoup, in 1949. Since this reform, the Japanese tax system has become significantly dependent on income taxation.

3 National bonds are classified into two categories, construction bonds and deficit-covering bonds, according to the purpose for which they are issued. Construction bonds are issued for raising funds for public capital infrastructure, such as roads and harbour facilities, and deficit-covering bonds are issued for other ordinary expenditures, such as personnel expenditures. The Fiscal Law provides only for the issuance of construction bonds (Article 4) since the issuance of deficit-covering bonds was regarded as one of the causes of serious inflation before the Second World War. A special law is therefore required in order to issue deficit-covering bonds.

4 The GTSRC was established as a permanent advisory organization to the Prime Minister in 1962. The GTSRC examines the current tax system and presents a proposal in answer to an enquiry from the Prime Minister once a year, and a long-term proposal at least one in three years. The Tax Bureau of the MOF supports the Cabinet Secretariat Office regarding the management of the GTSRC. The Tax Bureau actually decides the members of the GTSRC and creates drafts of proposals. About this role of the Tax Bureau, Mizuno Masaru wrote in his memoir that the Tax Bureau created a plan about the process of the discussion in the GTSRC and the details of the enquiry from the Prime Minister to the GTSRC considering what was in the mind of Prime Minister Nakasone about what should be discussed in the GTSRC. About members of the GTSRC, Prime Minister Nakasone requested that at least ten members who would play an active part in the GTSRC and not specialists in tax should be chosen as new members. The Tax Bureau decided on the new members and asked ten people to join the GTSRC as special members (Mizuno 1993: 50–1).

5 Takeshita Noboru, the Minister of Finance at that time, explained in his memoir that the resolution did not deny the possibility of the future introduction of a general consumption tax (Takeshita 2001: 318–19).

6 For instance, Vice-Secretary General Kanemaru Shin, who was a leader of kōkyō-jigyō (public works) zoku at that time, expressed his concern about an austere fiscal policy and cautiously accepted tax increases at a meeting of the three top executives of the LDP (the Secretary General of the LDP, the Chair of the PARC and the Chair of the EC) and executives of four major business organizations (the Federation of Economic Organizations, the Japan Committee for Economic Development, the Japan Federation of Employers' Associations and the Japan Chamber of Commerce and Industry) (*Asahi Shinbun*, 29 November 1984, evening edition).

7 At first, the LDP TSRC proposed taxation on office automation facilities (computers, word processors, photocopiers, pocket calculators, electric typewriters and facsimiles) from the 1984 fiscal year in 'the Major Line of Tax Reform of the 1984 Fiscal Year'. But the LDP TSRC abandoned this because of strong opposition from the business group.

8 According to Section 2 Article 56 of the Diet Law, when a bill is submitted to the HR, the Speaker of the HR passes it to a committee that has jurisdiction over it and, after deliberation by the committee, the Speaker of the HR passes it to the plenary session of the HR. When a bill is not voted in by the end of the session in which it was submitted, it is dropped (Article 68 of the Diet Law).

9 Mizuno Masaru, the Director General of the Tax Bureau at that time, admitted in his memoirs that executives of the government, the LDP and the MOF listened to opposition parties and sounded them out in order to find out their attitudes towards the deliberation on the package of tax reform bills in the Diet. Therefore, he wrote, when the LDP decided the 'Major Line of Structural Tax Reform' and the government submitted it to the cabinet meeting in June 1988, the opposition parties did not unite together to oppose the consumption tax (Mizuno 1993: 276).

10 The Special Committee reached agreement with respect to taxation on the founder's profit and taxation on the profit from sales of unlisted stocks (after which these stocks became listed stocks).

11 On the interim report, Mizuno Masaru wrote in his memoirs that the GTSRC decided that it would make no decision or suggest multiple options. With respect to which matters the LDP TSRC should decide on and which issues the decisions of the GTSRC should not be different from those of the LDP TSRC. Therefore, he wrote, the interim report of the GTSRC stated only the process of its discussion about a new indirect tax and presented its basic principles (Mizuno 1993: 217, 224).

12 Some interest groups were demanding that a zero-tax rate system should be adopted. In this system, a zero-tax rate is applied to non-taxable transaction and tax-exempt corporations do not have to pay the tax that is included in the price of items or services offered by taxable corporations. Consequently, when a tax-exempt corporation purchases items from a taxable corporation, the tax amount that is included in the price will be refunded. The MOF insisted that such a system should not be adopted, and it succeeded in adopting a simple tax rate system.

13 The invoice method involves calculating the tax amount by using compulsory invoices (written records of exchanges and transactions). The account method is calculates the tax amount by using the account books of individual firms. It was argued that the account method would cast less of a burden on firms since it would not require changes in their business procedures. On the other hand, it was argued that the invoice method would be helpful to clarify the profis of the firms and the transactions between firms. In the 'Major Line of Structural Tax Reform' the account method was adopted.

14 One executive of an LDP organization explained the details of this process in an interview: 'we took a lot of time to discuss in each LDP organization to give those who opposed the consumption tax an opportunity to express their opinions. . . . Although we obtained comprehensive delegation, the Chairs of division of the PARC and the Chair of the PARC negotiated and compromised with members. Indeed, you could say that such a procedure is time-consuming and not transparent, but it worked well with regard to the introduction of the consumption tax' (interview with an executive of the LDP organization, 8 April 2002).

15 In an interview with *Chūō Kōron*, Ishihara Nobuo, the Vice Cabinet Secretary at that time, explains that the political circumstances that surrounded the Takeshita Cabinet were very stable at the beginning. The Keiseikai and the Abe faction, he said, cooperated perfectly with each other because the Secretary General of the LDP, Abe Shintarō, who was the leader of the Abe faction, and Prime Minister Takeshita were very good friends. He pointed out that the Keiseikai and the Abe faction obtained an overwhelming majority of the LDP by cooperating with each other. (Ishihara 1996: 32.) The number of members of each faction (members of the HR and the HC) when the Takeshita Cabinet was formed were as follows: the Takeshita faction (Keiseikai) (120), the Miyazawa faction (89), the Abe faction (88), the Nakasone faction (81), the Kōmoto faction (31), other groups (21). The total number of LDP members of the HR and the HC was 446 (*Asahi Shinbun*, 7 November 1987).

16 Takeshita wrote some episodes in his memoirs that indicate his control over personnel matters in the LDP. He thought he had responsibility for Ministers of the second reshuffled Tanaka Cabinet (from 11 November 1974 to 9 December 1974) since he played a key role in appointing them. He compensated them for such a short term in office by appointing them as Ministers of other cabinets. As for Ministers of the Uno Cabinet (from 3 June 1989 to 10 August 1989), Prime Minister Uno asked him to create a list of Ministers for his Cabinet. Takeshita created it and all but one on the list were appointed as Ministers of

the Uno Cabinet. Again, Takeshita thought he should compensate them for such a short period in office, and he therefore appointed them as Ministers of other cabinets. (Takeshita 2001: 120–1).

17 One MOF executive described the cooperation of the MOF with the LDP TSRC in an interview: 'When the discussion in the Inner Committee reached a certain extent, we let one member of the Inner Committee suggest that it was time to decide a rough draft of the consumption tax system, and then we handed a draft to the Inner Committee. Of course, we negotiated key persons of the Inner Committee and the LDP TSRC beforehand. Before the Inner Committee was held, we informally negotiated with key members of the Inner Committee, such as Mr Yamanaka. We negotiated them one by one, face to face'(interview with an MOF executive, 13 August 2002). The details of deciding the rate of the consumption tax show intense negotiations by MOF executives. In his memoirs, Mizuno Masaru, the Director General of the Tax Bureau at that time, writes that the Minister's Secretariat, the Director General of the Budget Bureau and the Director General of the Tax Bureau persistently met the Chair of the LDP TSRC, Yamanaka, and asked him to adopt 5 per cent as the rate of the consumption tax (Mizuno 1993: 182).

18 The foreword by Takeshita to the memoirs written by Mizuno Masaru shows the close relationship between them. He referred to Mizuno as his comrade because they cooperated with each other and devoted themselves to putting the consumption tax into practice (Takeshita 1993: 3).

19 One MOF executive described this system in the process of the introduction of the consumption tax in an interview: 'When the consumption tax was discussed, all that we could do was to negotiate and to persuade key persons of the LDP TSRC. If we succeeded in persuading them and obtaining their support for our plans, the LDP as a whole supported us. But nowadays, it is not enough. To put it in an extreme way, if we could succeed in persuading Y. Sadanori, the LDP as a whole supported us. Mr Yamanaka silenced LDP members who presented objections to our plan. Now we cannot decide with whom we should negotiate and persuade beforehand' (interview with a MOF executive, 13 August 2002).

6 The financial crisis in Japan 1994–1998

1 The directive provided three cases in which banks should report to the MOF: (1) when the ratio of the current month or the estimated ratio in the three months thereafter was more than 90 per cent; (2) the month end ratio was more than 80 per cent and the marginal ratio for four months thereafter was more than 80 per cent; (3) other cases where, for instance, the increase of loans for the next four months was unusually large.

2 Those directives were revised later, in 1982 and in 1992. The directive of 1992 (Kihon Jikō Tsūtatsu) set: (1) the minimum solvency ratio (4 per cent); (2) the ratio of current assets to total deposits (at least 30 per cent); (3) the ratio of fixed assets for business use to net worth equity capital (less than 40 per cent); (4) the maximum dividend payout ratio (dividend payments divided by current profits, 40 per cent); (5) the maximum amount of bank lending to a single borrower as a percentage of own capital (20 per cent) (Rixtel 2002: 122).

3 Financial institutions were segmented according to the type of their business, such as long-term credit, trust business, foreign exchange business and securities business.

4 Article 65 of the Securities and Exchange Law prohibits banks from doing securities business (dealing, brokering, underwriting, distributing and selling securities). Since 1966 government bonds have been constantly issued. Banks and securities companies agreed that banks only underwrote them as a business accom-

panying banking business permitted by Article 5 of the Bank Law, and securities companies distributed them. After 1977, medium-term discount government bonds were issued, and banks wanted to sell them 'over the counter' as a business accompanying banking business permitted by the Article 5 of the Bank Law.

5 One ex-MOF executive explained in an interview: 'about the failure of banks, politicians did not intervene into such issues because they are too technical for politicians to understand . . . Therefore I did not explain about the failure of the two credit unions to politicians beforehand, I told only the Minister of Finance just before its announcement' (interview with an ex-MOF executive, 25 July 2001).

6 Takemura Masayoshi explained: 'On 1 December, a MOF executive told me that "the Bank of Japan, the MOF, the Tōkyō Metropolitan Government, and other financial facilities discussed this problem and made a final scheme. We have no choice other than this scheme"' (*The Proceedings of the Budget Committee of the House of Representatives*, 22 February 1995).

7 Japanese financial institutions had to pay higher interest rates compared with the financial institutions of other developed countries (such as the European Union and North American countries) when they raised funds in foreign financial markets. Such high interest rates were called the 'Japan premium'.

8 An MOF executive explained the details of the Sanyō's default: 'we knew there would be a default in a call market . . . But the Bank of Japan assured us we did not have to worry about it. The loan from Tōkyō Mitsubishi Bank, the Daiwa Bank and the NCB, amounting to 8 billion 500 million yen, was a collateral loan. The total amount of unsecured loan to the Gunma Shin'yō Kinko was only 1 billion yen. So we thought the effect of the Sanyō's default would not be so serious. Actually, its effect did not appear for the time being . . . I suppose many creditors of banks exploited Sanyō's default as an excuse to refuse to lend . . .' (interview with a MOF executive, 15 March 2001).

9 Tsuchida Masaaki, the Director General of the Banking Bureau at that time, explained the reasons why the first directive was not issued to the Jūsen and why the second directive did not include Sangyōshukisei at the Budget Committee of House of Representatives on 15 and 16 February 1996. He explained that the Jūsen were non-banks, not depositary institutions, and the MOF did not have the authority to regulate non-banks in order to keep their management sound according to the Regulation on Loan Industry Law. Therefore the MOF decided that it was not appropriate to take a rather drastic measure with respect to the Jūsen. Instead, the MOF advised the Jūsen to exercise self-restraint from giving loans to real estate businesses. As for the second directive, he pointed out that there were formal and informal systems by which the MOF and the MAFF could grasp the flow of funds of Shinren and Nōrinchūkin (*Proceedings of the Budget Committee of House of Representatives*, 15 and 16 March 1996).

10 Interview with an ex-MOF executive, 22 December 2000.

11 Katō Kōichi, the Secretary General at that time, explained the details of the memorandum at the Budgetary Committee of the House of Representatives on 16 February 1996. The Coordination Council of Ruling Coalition Parties had a hearing from founding banks and farm-related financial institutions, and farm-related financial institutions insisted that there was a memorandum in which founding banks promised to take responsibility for the reconstruction of the Jūsen. Katō Kōichi asked them to submit the memorandum and decided to publicize it (*Proceedings of the Budget Committee of the House of Representatives*, 16 February 1996).

12 The President of Jūtaku Loan Service (one of the Jūsen) admitted at the Budget Committee of the HR that the second reconstruction plan for Jūtaku Loan Service had been planned on the basis that the price of real estate would rise 25 per cent from 1992 to 2002 (*Proceedings of the Budget Committee of the House of Representatives*, 25 February 1996).

13 The LDP politician Etō Kōichi criticized Speaker Doi: 'the Speaker should show her decisive attitude by using police officers or Diet guards. How could we explain it to voters in our constituencies?' (*Asahi Shinbun*, 9 March 1996).

14 The NFP could not find a chance to stop the picketing until their candidate lost the by-election of the House of Councillors in Gifu prefecture on 24 March 1996.

15 One ex-Chief Executive Officer of a farm-related financial institution pointed out the lack of leadership in the LDP: 'Faction leaders, such as Mr Takeshita, Mr Hashimoto, Mr Nakasone, Mr Mitsuzuka, and Mr Miyazawa, did not take leadership in this case [the Jūsen problem]. So we [farm-related financial institutions] united to deal with this problem and worked on factions . . .' (interview with an ex-Chief Executive Officer of a farm-related financial institution, 2 August 2001).

16 It was reported that the DP was afraid that it would lose public support if it attended the deliberation in the Diet and tacitly permitted the injection of public funds to the LTCBJ (*Asahi Shinbun*, 13 September 1998).

17 One of the 'new policy-oriented politicians' explained the process of this case: 'the process of making the revised draft of the Financial Revitalization Bill was this: at first we discussed with members of the DP, such as Mr Edano, and we reported what we had decided to the PARC, then the PARC asked the Minister of Finance, Mr Miyazawa, his opinion. In the process from the PARC to Mr Miyazawa, the MOF intervened and MOF's idea was reflected in the opinions of the PARC and Mr Miyazawa. But after all they could not resist our draft' (interview with a member of the HR (member of the LDP), 1 August 2001).

7 The reform of the Ministry of Finance

1 On 4 February 1996, the LDP secretary General, Katō Kōichi, stated the necessity of MOF reform on a TV programme: 'the Banking Bureau and the International Finance Bureau should be integrated into a new agency, perhaps called the "Financial Agency", which should not have a broad range of authority of regulation on financial institutions' (*Asahi Shinbun*, 5 February 1996).

2 An Article 3 type organization (a committee similar to the Fair Trade Committee (FTC) according to Article 3 of the National Administrative Organization Law) has the authority to make a decision independently with respect to issues in its jurisdiction. On the other hand, an Article 8 type organization (a committee similar to the Securities and Exchange Surveillance Commission according to Article 8 of the National Administrative Organization Law) is subject to an Article 3 type organization and it is supposed to assist the Article 3 type organization. Therefore, an Article 3 type is regarded as more independent than an Article 8 type.

3 The Secretaries General of ruling coalition parties (the LDP, the SDPJ and the NHP) comprised the committee.

4 This issue was discussed at the meeting of the CAR on 5 November, and the split of the National Tax Administration Agency away from the MOF was abandoned.

5 One LDP executive who opposed Itō's proposal said: 'we and the MOF are now cooperating with each other and fighting against opposition parties in order to legislate the liquidation plan for the Jūsen. We cannot say to the MOF, "Now we are cooperating with each other, but after the Jūsen problem is settled, we will split your organization" . . . ' (*Asahi Shinbun*, 18 April 1996).

6 Such successive concessions to the NHP caused strong dissatisfaction among LDP members. The Chair of the Headquarters' Office on Administrative Reform of the LDP (HOAR), Mutō Yoshifumi, explained his difficult position at a general

meeting of the HOAR: 'Very regrettably the LDP has to form a ruling coalition. I would like to make the best efforts to negotiate with other ruling coalition parties in order to make our opinion prevail . . . ' (*Asahi Shinbun*, 21 November 1997).

7 One LDP politician explained the situation of the LDP at that time: 'There were several stances within the LDP. Some, such as S. Yasuhisa, insisted that the jurisdiction over financial policies should be split from the MOF. Some, such as Mr Yanagisawa, argued that the divisions of inspection and supervision of financial institutions should be separated from the MOF. I thought that the jurisdiction over financial policies should not be split from the MOF considering the management of the financial crisis' (interview with an LDP politician, 19 March 2001).

8 One LDP politician explained the atmosphere in the LDP at that time: 'When I and other LDP members of the study group refused to receive Chair Itō's draft, the Secretary General, Katō, warned us that such a behaviour would have a bad effect on the rate of approval of the LDP . . .' (interview with an LDP politician, 19 March 2001).

9 At the meeting of 18 September 1996, members of the Committee of Top Eight Executives of the LDP expressed their concern about the next general election that the LDP could not win it if they decided on an Article 8 type organization (*Asahi Shinbun*, 19 September 1996).

10 On 2 October 1998 the LDP agreed with the LP on the revision of the Credit Insurance Corporation, which the LP strongly demanded. The LDP cooperated with the LP and the SDPJ with respect to the National Railway's Debt Law. This law passed the HR on 2 October. On 10 November 1998 the LDP also agreed with the CGP on issuing gift certificates to each citizen.

11 One LDP executive criticized the reorganization of the MOF: 'reorganizing the MOF while a serious financial crisis is attacking the Japanese economy is just like reconstructing a fire station while a fire is breaking out . . .' (*Asahi Shinbun*, 18 September 1998.)

8 Conclusion

1 Most financial institutions had a section that was supposed to get information from and negotiate with the MOF. Those who were appointed to this section were called 'MOF-tan' abbreviating 'MOF tantōsha' since 'a person who is in charge of' is called 'tantōsha' in Japanese.

Bibliography

Aberbach, Joel D. and Bert A. Rockman, 'Image IV Revisited: Executive and Political Roles', *Governance*, vol. 1 no. 1, 1993, pp. 1–25.

—— and Robert D. Putnam, *Bureaucrats and Politicians in Western Democracies*, Harvard University Press, Cambridge MA and London, 1981.

Almond, Gabriel, 'The Return to the State', *The American Political Science Review*, vol. 82 no. 3, 1988, pp. 853–74.

Amakawa Akira, 'Senryō Seisaku to Kanryō no Taiō', in Shisō no Kagaku Kenkyūkai ed., *Kyōdō Kenkyū Nihon Senryōgun sono Hikari to Kage (Jōkan)*, Tokumashobō, Tōkyō, 1978.

Asahi Shinbun Keizaibu ed., *Kin'yū Dōran: Keizai System wa Saisei Dekiruka*, Asahi Shinbunsha, Tōkyō, 1999.

Asano, Ichirō ed., *Kokkai Jiten*, 3rd edn, Yūhikaku, Tōkyō, 1997.

Banno, Junji, Meiji Kenpō Taisei no Kakuritsu: Fukoku Kyōhei to Minryoku Kyūyō, Tōkyō Daigaku Shuppankai, Tōkyō, 1971.

Baumgarter, Frank R. and Bryan D. Jones, 'Agenda Dynamics and Policy Subsystem', *The Journal of Politics*, vol. 53 no. 4, 1991, pp. 1044–73.

—— *Agendas and Instability in American Politics*, University of Chicago Press, Chicago and London, 1993.

Beason, Dick and Jason James, *The Political Economy of Japanese Financial Markets: Myths Versus Reality*, Macmillan, London, 1999.

Beetham, David, *The Legitimation of Power*, Macmillan Education, Basingstoke, 1991.

Bendor, Jonathan and Terry M. Moe, 'An Adaptive Model of Bureaucratic Politics', *The American Political Science Review* vol. 79 no. 3 (1984), pp. 755–74.

Berger, Gordon Mark, *Parties out of Power in Japan: 1931–1941*, Princeton University Press, Princeton NJ, 1977.

Blais, André and Stéphane Dion eds, *The Budget Maximizing Bureaucrat: Appraisals and Evidence*, University of Pittsburgh Press, Pittsburgh PA, 1991.

Brown, Robert Jr., *The Ministry of Finance: Bureaucratic Practices and the Transformation of the Japanese Economy*, Quorum Books, Westport CT and London, 1999.

Calder, Kent E., 'Elites and Equalizing Role: ex Bureaucrats as Coordinators and Intermediaries in the Japanese Government-Business Relationship', *Comparative Politics*, vol. 21 no. 4, 1988a, pp. 370–403.

—— *Crisis and Compensation: Public Policy and Political Stability in Japan 1949–1986*, Princeton University Press, Princeton NJ, 1988b.

Callon, Scott, *Divided Sun: MITI and the Breakdown of Japanese High-Tech Industrial Policy 1975–1993*, Stanford University Press, Stanford CA, 1995.

Camerer, Colin, 'Individual Decision Making', in John H. Kagel and Alvin E. Roth eds, *The Handbook for Experimental Economics*, Princeton University Press, Princeton NJ, 1995.

Campbell, Colin and Graham K. Wilson, *The End of Whitehall: Death of a Paradigm?*, Blackwell, Oxford, 1995.

Carpenter, Daniel P., *The Forging of Bureaucratic Autonomy: Relations, Networks, and Policy Innovation in Executive Agencies, 1862–1928*, Princeton University Press, Princeton NJ, 2001a.

—— 'The Political Foundation of Bureaucratic Autonomy: A Response to Kernell', *Studies in American Political Development* 15, 2001b, pp. 113–22.

Cohen, Theodore (ed. by Herbert Passin), *Remaking Japan: The American Occupation as New Deal*, Free Press, New York, 1987.

Cowhey, Peter F. and Mathew D. McCubbins, *Structure and Policy in Japan and the United States*, Cambridge University Press, Cambridge, 1995.

Daika Kai ed., *Naimushōshi*, Hara Shobō, Tōkyō, 1981.

Dower, John W, *Yoshida Shigeru to Sono Jidai* (translated by Ōkubo Genji), Chūō Kōron Sha, Tōkyō, 1991.

—— *Embracing Defeat: Japan in the Aftermath of World War II*, Allen Lane, London, 1999.

Drewry, Gavin and Tony Butcher, *The Civil Service Today*, 2nd edn, Basil Blackwell, Oxford, 1991.

Dunleavy, Patrick, *Democracy, Bureaucracy and Public Choice: Economic Explanations in Political Science*, Harvester Wheatsheaf, New York and London, 1991.

—— and Brendan O'Leary, *Theories of the State: The Politics of Liberal Democracy*, Macmillan Education, Basingstoke, 1987.

Duus, Peter, *Party Rivalry and Political Change in Takshō Japan*, Harvard University Press, Cambridge MA, 1968.

Eckstein, Harry, 'Case Study and Theory in Political Science', in Roger Gomm, Martyn Hammerskey and Peter Foster eds, *Case Study Method: Key Issues, Key Texts*, Sage, London, and Thousand Oaks, New Delhi, 2000.

Evans, Peter B., Dietrich Rueschemeyer and Theda Skocpol eds, *Bringing the State Back In*, Cambridge University Press, Cambridge, 1985.

Garrett, John, *Managing the Civil Service*, Heinemann, London, 1980.

Gotō, *Shin'ichi, Kin'yū Kenkyūkai Sōsho, Kin'yūseido no Kaikaku to Tenbō*, Jichōsha, Tōkyō, 1992

Gotōda, Masaharu, 'Seiji to Gyōsei', in Meiji Gakuin Rippōkenkyūkai ed., *Genba Hōkoku: Nihon no Seiji Kōen to Tōron*, Shinzansha, Tōkyō, 1995.

Green, Donald P. and Ian Shapiro, *Pathologies of Rational Choice Theory: A Critique of Applications in Political Science*, Yale University Press, New Haven CT and London, 1994.

Hall, Peter A., *Governing the Economy: The Politics of State Intervention in Britain and France*, Oxford University Press, New York and Oxford, 1986.

—— 'The Movement from Keynesian to Monetarism: Institutional Analysis and British Economic Policy in the 1970s', in Sven Steinmo, Kathleen Thelen and Frank Longstreth eds, *Structuring Politics: Historical Institutionalism in Comparative Analysis*, Cambridge University Press, Cambridge, 1992.

—— and Rosemary C. R. Taylor, 'Political Science and the Three New Institutions', *Political Studies*, vol. 44, 1996, pp. 936–57.

Hammersley, Martyn, Roger Gomm and Peter Foster, 'Case Study and Theory', in Roger Gomm, Martyn Hammerskey and Peter Foster eds, *Case Study Method: Key Issues, Key Texts*, Sage, London, and Thousand Oaks, New Delhi, 2000.

Hartcher, Peter, *The Ministry: The Inside Story of Japan's Ministry of Finance*, HarperCollins Business, London, 1998.

Hashikawa, Bunzō, 'Kakushin Kamryō', in Kamijima Jirō, ed., *Gendon Nihon Shisō Takei Vol. 10: Kenvyoku no Shisō*, Chikumashobo, Tōkyō, 1965.

Hata, Ikuhiko, *Kanryū no Kenkyū: Fumetsu no Power 1868–1983*, Kōdansha, Tōkyō, 1983.

—— and Senzenki Kanryōsei Kenkyūkai eds, *Senzenki Nihon Kanryōsei no Seido Soshiki Jinji*, Tōkyō Daigaku Shuppankai, Tōkyō, 1981.

Hayashi, Shigeru and Tsuji Kiyoaki, *Nihon Naikakushiroku*, Daiichi Hōki Shuppan, Tōkyō, 1981.

Hays, Declan, *Japan's Big Bang: The Deregulation and Revitalization of the Japanese Economy*, Tuttle Publishing, Boston MA, 2000.

Heady, Bruce W., 'A Typology of Ministers: Implications for Minister-Civil Servant Relationships in Britain', in Mattei Dogan ed., *The Mandarins of Western Europe: The Political Role of Top Civil Servants*, Wiley, New York and London, 1975.

Hiwatari, Nobuhiro, *Sengo Nihon no Shijō to Seiji*, Tōkyō Daigaku Shuppankai, Tōkyō, 1991.

—— 'The Reorganization of Japan's Financial Bureaucracy: the Politics of Bureaucratic Structure and Blame Avoidance', in Hoshi Takeo and Hugh Patrick eds, *Crisis and Change in the Japanese Financial System*, Kluwer Academic, Boston MA and London, 2000.

Hood, Christopher, *The Art of the State: Culture, Rhetoric, and Public Management*, Clarendon Press, Oxford, 2000.

—— , Henry Rothstein and Robert Baldwin, *The Government of Risk: Understanding Risk Regulation Regimes*, Oxford University Press, Oxford, 2001.

Horne, James, *Japan's Financial Markets: Conflict and Consensus in Policymaking*, Allen & Unwin in association with the Australia-Japan Research Centre, Australian National University, Sydney and London, 1985.

House of Representitives, *The Proceedings of the Budget Committee of the House of Representatives*, House of Representatives, Tōkyō, 22 February 1995.

—— *The Proceedings of the Budget Committee of the House of Representatives*, House of Representatives, Tōkyō, 16 February 1996.

—— *The Proceedings of the Budget Committee of the House of Representatives*, House of Representatives, Tōkyō, 25 February 1996.

—— *The Proceedings of the Budget Committee of the House of Representatives*, House of Representatives, Tōkyō, 15/16 March 1996.

Ide, Yoshinori, 'Sengo Kaikaku to Nihon Kanryōsei: Kōmuin Seido no Sōritsu Katei', in Tōkyō Daigaku Shakai Kagaku Kenkyūjo ed., *Sengo Kaikaku 3: Seiji Katei*, Tōkyō Daigaku Shuppankai, Tōkyō, 1974.

—— *Nihon Kanryōsei to Gyōsei Bunka: Nihon Gyōsei Kokkaron Josetsu*, Tōkyō Daigaku Shuppankai, Tōkyō, 1982.

Ihori, Toshihiro, 'Zaisei Seisaku ni Tsuite', in Ōno Yoshiyasu and Yoshihara Hiroshi eds, *Keizai Seisaku no Tadashii Kangaekata*, Tōkyō Keizai Shinpōsha, Tōkyō, 1999.

—— and Doi Takerō, *Nihon Seiji no Keizai Bunseki*, Bokutakusha, Tōkyō, 1998.

Iio, Jun, 'Seijiteki Kanryō to Gyōseiteiki Seijika: Gendai Nihon no Seikan Yūgō Katei', *Nihon Seiji Gakkai Nenpō*, 1995, pp. 135–49.

Inatsugu, Hiroaki, *Nihon no Kanryō Jinji System*, Tōkyō Keizai Shinpōsha, Tōkyō, 1996.

Inoguchi, Takashi and Iwai Yasunobu, *Zokugiin no Kenkyū: Jimintō Seiken wo Gyūjiru Shuyakutachi*, Nihon Keizai Shinbunsha, Tōkyō, 1987.

Iseri, Hirofumi, *Habatsu Saihensei*, Chūō Kōron Sha, Tōkyō, 1988.

Ishida, Takeshi, *Sengo Nihon no Seiji Taisei*, Miraisha, Tōkyō, 1961.

Ishihara, Nobuo, Heisei no Shushō Kantei, *Chūō Kōron*, December 1996, pp. 28–53.

Ishikawa Masumi, *Data Sengoshi*, Iwanami Shoten, Tōkyō, 1984.

—— and Hirose Michisada, *Jimintō: Chōki Shihai no Kōzō*, Iwanami Shoten, Tōkyō, 1989.

Itō, Daiichi, *Gendai Nihon Kanryōsei no Bunseki*, Tōkyō Daigaku Shuppankai, Tōkyō, 1980.

Itō, Mitsuharu, *Nihon Keizai no Henyō: Rinri no Sōshitsu wo Koete*, Iwanami Shoten, Tōkyō, 2000.

Jin'no, Naohito, *System Kaikaku no Seiji Keizaigaku*, Iwanami Shoten, Tōkyō, 1998.

Jiyūkokumihsha ed., *Gendai Yōgo no Kiso Chishiki*, Jiyukokuminsha, Tōkyō, 2002.

Johnson, Chalmers, 'The Institutional Foundations of Japanese Industrial Policy', in Claude E. Barfield Jr and William A. Scambra ed., *The Politics of Industrial Policy: a Conference Sponsored by the American Enterprise Institute for Public Policy Research*, AEI Press, Washington DC, 1986.

Kabashima, Ikuo, 'Shintō no Tōjō to Jimintō Ittō Yūi Taisei no Hōkai', *Leviathan*, 15, 1994, pp. 7–31.

—— '98 nen San'insen: Jimintō wa Naze Maketanoka', *Leviathan*, 25, 1999, pp. 78–102.

—— and Takenaka Yoshihiko, *Gendai Nihonjin no Ideology*, Tōkyō Daigaku Shuppankai, Tōkyō, 1996.

Karube, Kensuke and Nishino Tomohiko, *Kenshō Keizai Shissei: Dare ga Nani wo Naze Machigaetaka*, Iwanami Shoten, Tōkyō, 1999.

Kasza, Gregory J., *The State and the Mass Media in Japan, 1918–1945*, University of California Press, Berkeley CA, Los Angeles, London, 1988.

Katō, Junko, 'Shin Seidoron wo Meguru Ronten: Rekishiteki Approach to Gōriteki Sentaku Riron', *Leviathan*, 15, 1994, pp. 176–82.

—— 'Review Article: Institutions, and Rationality in Politics – Three Varieties of Neo-Institutionalists', *British Journal of Political Science*, vol. 26, 1996, pp. 553–82.

—— *Zeisei Kaikaku to Kanryōsei*, Tōkyō Daigaku Shuppankai, Tōkyō, 1997.

Katz, Richard, *Japan, the System that Soured: the Rise and Fall of the Japanese Economic Miracle*, M. E. Sharp, Armonk NY and London, 1998.

Kavanagh, Dennis, *The Reordering of British Politics: Politics after Thatcher*, Oxford University Press, Oxford, 1997.

Kawahito, Sadafumi, 'Seniority Rule to Habatsu: Jimintō ni okeru Jinji Haibun no Henka', *Leviathan*, winter 1996, pp. 111–45.

Kawakita, Takao, 'Ōkurashō Kenkyū: Ōkurashō wa Kaikaku Sarerunoka', *Gekkan Kankai*, August 1999, pp. 230–40.

—— *Zaimushō de Naniga Kawaruka*, Kōdansha, Tōkyō, 2000.

174   *Bibliography*

Kawnto Sadafumi, 'Seniority Rule to Habatsu: Jimintōni Okeru Jinji Haibun no Henka', *Leviathan*, Winter 1996.

Kazami, Akira, *Konoe Naikaku*, Nihon Shuppan Kyodo Kabushikikaisha, Tōkyō, 1997.

Keehn, Edward B., 'Managing Interests in the Japanese Bureaucracy: Informality and Discretion', *Asian Survey*, vol. 30 no. 11, 1990, pp. 1021–37.

Kernell, Samuel, 'Rural Free Delivery as a Critical Test of Alternative Models of American Political Development', *Studies in American Political Development*, 15, 2001, pp. 103–12.

Kim, Hyung-Ki, Muramatsu Michio, T. J. Pempel and Yamamura Kōzō eds, *The Japanese Civil Service and Economic Development: Catalysts of Change*, Clarendon Press, Oxford, 1995.

King, Desmond, *Actively Seeking Work?: The Politics of Unemployment and Welfare Policy in the United States and Great Britain*, University of Chicago Press, Chicago and London, 1995.

Kinoshita, Kazuo, *Zeisei Chōsakai: Sengo Zeisei Kaikaku no Kiseki*, Zeimu Keirikyōkai, Tōkyō, 1992.

Kishi, Nobuo, *Kenshō Ōkurashō Hōkai: Kenryoku no Kyotō wo Osotta Zettai Zetsumei no Kiki*, Tōkyō Keizai Shinpōsha, Tōkyō, 1996.

Kishiro, Yasuyuki, *Jimintō Zeisei Chōsakai*, Tōkyō Keizai Shinpōsha, Tōkyō, 1995.

Kitaoka, Shin'ichi, *Jimintō: Seikentō no 38 nen*, Yomiuri Shinbunsha, Tōkyō, 1995.

Koh, B. C., *Japan's Administrative Elite*, University of California Press, Berkeley CA, Los Angeles, Oxford, 1989.

Krauss, Ellis S., 'Japanese Parties and Parliament: Changing Leadership Roles and Role Conflict', in Terry Edward MacDougall ed., *Political Leadership in Contemporary Japan*, Centre for Japanese Studies, University of Michigan, Ann Arbor MI, 1982.

Large, Stephen S., *Emperor Hirohito and Showa Japan: A Political Biography*, Routledge, London, 1992.

Mabuchi, Masaru, *Ōkurashō Tōsei no Keizaigaku*, Chūō Kōron Sha, Tōkyō, 1994.

—— *Ōkurashō wa Naze Oitsumeraretanoka: Seikan Kankei no Henbō*, Chūō Kōron Sha, Tōkyō, 1997.

March, James G. and Johan P. Olsen, 'The New Institutionalism: Organizational Factors in Political Life', *The American Political Science Review*, vol. 78 no. 3, 1984, pp. 734–49.

—— *Rediscovering Institutions: The Organizational Basis of Politics*, Free Press, Maxwell Macmillan, New York and Oxford, 1989.

Matsuda, Horoshi, *Kōshoku Tsuihō: Sandai Purge no Kenkyū*, Tōkyō Daigaku Shuppankai, Tōkyō, 1996.

Matsumoto, Masao, *Seiji Ishiki Zusetsu: Seitō Shizi Sedai no Taijō*, Chūō Kōron Shinsha, Tōkyō, 2001.

Mezey, Michael, 'Classifying Legislatures', in Philip Norton ed., *Legislatures*, Oxford University Press, Oxford, 1990.

Mikuriya, Takashi, *Nihon no Kindai 3: Meiji Kokka no Kansei: 1890–1905*, Chūō Kōron Shinsha, Tōkyō, 2001.

Minobe Tatsukichi, 'Waga Gikai Seido no Zento', *Chūōkōron*, January 1934.

Miyake, Ichirō, *Nihon no Seiji to Senkyo*, Tōkyō Daigaku Shuppankai, Tōkyō, 1995.

Mizuno, Masaru, *Shuzei Kyokuchō no 1300 nichi: Zeisei Bappon Kaikaku eno Ayumi*, Ōkura Zaimukyōkai Zei no Shirube Sōkyoku, Tōkyō, 1993.

Mizutani, Mitsuhiro, *Nihon no Kindai 13: Kanryō no Fūbō*, Chūō Kōron Shinsha, Tōkyō, 1999.

Moe, Terry M., 'The New Economics of Organization', *The American Journal of Political Science*, vol. 28, 1984, pp. 739–77.

Mulgan, Aurelia George, *Japan's Failed Revolution: Koizumi and the Politics of Economic Reform*, Asia Pacific Press, Canberra, 2002.

Murakawa, Ichirō, 'Jimintō Zeisei Chōsakai', in Uchida Kenzō ed., *Keizai Seisaku Kettei Katei no Kenkyū*, Nihon Keizai Kenkyū Centre, Tōkyō, 1986.

Muramatsu, Michio and Ellis S. Krauss, 'Bureaucrats and Politicians in Policymaking: The Case of Japan', *The American Political Science Review*, vol. 78 no. 1, 1984, pp. 126–46.

—— 'The Conservative Policy Line and the Development of Patterned Pluralism', in Murakami Yasusuke, Hugh T. Patrick, Inoguchi Takashi *et al.* eds, *The Political Economy of Japan vol. 1 The Domestic Transformation*, Stanford University Press, Stanford CA, 1987.

Naiseishi Kenkyūkai, *Naiseishi Kenkyū Shiryō vol. 24: Hoshino Naoki Danwa Sokkiroku*, Naiseishi Kenkyūkai, Tōkyō, 1964a.

—— *Naiseishi Kenkyū Shiryō vol. 25: Aoki Tokuzō Danwa Sokkiroku*, Naiseishi Kenkyūkai, Tōkyō, 1964b.

—— *Naiseishi Kenkyū Shiryō vol. 93: Matsukuma Hideo Danwa Daiikkai Sokkiroku*, Naiseishi Kenkyūkai, Tōkyō, 1971.

Nakakita, Tōru and Takabe Seiichi, *Jūsen no Yami*, Asahi Shinbunsha, Tōkyō, 1996.

Nihon Keizai Shinbunsha ed., *Jimintō Seichōkai*, Nihon Keizai Shinbunsha, Tōkyō, 1983.

—— *Kanryō: Kishimu Kyodai Kenryoku*, Nihon Keizai Shinbunsha, Tōkyō, 1994.

—— *Kin'yū Meisō no 10 nen: Kiki wa Naze Fusegenakatta noka*, Nihon Keizai Shinbunsha, Tōkyō, 2000.

Nihon Kokumin Seidoshi Kenkyūkai ed., *Kanri Kōmuin Seido no Hensen*, Daiichi Hōki, Tōkyō, 1989.

Nishimura, Yoshimasa, *Kin'yū Gyōsei no Haiin*, Bungei Shunjū, Tōkyō, 1999.

Nishino, Tomohiko, *Kenshō Keizai Meisō: Naze Kiki ga Tsuzukunoka*, Iwanami Shoten, Tōkyō, 2001.

Noguchi, Yukio, *1940 nen Taisei: Saraba 'Senji Keizai'*, Tōkyō Keizai Shinpōsha, Tōkyō, 1995.

Nonaka, Naoto, *Jimintō Seikenka no Seiji Elite: Shin Seidoron niyoru Nichifutsu Hikaku*, Tōkyō Daigaku Shuppankai, Tōkyō, 1995.

—— 'Senzo Gaeri?: Renritsu Seiken Jidai ni Okeru Seisaku Katei no Hen'yō', *Leviathan*, Summer 1998, pp. 37–67.

Nordlinger, Eric A., *On the Autonomy of the Democratic State*, Harvard University Press, Cambridge MA and London, 1981.

North, Douglass C., *Institutions, Institutional Change and Economic Performance*, Cambridge University Press, Cambridge, 1990.

Okada, Akira, *Gendai Nihon Kanryōsei no Seiritsu Katei: Sengo Senryōki ni okeru Gyōsei Seido no Saihensei*, Hōsei Daigaku Shuppanbu, Tōkyō, 1994.

Ōkurashō Shōwa Zaiseishi Henshūshitsu ed., *Shōwa Zaiseishi*, Tōkyō Keizai Shinpōsha, Tōkyō, 1956.

Ōkurashō Zaiseishishitsu, *Ōkurashōshi: Meiji Taishō Shōwa*, Ōkura Zaimu Kyōkai, Tōkyō, 1998.

—— *Shōwa Zaiseishi: Shōwa 27nen-48 nendo* vol. 10, Kin'yū 2, Tōyōkeizai Shinpōsha, Tōkyō, 1991.

Olsen, Johan P. and B. Guy Peters, 'Learning from Experience?', in Johan P. Olsen and B. Guy Peters eds, *Lessons from Experience: Experiential Learning in Administrative Reforms in Eight Democracies*, Scandinavian University Press, Oslo and Oxford, 1996.

Ōtake, *Hideo, Nihon Seiji no Tairitsujiku: 93 nen Ikō no Seikai Saihen no Nakade*, Chūō Kōron Shinsha, Tōkyō, 1999.

—— ed., *Seikai Saihen no Kenkyū: Shin Senkyo Seido niyoru Sōsenkyo,* Yūhikaku, Tōkyō, 1997.

Ozaki, Mamoru, *Uwagaki Hozon: Moto Ōkura Kanryō no Hitorigoto*, Tokuma Shoten, Tōkyō, 1999.

Ozaki, Tetsuji and Okuno Masahiro, 'Gendai nihon no Keizai System to sono Rekishiteki Genryū', in Ozaki Tetsuji and Okuno Masahiro eds, *Gendai Nihon Keizai System no Genryū*, Nihon Keizai Shinbunsha, Tōkyō, 1993.

Page, Edward C., *Political Authority and Bureaucratic Power: A Comparative Analysis*, 2nd edn, Harvester Wheatsheaf, New York and London, 1992.

Park, Young H., *Bureaucrats and Ministers in Contemporary Japanese Government*, Institute of East Asian Studies, University of California, Berkeley CA, 1986.

Parsons, D. Wayne, *Public Policy: An Introduction to the Theory and Practice of Policy Analysis*, Elger, Aldershot, 1995.

Pempel, T. J., *Regime Shift: Comparative Dynamics of the Japanese Political Economy*, Cornell University Press, Ithaca NY and London, 1998.

—— ed., *Uncommon Democracies: the One Party Dominant Regimes*, Cornell University Press, Ithaca NY, 1990.

Peters, B. Guy, 'The Problem of Bureaucratic Government', *The Journal of Politics*, vol. 43, 1981, pp. 45–82.

—— *Institutional Theory in Political Science: the 'New Institutionalism'*, Pinter, London, 1999.

Pierson, Paul, 'Increasing Returns, Path Dependence and the Study of Politics', *The American Political Science Review*, vol. 94 no. 2, 2000a, pp. 251–67.

—— 'Not Just What, but When: Timing and Sequence in Political Processes', *Studies in American Political Development*, 14, 2000b, pp. 72–92.

Ramseyer, J. Mark and Frances McCall Rosenbluth, *Japan's Political Marketplace*, Harvard University Press, Cambridge MA and London, 1993.

Reed, Steven R. and Sakamoto Takayuki, 'Gōriteki Sentakuron: Gōiten wo Motomete', *Leviathan*, 19, 1996, pp. 105–25.

Rhodes, Rod, 'The Civil Service', in Anthony Seldon ed., *The Blair Effect: The Government (1997–2001),* Little Brown, London, 2001.

Richards, David, *The Civil Service: under the Conservatives 1979–1997 Whitehall's Political Poodles?,* Sussex Academic Press, Brighton, 1997.

—— 'The Conservatives, New Labour and Whitehall: a Biographical Examination of the Political Flexibility of the Mandarin Cadre', in Kevin Theakston ed., *Bureaucrats and Leadership*, Macmillan, Basingstoke, 2000.

Richardson, Bradley M., 'Policymaking in Japan: An Organizing Perspective', in T. J. Pempel ed., *Policymaking in Contemporary Japan*, Cornell University Press, Ithaca NY and London, 1977.

—— *Japanese Democracy: Power Coordination and Performance*, Yale University Press, New Haven CT and London, 1997.

Rixtel, Adrian van, *Informality and Monetary Policy in Japan: The Political Economy of Bank Performance*, Cambridge University Press, Cambridge, 2002.

Rose, Richard, 'The Political Status of Higher Civil Servants in Britain', in Ezra N. Suleiman ed., *Bureaucrats and Policy Making: A Comparative Overview*, Holms and Meier, New York and London, 1984.

Roth, Alvin E., 'Introduction to Experimental Economics', in John H. Kagel and Alvin E. Roth ed., *The Handbook of Experimental Economics*, Princeton University Press, Princeton NJ, 1995.

Rothacher, Albrecht, *The Japanese Power Elite*, St Martin's Press Macmillan, New York and Basingstoke, 1993.

Saeki, Yoshimi, *Jūsen to Nōkyō*, Nōrin Tōkei Kyōkai, Tōkyō, 1997.

Sakakibara, Eisuke, *Nihon wo Enshutsu suru Shin Kanryōzō*, Yamateshobō, Tōkyō, 1977.

Sasaki Suguru, *Shishi to Kanryō: Meiji wo Sōgyōshita Hitobito*, Kōdansha, Tōkyō, 2000.

Sasaki, Takeshi, Yoshida Shin'ichi, Yamamoto Shūji and Tanibuchi Masaki eds, *Daigishi to Kane: Seiji Shikin Zenkoku Chōsa Hōkoku*, Asahi Shinbunsha, Tōkyō, 1999.

Satō, Seizaburō, Shin Ittō Yūisei no Kaimaku, *Chūō Kōron*, April 1997, pp. 170–83.

—— and Matsuzaki Tetsuhisa, *Jimintō Seiken*, Chūō Kōron Sha, Tōkyō, 1986.

Schaede, Ulrike, 'The "Old Boy" Network and Government-Business Relationships in Japan', *Journal of Japanese Studies*, vol. 21 no. 2, 1995, pp. 293–317.

Schmidt, Vivien A., *From State to Market?: the Transformation of French Business and Government*, Cambridge University Press, Cambridge, 1996.

Shibagaki, Kazuo, ' "Keizai Shin Taisei" to Tōseikai: sono Rinen to Genjitsu', in Tōkyō Daigaku Shakai Kagaku Kenkyūjo ed., *Fascism ki no Kokka to Shakai 2: Senji Nihon Keizai*, Tōkyō Daigaku Shuppankai, Tōkyō 1979.

Shimizu, Tadashi, Akashi Shūo and Mito Hironari, *Kenshō Jūsen: sono Ura to Omote wo Surudoku Tsuikyū*, Kenshūsha, Tōkyō, 1996.

Shūgiin, and Sangiin eds, *Gikaiseido Hyakunen Shi: Teikokugikai Shi Jōkan*, Ōkurashō Insatsukyoko, Tōkyō, 1990.

Silberman, Bernard S., 'The Bureaucratic Role in Japan, 1900–1945: The Bureaucrat as Politician', in Bernard S. Silberman and H. D. Harootunian eds, *Japan in Crisis: Essays on Taisho Democracy*, Princeton University Press, Princeton NJ, 1974.

—— *Cages of Reason: the Rise of the Rational State in France, Japan, the United states and Great Britain*, University of Chicago Press, Chicago and London, 1993.

Simon, A. Herbert, 'Human Nature in Politics: The Dialogue of Psychology with Political Science', *The American Political Science Review*, vol. 79 no. 2, 1985, pp. 293–304.

Smith, Brian C., *Bureaucracy and Political Power*, Wheatsheaf, St Martin's Press, Brighton and New York, 1988.

Smith, Martin J., *The Core Executive in Britain*, Macmillan, Basingstoke, 1999.

Spaulding Jr, Robert M., *Imperial Japan's Higher Civil Service Examinations*, Princeton University Press, Princeton NJ, 1967.

—— 'Japan's "New Bureaucrats" 1932–45', in George M. Willson ed., *Crisis Politics in Prewar Japan: Institutional and Ideological Problems of the 1930s*, Sophia University, Tōkyō, 1970.

—— 'The Bureaucracy as a Political Force, 1920–45', in James William Morley ed., *Dilemmas of Growth in Prewar Japan*, Princeton University Press, Princeton NJ, 1971.

—— 'The Bureaucracy as a Political Force, 1920–45, in James William Morley, ed., *Dilemmas of Growth in Prewar Japan*, Princeton University Press, Princeton NJ, 1974.

Steinmo, Sven, *Taxation and Democracy: Swedish, British and American Approaches to Financing the Modern State,* Yale University Press, New Haven CT and London, 1993.

——, Kathleen Thelen and Frank Longstreth eds, *Structuring Politics: Historical Institutionalism in Comparative Analysis*, Cambridge University Press, Cambridge, 1992.

Stockwin, J. A. A. ed., *Dynamic and Immobilist Politics in Japan*, Macmillan in association with St Antony's College, Basingstoke, 1988.

—— 'Reforming Japanese Politics: Highway of Change or Road to Nowhere?', in Purnendra Jain and Inoguchi Takashi eds, *Japanese Politics Today: Beyond Karaoke Democracy?,* Macmillan Education Australia, Melbourne, 1997.

—— *Governing Japan: Divided Politics in a Major Economy*, 3rd edn, Blackwell, Oxford 1999.

Suleiman, Ezra N., 'From Right to Left: Bureaucracy and Politics in France', in Ezra N. Suleiman ed. *Bureaucrats and Policy Making: A Comparative Overview*, Holmes and Meier, New York and London, 1984.

Suzuki, Motoshi, 'Gōriteki Sentaku Shin Seidoron ni yoru Nihon Seiji Kenkyū no Hihanteki Kōsatsu', *Leviathan*, 19, 1996, pp. 86–104.

Takeshita, Noboru, 'Foreword', in Mizuno Masaru, *Shuzei Kyokuchō no Sen Sanbyaku Nichi: Zaisei Kaikaku eno Ayumi*, Ōkura Zaomu Kyōkai Zei no Shirube Sōkyoku, Tōkyō, 1993.

—— *Seiji towa Nanika*, Kōdansha, Tōkyō, 2001.

Tanaka, Aiji, 'Seitō Shijinashisō no Ishiki Kōzō: Seitō Shiji Gainen Saikentō no Shiron', *Leviathan*, 20, 1997, pp. 101–29.

Taniguchi, Masaaki, 'Ukabiagatta Seiji Shikin System no Mondaiten', in Sasaki Takeshi,, Yoshida Shin'ichi, Taniguchi Masaaki and Yamamoto Shūji eds, *Daigishi to Kaue: Seiji Shikui Zeukoku Chōsa Hōkoku*, Asahi Shinbunsha, Tōkyō, 1999.

Tawara Sōichirō, *Kyodai na Rakujitsu: Ōkura Kanryō Haisō no 850 nichi*, Bungei Shunjū, Tōkyō, 1998.

Teranishi Jūrō, *Nihon no Keizai Hatten to Kin'yū*, Iwanami Shoten, Tōkyō, 1982.

Thelen, Katheleen, 'Historical Institutionalism in Comparative Politics', Annual Review of Political Science, vol. 2, 1999, p. 382.

—— and Sven Steinmo, 'Historical Institutionalism in Comparative Politics', in Sven Steinmo, Kathleen Thelen and Frank Longstreth eds, *Structuring Politics: Historical Institutionalism in Comparative Analysis*, Cambridge University Press, Cambridge, 1992.

Tomohito, Shinoda, 'Japan's Decision Making under the Coalition Governments', *Asian Survey*, vol. 7, 1998, pp. 703–23.

Toshikawa, Takao, 'Ōkurashō Fukkatsu no Uchimaku', *Chūō Kōron*, May 1999, pp. 72–83.

Tsuji, Kiyoaki, 'Kanryōkikō no Onzon to Kyōka', in Oka Yoshitake ed., *Gendai Nihon no Seiji Katei*, Iwanami Shoten, Tōkyō, 1958.

—— *Shinpan Nihon Kanryōsei no Kenkyū*, Tōkyō Daigaku Shuppankai, Tōkyō, 1969.

Uchida, Kenzō, Kanazashi Masao and Fukuoka Masayuki eds, *Zeisei Kaikaku wo Meguru Seiji Rikigaku*, Chūō Kōron Sha, Tōkyō, 1988.

Umezawa, Shōhei, *Yatō no Seisaku Katei*, Asahi Shobō, Tōkyō, 2000.

Ushio, Shinoda, *Ōkura Jimujikan no Tatakai: Saitō Jidai Meisō no 701 nichi*, Tōkyō Keizai Shinpōsha, Tōkyō, 1995.

Wildavsky, Aaron B., *Budgeting: a Comparative Theory of Budgetary Process*, revised edn, Transaction Books, New Brunswick and Oxford, 1986.

Woodall, Brian, *Japan under Construction: Corruption, Politics and Public Works*, University of California Press, Berkeley CA and Oxford, 1996.

Wright, Maurice, *Japan's Fiscal Crisis: The Ministry of Finance and the Politics of Public Spending 1975–2000*, Oxford University Press, Oxford, 2002.

Yamaguchi, Jirō, 'Gendai Nihon no Seikan Kankei: Nihongata Giin Naikakusei ni okeru Seiji to Gyōsei wo Chūshin'ni', *Nihon Seiji Gakkai Nenpō*, 1995, pp. 151–72.

—— and Seikatsu Keizai Kenkyūsho ed., *Sōdai na Seijiteki Jikken?: Renritsu Seiji Dōjidai no Kenshō*, Asahi Shinbunsha, Tōkyō, 1997.

Yamamura, Katsurō, 'Keizai Kanryō: Ōkurashō Kikō to Yakuwari', in Hosoya Chihiro, Saitō Makoto, Imai Seiichi and Rōyama Michio eds *Nichibei Kankeishi 2: Kaisen ni Itaru 10 nen (1931–41)*, Tōkyō Daigaku Shuppankai, Tōkyō 1971.

Yoshida, Shin'ich and Yamamoto Shūji, 'Giin no Ugokasu Cost', in Sasaki Tekeshi, Yoshida Shin'ichi, Tamiguchu Masaki and Yamamoto Shūji eds, *Daigishi to Kame: Seji Shikin Zenkoku Chōsa Hōkuku*, Asahi Shinbunsha, Tōkyō, 1999.

Yoshikawa, Hiroshi, *Tenkanki no Nihon Keizai*, Iwanami Shoten, Tōkyō, 1999a.

—— 'Nihon Keizai no Seichōryoku', in Ōno Yoshiyasu and Hoshikawa Hiroshi eds, *Keizai Seisaku no Tadashii Kangaekata*, Tōkyō Keizai Shinpoōsha, Tōkyō, 1999b.

Yoshino, Shinji, *Shōkō Gyōsei no Omoide*, Shōkō Seisaku Kankōkai, Tōkyō, 1962.

Zysman, John, *Governments, Markets and Growth: Financial Systems and the Politics of Industrial Change*, Robertson, Oxford, 1983.

Index

Page references in italics indicate figures and tables.